IGI PUBLISHING
WWW.IGI-GLOBAL.COM

CALL FOR ARTICLES

International Journal of Distance Education Technologies

An official publication of the Information Resources Management Association

MISSION:

The *International Journal of Distance Education Technologies* (IJDET) publishes original research articles of distance education four issues per year. IJDET is a primary forum for researchers and practitioners to disseminate practical solutions to the automation of open and distance learning. This journal is targeted to academic researchers and engineers who work with distance learning programs and software systems, as well as general participants of distance education.

ISSN 1063-8016
eISSN 1533-8010
Published quarterly

COVERAGE/MAJOR TOPICS:

Topics to be discussed in this journal include (but are not limited to) the following:
- Technology enhanced learning
- Ubiquitous learning
- Intelligent and adaptive learning
- Pedagogical issues
- Social learning
- Distance learning for culture and arts
- Virtual worlds and serious games for distance education

Submissions should be submitted through the following web site:
http://www.ijdet.com

Inquiries should be directed to the attention of:
Fuhua Lin, Professor
Editor-in-Chief
Email: oscarl@athabascau.ca

Ideas for Special Theme Issues may be submitted to the Editor-in-Chief.

Please recommend this publication to your librarian. For a convenient easy-to-use library recommendation for. please visit:
http://www.igi-global.com/IJDET

INTERNATIONAL JOURNAL OF DISTANCE EDUCATION TECHNOLOGIES

April-June, 2013 Vol. 11, No. 2

Table of Contents

SPECIAL ISSUE ON EMOTIONAL INTELLIGENCE FOR ONLINE LEARNING

GUEST EDITORIAL PREFACE

i   *Maiga Chang, School of Computing and Information Systems, Athabasca University, Athabasca, AB, Canada*
    Rita Kuo, Knowledge Square Inc., Taiwan
    Li Zhang, School of Computing, Engineering, and Information Sciences, University of Northumbria, Newcastle, UK

RESEARCH ARTICLES

1   **Recognizing Student Emotions using Brainwaves and Mouse Behavior Data**
    Judith Azcarraga, Center for Empathic Human-Computer Interactions, De La Salle University, Manila, Philippines
    Merlin Teodosia Suarez, Center for Empathic Human-Computer Interactions, De La Salle University, Manila, Philippines

16 **Towards Computational Fronesis:Verifying Contextual Appropriateness of Emotions**
    Michal Ptaszynski, High-Tech Research Center, Hokkai-Gakuen University, Sapporo, Hokkaidō, Japan
    Pawel Dybala, Department of Information and Management Science, Otaru University of Commerce, Sapporo, Hokkaidō, Japan
    Michal Mazur, Graduate School of Information Science and Technology, Hokkaido University, Sapporo, Hokkaidō, Japan
    Rafal Rzepka, Graduate School of Information Science and Technology, Hokkaido University, Sapporo, Hokkaidō, Japan
    Kenji Araki, Graduate School of Information Science and Technology, Hokkaido University, Sapporo, Hokkaidō, Japan
    Yoshio Momouchi, Department of Electronics and Information Engineering, Faculty of Engineering, Hokkai-Gakuen University, Sapporo, Hokkaidō, Japan

48 **Towards a Semantic-Based Approach for Affect and Metaphor Detection**
    Li Zhang, School of Computing, Engineering and Information Sciences, Northumbria University, Newcastle, UK
    John Barnden, School of Computer Science, University of Birmingham, Birmingham, UK

66 **Using Emotional Intelligence in Training Crisis Managers: The Pandora Approach**
    Lachlan Mackinnon, School of Computing & Mathematical Sciences, Old Royal Naval College, University of Greenwich, London, UK
    Liz Bacon, School of Computing & Mathematical Sciences, Old Royal Naval College, University of Greenwich, London, UK
    Gabriella Cortellessa, Consiglio Nazionale delle Ricerche-Istituto di Scienze e Tecnologie della Cognizione, Rome, Italy
    Amedeo Cesta, Consiglio Nazionale delle Ricerche-Istituto di Scienze e Tecnologie della Cognizione, Rome, Italy

96 **Affective Realism of Animated Films in the Development of Simulation-Based Tutoring Systems**
    Hiran B. Ekanayake, Stockholm University, Sweden & University of Skövde, Sweden & Department of Computation and Intelligent Systems, University of Colombo School of Computing, Colombo, Sri Lanka
    Uno Fors, Department of Computer and Systems Sciences, Stockholm University, Stockholm, Sweden
    Robert Ramberg, Department of Computer and Systems Sciences, Stockholm University, Stockholm, Sweden
    Tom Ziemke, School of Humanities & Informatics, University of Skövde, Skövde, Sweden
    Per Backlund, School of Humanities & Informatics, University of Skövde, Skövde, Sweden
    Kamalanath P. Hewagamage, University of Colombo School of Computing, Colombo, Sri Lanka

110 **Words that Fascinate the Listener: Predicting Affective Ratings of On-Line Lectures**
    Felix Weninger, Institute for Human-Machine Communication, Technische Universität München, Munich, Germany
    Pascal Staudt, Institute for Human-Machine Communication, Technische Universität München, Munich, Germany
    Björn Schuller, Institute for Human-Machine Communication, Technische Universität München, Munich, Germany

IJDET is indexed or listed in the following: ABI/Inform; ACM Digital Library; Aluminium Industry Abstracts; Australian Education Index; Bacon's Media Directory; Burrelle's Media Directory; Cabell's Directories; Ceramic Abstracts; Compendex (Elsevier Engineering Index); Computer & Information Systems Abstracts; Corrosion Abstracts; CSA Civil Engineering Abstracts; CSA Illumina; CSA Mechanical & Transportation Engineering Abstracts; DBLP; DEST Register of Refereed Journals; EBSCOhost's Academic Search; EBSCOhost's Academic Source; EBSCOhost's Business Source; EBSCOhost's Computer & Applied Sciences Complete; EBSCOhost's Computer Science Index; EBSCOhost's Computer Source; EBSCOhost's Current Abstracts; EBSCOhost's Science & Technology Collection; Electronics & Communications Abstracts; Engineered Materials Abstracts; ERIC – Education Resources Information Center; GetCited; Google Scholar; INSPEC; JournalTOCs; KnowledgeBoard; Library & Information Science Abstracts (LISA); Materials Business File - Steels Alerts; MediaFinder; Norwegian Social Science Data Services (NSD); PsycINFO®; PubList.com; SCOPUS; Solid State & Superconductivity Abstracts; The Index of Information Systems Journals; The Standard Periodical Directory; Ulrich's Periodicals Directory

GUEST EDITORIAL PREFACE

Special Issue on Emotional Intelligence for Online Learning

Maiga Chang, School of Computing and Information Systems, Athabasca University, Athabasca, AB, Canada

Rita Kuo, Knowledge Square Inc., Taiwan

Li Zhang, School of Computing, Engineering, and Information Sciences, University of Northumbria, Newcastle, UK

The detection of affect from multimodal channels and emotion generation bring research from different disciplines (such as cognitive, social, computer, mathematical and biological science) together. Various artificial intelligence techniques and bio-inspired approaches are used to interpret affect from verbal and non-verbal communications.

Emotions play an important role when users engage in career training, or learning situations. Such research is significantly beneficial to the development of intelligent tutoring systems which are capable of interpreting social relationships, contexts, general mood and emotion, sensing or reasonably predicating others' inter-conversion, identifying its role and participating intelligently in open-ended interactions.

Many intelligent tutoring systems have been developed and used to support students' learning. Good online learning systems require emotional communications happened in-between the tutors and the learners. Emotion is one of the most important factors that influence how people making decision. How to develop a system which can identify user's emotion and/or present its feelings to the user according to user's words, behaviors, and performance in online learning is definitely an important, a very helpful as well an interesting research topic.

The purpose of this special issue is to explore how models, theories, and solutions of emotion intelligence can be used in online learning and what benefits users can receive from such emotion intelligence-embedded systems and agents. This issue covers two aspects of emotion intelligence for learning: emotion recognition methods and applications.

For emotion recognition methods, first of all, Ms. Azcarraga and Dr. Suarez propose the use of Brainwaves (EEG signals) and mouse behavior together while doing emotion recognition. They find combining the accuracy in predicting academic emotions substantially increases if the extracted features from EEG signals and mouse click behaviors are taken into consideration at the same time. Dr. Ptaszynski and colleagues at the second article propose a new method for doing contextual affect analysis. They develop two systems, ML-Ask and CAO, for enhancing human-computer interactions with human-agent based dialogs. Dr. Zhang and Prof. Barnden at the third article propose a method to detect emotions from open-ended virtual improvisational contexts. They employ latent semantic analysis to find the hidden semantics from emotional expressions to improve the performance of emotion recognition results. The results show that the proposed method performs fair when compared with the results annotated by human grader.

For emotion recognition applications, Dr. Mackinnon and colleagues at the fourth article use a behavioral modeling component to detect the stress levels of the trainees as well as to impose variable stress on trainees, so their decision-making, behavior and performance can be done and assessed under stress. Dr. Ekanayake and colleagues compare users' reacting emotions measured from galvanic skin responses when they are watching films with real actors based scenarios and animated characters based scenarios. They find that no significant difference between the mean skin conductance responses (SCR) scores of the two groups, which means both types of scenarios are equally capable of triggering psychophysiological activity of subjects. This finding is important for us to consider the use of animated characters in simulation-based tutoring systems. The last article, Mr. Weninger and colleagues use 843 transcripts of TED talks and ask participants to rate the lectures by with predefined emotion tags. They identify ten most discriminative words for each predefined emotion tags at the end. These words may be very useful for learning systems to recognize the posts of student discussions.

Maiga Chang
Rita Kuo
Li Zhang
Guest Editors
IJDET

Introducing the Newest Additions to IGI Global's
Premier Journal Collection 2013

 International Journal of Pharmacology
and Pharmaceutical Technology

Editor(s)-in-Chief: Karthikeyan M. (Al Shifa College of Pharmacy, India)

 International Journal of Conceptual
Structures and Smart Applications

Editor(s)-in-Chief: Simon Polovina (Sheffield Hallam University, UK)
and Simon Andrews (Sheffield Hallam University, UK)

 International Journal of Monitoring and
Surveillance Technologies Research

Editor(s)-in-Chief: Nikolaos Bourbakis (Wright State University, USA), Konstantina S. Nikita (National
Technical University of Athens, Greece) and Ming Yang (Southern Polytechnic State University, USA)

 International Journal of Surface Engineering
and Interdisciplinary Materials Science

Editor(s)-in-Chief: J. Paulo Davim (University of Aveiro, Portugal)

 International Journal of Robotics
Applications and Technologies

Editor(s)-in-Chief: Dan Zhang (University of Ontario Institute of Technology, Canada)

 International Journal of
Software Innovation

Editor(s)-in-Chief: Roger Y. Lee (Central Michigan University, USA)
and Lawrence Chung (The University of Texas at Dallas, USA)

 International Journal of Privacy and
Health Information Management

Editor(s)-in-Chief: Muaz A. Niazi (Bahria University, Pakistan)

www.igi-global.com/journals

Recognizing Student Emotions using Brainwaves and Mouse Behavior Data

Judith Azcarraga, Center for Empathic Human-Computer Interactions, De La Salle University, Manila, Philippines

Merlin Teodosia Suarez, Center for Empathic Human-Computer Interactions, De La Salle University, Manila, Philippines

ABSTRACT

Brainwaves (EEG signals) and mouse behavior information are shown to be useful in predicting academic emotions, such as confidence, excitement, frustration and interest. Twenty five college students were asked to use the Aplusix math learning software while their brainwaves signals and mouse behavior (number of clicks, duration of each click, distance traveled by the mouse) were automatically being captured. It is shown that by combining the extracted features from EEG signals with data representing mouse click behavior, the accuracy in predicting academic emotions substantially increases compared to using only features extracted from EEG signals or just mouse behavior alone. Furthermore, experiments were conducted to assess the prediction accuracy of the system at points during the learning session where several of the extracted features significantly deviate in value from their mean. The experiments confirm that the prediction performance increases as the number of feature values that deviate significantly from the mean increases.

Keywords: Affect Recognition, Brainwaves, Electroencephalography (EEG), Mouse Behavior, Tutoring Systems

INTRODUCTION

Students experience various emotions while engaged in learning. Such emotions, also referred to as academic emotions (Pekrun, 2002), may affect the flow of learning as well as the motivation to continue with the learning task. This has been the challenge for the human tutors and even for those who develop intelligent tutoring systems (ITS). Indeed, effective tutors, whether human tutors or computer-based intelligent tutoring systems, are those who are not only aware of the cognitive needs of the students but also of their affective needs.

With this in mind, recent research projects in the area of ITS have tried to address not only the cognitive needs of students but their affective needs as well. Such affective systems, also referred to as *affective tutoring systems*, consider the effect of emotions in the learning process of a learner as well as the typical emotional patterns under different learning scenarios. Academic

DOI: 10.4018/jdet.2013040101

emotions typically experienced by a learner while using a tutoring system are *confidence* (Arroyo et al., 2009; Azcarraga et al., 2011a, 2011b, 2011c; Ibañez et al., 2011), *excitement* (Arroyo et al., 2009; Azcarraga et al., 2011a, 2011b, 2011c; Ibañez et al., 2011), *frustration* (Arroyo et al., 2009; Azcarraga et al., 2011a, 2011b, 2011c; Burleson, 2006; Ibañez et al., 2011), *interest* (Arroyo et al., 2009; Azcarraga et al., 2011a, 2011b, 2011c; D'Mello & Graesser, 2009; Ibañez et al., 2011; Kapoor, Burleson & Picard, 2007) , *flow/engagement* (D'Mello & Graesser, 2009; Stevens, Galloway & Berka, 2007), *boredom* (D'Mello & Graesser, 2009) and *confusion* (D'Mello & Graesser, 2009).

Affective tutoring systems are capable of recognizing student affect based on tutorial information complemented with the user profile. Furthermore, these systems sometimes also include a combination of facial expression, gesture and physiological signals. In (Arroyo et al., 2009), affective states such as *confident, frustrated, excited* and *interested* are predicted with high accuracy using special devices such as a camera to capture facial expression, posture chair to monitor the level of engagement, pressure-sensitive mouse and skin-conductance sensor. Similarly, Burleson (2006) uses the same set of devices in order to predict student *frustration* and the *need for help.* Moreover, tutorial information such as conversational cues, posture and facial features are used in *Autotutor* to predict *boredom, flow/engagement, confusion* and *frustration* (D'Mello & Graesser, 2009).

Another physiological sensor also explored in detecting student emotions is the EEG sensor which reads brainwaves. Such a device can measure the electrical activity in the brain induced by the electro-chemical processes related to the firing of neurons. Negative emotions, such as "disgust" were found to be associated with right-sided activation in the frontal and anterior temporal regions whereas "happiness" was found to be associated with left-sided activation in the anterior temporal region (Davidson, 2000). Nevertheless, whether a given spike in neuron activities as captured by an EEG sensor is indeed induced by some emotion cannot be ascertained. Muscle movements near the eyes and forehead are typical noise/artifacts in EEG recording. Various other artifacts may also get (wrongly) captured. As explained later, serious care must be given to pre-processing EEG data in order to increase its signal-to-noise ratio and at some point be able to isolate segments of EEG signals, over some sustained period.

Past researches have used brainwaves information to measure user alertness and cognitive workload (Sanei & Chambers, 2007), while others have used these to predict the stress level (Heraz et al., 2009) and emotional dimensions (pleasure, valence, arousal and dominance) (Frantzidis et al., 2010; Heraz, Razaki, & Frasson, 2007). In Stevens, Galloway, & Berka (2007), the student's level of frustration, distraction and cognitive workload were observed while the student is engaged in different activities in a multimedia-learning environment.

Similarly, in the previous work of the authors (cf. Azcarraga et al., 2010), the level of problem difficulty faced by academic achievers is predicted based on brainwaves. Those who assessed the problems as easy tended to have higher excitement level compared to those who found the tasks to be difficult. Moreover, those who experienced difficulty with the problems tended to be more frustrated.

Other research efforts have been directed at detecting student affective states while using some learning environment with various sensors connected to the head or body of the learner (Azcarraga et al., 2011a, 2011b, 2011c; Chanel, 2009; Ibañez et al., 2011). In Chanel (2009), classification based on EEG led to a higher accuracy for the assessment of the valence dimension of emotions as compared to the peripheral features from GSR, temperature, BVP, HR and respiration. Also, emotion valence and arousal prediction have improved when EEG features are combined with these peripheral features.

The problem with many of these physiological sensors, aside from being expensive, is that they sometimes interfere with the natural learning environment of the student. Their obtrusive nature might affect the cognitive processes and may also result in poor prediction of the true academic emotion of the learner. One device that may capture affect-related information and is non-obtrusive is a computer mouse. A computer mouse may be a standard input mouse or a special one that is sensitive to the hand pressure and possibly also sensitive to other physiological manifestations. The use of a pressure-sensitive mouse in a tutoring scenario has been explored in Arroyo et al. (2009), Burleson (2006), Kapoor, Burleson, and Picard (2007). In yet another research, a biometric mouse that captures user biometrics was explored in Kaklauskas et al. (2011) to measure a user's emotional state and productivity. This special mouse device can capture physiological behavior based on skin conductance, amplitude of hand tremble and skin temperature, and motor behavior based on mouse pressure, speed and acceleration of mouse pointer movement, scroll wheel turns, right- and left-click frequency.

In fact, even a standard mouse may provide useful information about a user's emotional state and interest, as demonstrated in Scheirer et al. (2001) and Zimmerman et al. (2003). Scheirer et al. (2001) investigated various mouse behavior patterns such as the mouse movement when users were presented with frustration-eliciting events while playing a game. The reason, it seems, is that a person's emotions and mood may affect not only his/her physiological manifestations but also his/her motor movements (Zimmermann et al., 2003)

In this study, a standard input mouse was used to capture hand motor behavior in detecting student affective states such as *confidence, excitement, frustration* and *interest*. Mouse behavior information such as the number of clicks, the duration of each click and the distance traveled by the mouse were taken as features to classify the four affective states. We compare the prediction accuracy when using solely mouse information with the accuracy when brainwaves information were used as supplementary features.

EXPERIMENTAL SET-UP

Twenty-five computer science undergraduate students (14 male and 11 female) aged 17 to 21, all mentally healthy and all right-handed, were asked to participate in the experiment (Ibañez, Lim & Lumanas, 2011). All had already taken an intermediate algebra course. During the experiment, they were asked to learn the tutoring software *Aplusix* that teaches algebra (Nicaud, Bouhineau, & Huguet, 2002). The participants were asked to solve 4 algebra equations of different difficulty levels for a period of 15 minutes. The tutorial session was designed so as to elicit a variety of emotions, including frustration and excitement, by having a wide range of difficulty levels. While using the software, their brainwaves were captured using an EEG sensor attached to their head. Moreover, the details of their mouse clicks, click duration and movement were automatically captured and stored in 2 different mouse log files - one for the clicks and duration and another for the movement.

The EEG sensor that was used in the experiment is the *Emotiv EPOC* headset, a commercially available EEG sensor typically used for gaming purposes. The *Emotiv EPOC* is equipped with 14 channels (AF3, F7, F3, FC5, T7, P7, O1, O2, P8, T8, FC6, F4, F8, AF4) according to the international standard 10-20 locations. The experiment was conducted in a quiet room to avoid external noise that may affect the signals. Further, the EEG sensor was regularly checked if it is well attached and its signals are well captured by the computer connected thru a USB terminal. A special service program was written to automatically capture the raw EEG signals coming from each of the channels.

Prior to the actual learning session, the "resting-state" EEG signals of each subject were measured by asking them to relax and close their eyes for a period of 3 minutes. These resting-state EEG signals were used as baseline measures, following the methodology described in (Davidson et al., 1990; Tomarken et al., 1992).

The participants were then given brief instructions on how to use the software and the self-report window. While solving algebra equations, an emotion annotation window automatically pops up every 2 minutes in which the participant can conveniently report the level of intensity of each of the 4 emotions (*confidence, excitement, frustration* and *interest*) using a sliding bar with values from 1 to 100 for each of the four emotions. This part of the experiment has been pre-tested with students to check whether they get irritated or stressed by the self-report pop-up window every two minutes, and whether a period of two minutes is not too often for them. The feedback has consistently been that the sliding bars are intuitive and natural enough to use and that they are not negatively affected when being asked to rate the intensity of their emotion. The two-minute interval is also not too often for them. Indeed, 120 seconds is quite a long period when one is using a learning system on screen.

DATA PREPARATION AND RESULTS

Two EEG recordings were collected from each subject: one from the resting-state period and one from the tutorial session. During the resting-state period, the values of each EEG channel for each subject were averaged. The average value serves as the baseline EEG of that particular subject, for the given channel (Davidson et al., 1990; Tomarken et al., 1992). Guided by the methodology in psycho-physiological research on emotion (cf. Davidson et al., 1990), the raw EEG channel values taken during the tutorial session were processed and filtered by computing the difference between the raw value of the channels and the mean value of corresponding channels from the baseline (resting-state) data. These differences were then normalized. Figure 1 provides an illustration of a sample baseline value.

Figure 1. Baseline of a student for the AF3 sensor channel representing the average EEG value for the AF3 channel measured during the resting-state period. The EEG signals for the same channel measured during the tutorial period is super-imposed on the graph. Note that in this case, the AF3 signal stays mostly below the baseline value, or the resting-state EEG, during the entire length of the tutorial session.

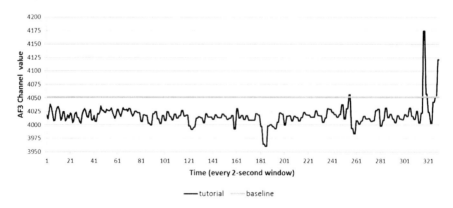

According to psycho-physiological litera-ture (Levenson, 1998; Ekman, 1984), emotions persist for about 0.5 to 4 seconds. Guided by this, we used 2-second window samples. All the pre-processed EEG data, mouse data, and self-reported emotion tag were carefully syn-chronized, merged and uniformly segmented into 2-second windows with 1-second overlap. Each segment was treated as a single instance in each subject's dataset. The full dataset had a total of 17 features: 14 for the EEG channels and 3 for mouse behavior (number of clicks, distance travelled, click duration). The most dominant self-reported emotion serves as the tag for each recorded instance. The most dominant emotion is identified as the emotion with the highest intensity value among the 4 emotions. In case there are two or more emotions with the same highest value, the most dominant emotion in the previous instance is chosen.

Mouse activities such as click duration and movement were automatically captured by a service program and stored in two different mouse log files. Raw values such as the x- and y-positions of the mouse were stored. Moreover, the button, left or right, that was clicked and the duration of such click were also stored in a separate file. The button that was clicked and the duration of the click every 2 seconds with 1 second overlap were computed. In addition, the spatial (Euclidean) distance travelled by the mouse every 2 seconds is computed.

From the 25 subjects, data from only 16 students were found to be useful, given the stringent conditions we set in terms of balanc-ing the data for all the four different emotions. Subjects with very few outlier features were eliminated. All the instances or data points for each student are combined and balanced ac-cording to emotions. The number of instances for each emotion is the same. Moreover, the number of instances for each subject for that particular emotion is also the same. Thus, no participant has more instances than the others for any emotion.

Balanced student instances and emotions were generated in each dataset (to be discussed in the next section) in order to avoid any bias in classifying emotions, which is a required data preparation step for Multi-Layered Perceptrons (MLP). MLPs require datasets to be balanced, otherwise the more MLP will tend to classify most instances as belonging to the most com-mon emotion, i.e. the emotion with the most number of instances.

In predicting academic emotions, perfor-mance measures such as Precision, Recall and F-Measure were used. Such measures were based on the computed True Positive (tp), False Positive (fp), True Negative (tn) and False Negative (fn). These are the standard metrics for MLP and Support Vector Machines (SVM).

Precision is the probability that a class A is true among all that have been classified as class A. This is also referred to as the Positive Predictive Value (PPV):

$$\text{Precision (P)} = \frac{tp}{(tp+fp)} \qquad (1)$$

Recall is the proportion of examples which were classified as class A among all instances of class A. This is also referred to as the True Positive Rate or Sensitivity:

$$\text{Recall (R)} = \frac{tp}{(tp+fn)} \qquad (2)$$

F-Measure is the combined computation of precision and recall. This is the harmonic mean of Precision and Recall in which both are evenly weighted:

$$\text{F-Measure (FM)} = \frac{(2 * \text{Precision} * \text{Recall})}{(\text{Precision} + \text{Recall})} \qquad (3)$$

These 3 performance measures were used to assess the performance of classification models, MLP and SVM. MLP is a feed-forward artificial neural network that can be trained in a supervised manner to map a given input set to output set (Haykin, 2008; Hornik, Stinchcombe

& White, 1989; Rumelhart, Hinton & Williams, 1986). The input-output mapping need not be known to the user, but numerous examples of the correct input-output pairs must be available so that the network can learn to make the proper association. It has been proven in Hornik, Stinchcombe, and White (1989) that MLPs are universal approximators – that is, some MLP can be trained to learn any mathematical function, possibly non-linear, between input and output sets, except that it is not known how many hidden units would be needed for every input-output mapping to be learned. In other words, any underlying mathematical function between input features and some set of output states or categories can be approximated by a MLP. Because the relationship between EEG signals and emotions is still largely unknown, the general approximation capability of MLPs is clearly attractive.

The SVM is also a universal constructive learning procedure that is based on the statistical learning theory (Vapnik, 1995). It is "universal" since it can be used to learn a variety of representations such as neural networks, radial basis functions, and so on (Cherkassky & Mulier, 2007). It has been shown to be a powerful classifier that has the statistical basis for arriving at optimal hyperplanes that would separate the data into their respective categories (Cherkassky

& Mulier, 2007). An SVM model provides a representation of data points in space that are mapped so that the examples of the separate categories are divided by a clear gap that is as wide as possible. Indeed, some initial results on emotional assessment are reported to have been based on SVM (Chanel, 2009).

WEKA, a machine learning tool for feature classification (Hall et al., 2009), was used. Table 1 presents the performance of each model using a 10-fold cross validation technique for testing and validating the data. When using 10-fold cross validation, the training based on the train set and the classification based on the test set is run 10 times. For each of the 10 runs, the dataset is randomly partitioned in such a way that a sample is isolated as a test set (10% of the entire dataset), while the rest (90% of the entire dataset) are used for training. The sample test set is then replaced with a new sample set for the second iteration, and the remaining samples are used as training set. This is done 10 times per run, and the average performance for recall, precision, and f-measure are averaged over 10 runs. For MLP and SVM classifiers, this technique is the standard way of measuring classification performance.

Based on the results in Table 1, MLP seems to perform generally better than SVM particularly when brainwaves features are used in the

Table 1. Performance results of multi-layered perceptrons (MLP) and support vector machines (SVM)

Classifier	Dataset	Brainwaves Only			Mouse Only			Brainwaves + Mouse		
		P	R	FM	P	R	FM	P	R	FM
MLP	Confidence	0.48	0.38	0.42	0.33	0.17	0.23	0.54	0.49	0.51
	Excitement	0.54	0.55	0.54	0.33	0.3	0.31	0.58	0.63	0.6
	Frustration	0.54	0.5	0.52	0.32	0.21	0.25	0.6	0.57	0.59
	Interest	0.59	0.73	0.65	0.32	0.62	0.42	0.72	0.75	0.73
SVM	Confidence	0.27	0.15	0.2	0.3	0.21	0.25	0.35	0.25	0.29
	Excitement	0.42	0.45	0.43	0.19	0.01	0.01	0.41	0.41	0.41
	Frustration	0.37	0.36	0.36	0.32	0.51	0.39	0.44	0.4	0.42
	Interest	0.37	0.52	0.43	0.33	0.55	0.41	0.44	0.61	0.51

classification. In both cases, the classification performance has consistently increased when brainwaves features are complemented with mouse behavior information. It can also be observed that among the four emotions, whether using MLP or SVM, *interest* was predicted most accurately for all the 3 modalities. Using f-measure as the main basis for classification performance, the comparative performance show f-measures for brainwaves only of 0.43 for SVM and 0.65 for MLP, for mouse only of 0.41 for SVM and 0.42 for MLP, and for the combination of brainwaves and mouse, the f-measure is 0.51 for SVM and as high as 0.73 for MLP. This is a significant finding because *interest* may be highly correlated with engagement which is an essential factor for student motivation. Note that in the succeeding sections, we will see that the classification performance for all emotions would increase once we restrict the classification to only those instances when features values have been noted to be "special", in that they deviate in a major way from the rest of the feature values.

SELECTIVE PREDICTION

Six different datasets were formed based on the percentage of so-called feature "outliers" (Azcarraga et al., 2011c). Azcarraga et al. (2011c) considers some feature values to be "special", signifying that something caused to be distinct from the other features values. These special feature values are referred to as an "outlier" if they deviate by at least one standard deviation from the mean. To be precise, a feature value v_f is an "outlier" if it deviates from the mean μ_f by at least one standard deviation, denoted by σ_f, as defined in (4). Means and standard deviations are computed per feature and per subject/student. Figure 2 provides an illustration of outlier data points:

$$v_f > \mu_f + \sigma_f$$
$$v_f < \mu_f - \sigma_f \qquad (4)$$

Figure 2. A feature value is treated as special and is considered an "outlier" if it deviates in value by at least one standard deviation from the mean

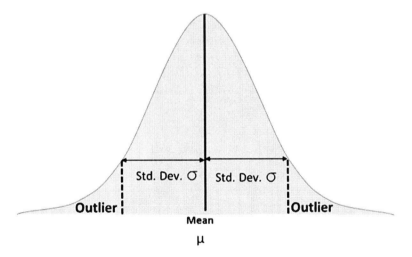

Feature values that are *outliers* for each instance are thus counted. Based on this number, different datasets were formed as described in Table 2. The full dataset (or Dataset 0) contains the instances from all the 16 subjects. Dataset 10 consists of only those instances where at least 10% of the feature values are outlier values. Dataset 25 consists of only those instances where at least 25% of the feature values are outlier values, and so on. Each dataset may contain multiple samples from a single subject.

Each dataset was balanced by ensuring that the number of instances for each emotion is the same. This is to avoid any bias that would severely affect the classification of MLP (This is not an issue for SVM). For Dataset 60, only 15 subjects were included since 1 subject did not have instances that had at least 60% outlier features.

For each dataset classification accuracy of each modality, whether brainwaves or mouse, as well as of their combination is analyzed using MLP and SVM models. The performance of the full dataset (Dataset 0) is shown in Table 1. As what was observed in Table 1, Table 3 also shows that even for the individual datasets, the same comparative performance results are observed when we compare the performance of each modality (i.e. mouse only, brainwaves only, and mouse plus brainwaves). Classification based on brainwaves sensor data was consistently and significantly better than when based on just the data from mouse behavior. The results of Table 3 which present the average for all the four emotions very clearly show that

the classification performance improves when data from both the EEG sensors and the mouse clicks are combined.

Using different datasets which are formed according to the number of outlier features, it is also very interesting to note that the results clearly show that the prediction accuracy increases when instances in a dataset have feature values that deviate significantly from their mean values of a given subject. It should be emphasized that such "outlier" feature values that deviate significantly from the mean baseline figure may indicate that the EEG is picking up something unusual or the mouse is being handled or clicked somewhat differently (Azcarraga et al., 2011c). The findings not only show that there are significant increase in the prediction accuracy when the predictions are made once outliers are detected. More importantly, the results clearly show that as the number of outliers increase (from 0% to 10% to 25%, to 33%, to 50%, to 60%), the prediction accuracy based on MLP systematically increases from 61% to 70% to 77% to 82% to 88% to 92%. The SVM results, although registering lower prediction accuracies, also show the very same trend. Figure 3(a) describes such trend.

Figure 3(a) and Table 3 clearly show that the classification performance increases for datasets composed of only instances that deviate (by at least one standard deviation) from the mean. As the datasets become more and more restrictive (10% outliers, 33% outliers, and so on), the classification performance also increases. There is clear evidence that when classification is at-

Table 2. Datasets for emotion classification

Dataset	No. of Outlier Features	No. of Students	No. of Instances per Emotion
Dataset 0	0 or more (0%)	16	3,600
Dataset 10	2 or more (10%)	16	2,250
Dataset 25	4 or more (25%)	16	650
Dataset 33	6 or more (33%)	16	325
Dataset 50	8 or more (50%)	16	260
Dataset 60	10 or more (60%)	15	165

Table 3. Average of all emotions for each dataset

Classifier	Dataset	Brainwaves Only			Mouse Only			Brainwaves + Mouse		
		P	R	FM	P	R	FM	P	R	FM
MLP	Dataset 0	0.53	0.54	0.53	0.33	0.33	0.3	0.61	0.61	0.61
	Dataset 10	0.65	0.64	0.64	0.38	0.38	0.35	0.7	0.7	0.7
	Dataset 25	0.75	0.75	0.75	0.42	0.44	0.43	0.77	0.77	0.77
	Dataset 33	0.79	0.79	0.79	0.46	0.46	0.46	0.82	0.82	0.82
	Dataset 50	0.86	0.86	0.86	0.46	0.44	0.44	0.88	0.88	0.88
	Dataset 60	**0.88**	**0.88**	**0.88**	**0.48**	**0.49**	**0.47**	**0.92**	**0.92**	**0.92**
SVM	Dataset 0	0.36	0.37	0.36	0.28	0.32	0.27	0.41	0.42	0.41
	Dataset 10	0.4	0.4	0.4	0.28	0.34	0.24	0.45	0.45	0.44
	Dataset 25	0.47	0.47	0.46	0.37	0.37	0.33	0.53	0.53	0.53
	Dataset 33	0.57	0.56	0.56	0.35	0.34	0.32	0.57	0.56	0.56
	Dataset 50	0.62	0.6	0.61	0.35	0.32	0.31	0.63	0.62	0.62
	Dataset 60	**0.65**	**0.65**	**0.64**	**0.24**	**0.31**	**0.26**	**0.66**	**0.65**	**0.65**

Figure 3. (a) Performance of MLP and SVM on different modalities for the different datasets that were generated based on the number of outlier values. As the number of outliers increases, the classification performance for both MLP and SVM also increases. (b) Performance of MLP and SVM on different modalities for all datasets with the same sample size (165 instances).

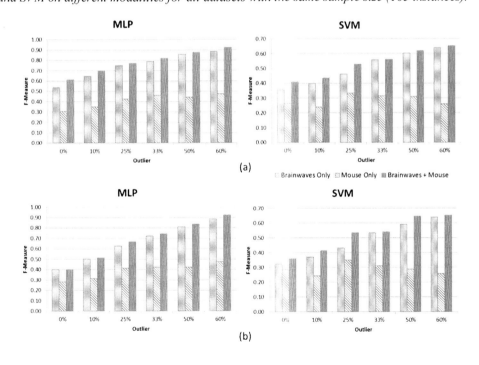

tempted at only those instances when a good number of the instances deviate "significantly" from the mean, then the performance would tend to increase. It can be said, however, that the sample sizes of these datasets vary, and the decreasing sample size might in fact be in the reason why the performance increases.

In general, we expect large sample sizes to give better performance rates, so it is quite unlikely that the smaller sample size of datasets 50 and 60, for example, is the reason why the classification performance rates for these datasets are higher. But just the same, in order to establish whether indeed it is the smaller sample size that causes the classification performance rates to increase, new datasets for 0%-50% outliers were generated having the same sample size as that of 60% outlier dataset. Since Dataset 60 (with 60% or more outliers) contains 165 instances, all the other datasets (0, 10, 25, 33, 50) were also randomly sampled so that each would also have 165 samples each. Note that each of the datasets still had all the 16 students, and the random sampling had to do with the selection of instances per student in order to have the uniform sample size of 165. Figure 3(b) shows the performance of MLP and SVM

on these datasets with uniform sample size. Table 4 presents the average of all emotions for such datasets. Both Figure 3(a) and Table 3 confirm the same results as Figure 3(b) and Table 4 – that the classification performance is better when restricted to a higher number of outliers. Note that as expected, the results for datasets 0, 10, 25, 33, and 50, in the case of the uniform sample size of 165, are lower than those when all the instances were included (i.e. larger sample sizes).

These findings have serious and important implications. The findings imply that in designing an affective learning system, the system should try to predict academic emotion only at those instances when many of the EEG signals deviate significantly from the baseline values or when the mouse is being handled or clicked somewhat differently. Otherwise, prediction may not be as dependable. In other words, it can be visualized that affective tutoring systems to be designed in the future may have physiological sensors (e.g. EEG, skin conductance, posture, heart rate), as well as tracking systems that monitor mouse usage, and other system-specific logs, so that when these sensors and tracking systems are picking up signals that are

Table 4. Average of all emotions for each dataset (same sample size as dataset 60)

Classifier	Dataset	Brainwaves Only			Mouse Only			Brainwaves + Mouse		
		P	R	FM	P	R	FM	P	R	FM
MLP	Dataset 0	0.40	0.40	0.40	0.29	0.31	0.28	0.40	0.40	0.40
	Dataset 10	0.50	0.50	0.50	0.33	0.35	0.32	0.51	0.52	0.51
	Dataset 25	0.63	0.63	0.63	0.42	0.42	0.41	0.67	0.67	0.67
	Dataset 33	0.73	0.72	0.72	0.47	0.45	0.42	0.74	0.74	0.74
	Dataset 50	0.81	0.81	0.81	0.42	0.45	0.42	0.84	0.84	0.83
	Dataset 60	**0.88**	**0.88**	**0.88**	**0.48**	**0.49**	**0.47**	**0.92**	**0.92**	**0.92**
SVM	Dataset 0	0.33	0.33	0.32	0.31	0.32	0.29	0.37	0.37	0.36
	Dataset 10	0.37	0.37	0.37	0.26	0.34	0.24	0.42	0.43	0.41
	Dataset 25	0.44	0.44	0.43	0.39	0.39	0.35	0.54	0.54	0.54
	Dataset 33	0.54	0.54	0.54	0.35	0.34	0.31	0.54	0.54	0.54
	Dataset 50	0.62	0.58	0.59	0.32	0.34	0.29	0.66	0.64	0.65
	Dataset 60	**0.65**	**0.65**	**0.64**	**0.24**	**0.31**	**0.26**	**0.66**	**0.65**	**0.65**

out of the ordinary, then the emotion prediction system can be launched in order to determine the academic emotion of the user.

Depending on the predicted emotion, the appropriate learning modules are then offered to the user. If the system, for example, determines that the learner is *confused*, but otherwise is still quite engaged, then modules that backtrack a little bit on the subject matter and that provide clarifications may then be presented. When the learner is determined to be *frustrated*, the level of difficulty of the learning task may be lowered, and a diagnostic system may be launched in order to understand better the source of errors so that appropriate remediation may be inserted in the learning session. Or, if the system starts to detect *boredom*, then perhaps the entire interface may be altered, or the nature of the learning task and activity may be altogether revised, such as shifting to a video presentation or animation-enriched tutorial, or a shift to paper-and-pencil drill, or even for the system to suggest "this might be a good time for a short break --- would you like to return in 5 minutes?".

Table 5 gives the details of the *precision*, *recall* and *f-measures* according to specific emotion category for MLP and SVM. The results, indeed, confirm the earlier findings reported in (Azcarraga et al.,, 2011c) which reported only performance measures using MLP. Prediction accuracy indeed increases as the number of outlier feature values increases. Moreover, the tables clearly show that the classification accuracy significantly improves when data from brainwaves and mouse behavior are combined. These conclusions can be made whether using MLP or SVM.

At this point, it is important to stress that as far as the current results are concerned, classifying academic emotions based only on mouse features seems to be ineffective. We were hoping that mouse behavior alone could give better prediction accuracies. Unfortunately, this was not the case. Perhaps there is a need to look for more pertinent mouse click features, or some more complex feature selection and feature transformation need to be done prior to feeding mouse click features for classification.

The results, however, clearly also indicate that when features based on mouse behavior are combined with brainwaves features, classification accuracy based on *F-Measure* significantly improve. Accuracy rates reach to 97% when brainwaves and mouse behavior data are combined in predicting *interest*. And accuracy is really higher for instances with many features (as much as 60%) have with outlier values (where outlier values means the value deviate more than one standard deviation from mean).

SUMMARY AND CONCLUSION

Twenty five (25) undergraduate students were asked to use a math learning software while an EEG sensor was attached to their heads to capture their brainwaves. At the same time, their mouse behavior, such as the number of clicks, duration of each click, and the distance traveled by the mouse, were also automatically captured. Brainwaves were carefully synchronized with the mouse behavior signals. During the experiment, each subject regularly reported the level of each emotion (*confidence, excitement, frustration* and *interest*). The self-reported emotion serves as the tag for the corresponding data point. From the 25 subjects, the data from only 16 were found to be useful due to some data balancing-related issues which are critical for classifying emotions using the MLP computational model.

Different datasets were generated according to the number of outlier features. A feature value is considered an *outlier* if it exceeds by one standard deviation from the mean of that particular feature and for that particular subject. Using MLP and SVM models in classifying *confidence, excitement, frustration* and *interest*, it is shown that the prediction accuracy based on f-measure increases significantly when instances in a dataset have increased number of

Table 5. Performance of MLP and SVM

Dataset	Emotion	Brainwaves Only			Mouse Only			Brainwaves + Mouse		
		P	R	FM	P	R	FM	P	R	FM
MLP										
Dataset 10	Confidence	0.55	0.58	0.56	0.28	0.21	0.24	0.6	0.61	0.61
	Excitement	0.66	0.64	0.65	0.41	0.17	0.24	0.69	0.68	0.68
	Frustration	0.67	0.58	0.62	0.42	0.38	0.4	0.69	0.69	0.69
	Interest	0.7	0.78	0.74	0.4	0.76	0.52	0.82	0.83	0.82
Dataset 25	Confidence	0.67	0.67	0.67	0.31	0.18	0.22	0.73	0.7	0.71
	Excitement	0.77	0.71	0.74	0.44	0.53	0.48	0.74	0.77	0.76
	Frustration	0.72	0.75	0.73	0.35	0.39	0.37	0.76	0.72	0.74
	Interest	0.84	0.87	0.86	0.59	0.67	0.63	0.84	0.9	0.87
Dataset 33	Confidence	0.78	0.72	0.75	0.39	0.31	0.35	0.76	0.79	0.78
	Excitement	0.71	0.83	0.76	0.37	0.39	0.38	0.78	0.86	0.82
	Frustration	0.77	0.73	0.75	0.39	0.41	0.4	0.83	0.71	0.76
	Interest	0.9	0.87	0.89	0.67	0.73	0.7	0.91	0.92	0.91
Dataset 50	Confidence	0.83	0.8	0.81	0.41	0.41	0.41	0.85	0.8	0.82
	Excitement	0.8	0.89	0.84	0.3	0.25	0.27	0.85	0.94	0.89
	Frustration	0.85	0.8	0.83	0.39	0.52	0.44	0.87	0.87	0.87
	Interest	0.94	0.93	0.94	0.73	0.57	0.64	0.94	0.89	0.91
Dataset 60	Confidence	0.84	0.82	0.83	0.55	0.36	0.44	0.93	0.84	0.89
	Excitement	0.85	0.83	0.84	0.29	0.25	0.27	0.87	0.96	0.91
	Frustration	0.89	0.89	0.89	0.55	0.59	0.57	0.94	0.91	0.93
	Interest	0.95	1	0.98	0.54	0.75	0.62	0.95	0.98	0.97
SVM										
Dataset 10	Confidence	0.37	0.31	0.34	0.38	0.02	0.04	0.44	0.25	0.32
	Excitement	0.39	0.37	0.38	0.03	0	0	0.41	0.37	0.39
	Frustration	0.38	0.44	0.41	0.34	0.71	0.46	0.44	0.59	0.5
	Interest	0.45	0.48	0.46	0.35	0.64	0.45	0.49	0.59	0.54
Dataset 25	Confidence	0.45	0.33	0.38	0.34	0.05	0.09	0.48	0.39	0.43
	Excitement	0.44	0.63	0.52	0.46	0.46	0.46	0.58	0.48	0.52
	Frustration	0.49	0.47	0.48	0.35	0.63	0.45	0.5	0.54	0.52
	Interest	0.51	0.44	0.47	0.33	0.33	0.33	0.57	0.73	0.64
Dataset 33	Confidence	0.51	0.5	0.51	0.38	0.14	0.2	0.49	0.5	0.49
	Excitement	0.52	0.44	0.48	0.32	0.26	0.29	0.54	0.44	0.48
	Frustration	0.49	0.6	0.54	0.34	0.71	0.46	0.49	0.59	0.53
	Interest	0.75	0.69	0.72	0.37	0.28	0.32	0.76	0.73	0.74

continued on following page

Table 5. Continued

Dataset	Emotion	Brainwaves Only			Mouse Only			Brainwaves + Mouse		
		P	R	FM	P	R	FM	P	R	FM
Dataset 50	Confidence	0.41	0.47	0.44	0.49	0.18	0.26	0.45	0.49	0.47
	Excitement	0.54	0.6	0.57	0.21	0.22	0.21	0.52	0.58	0.55
	Frustration	0.67	0.58	0.62	0.34	0.42	0.38	0.69	0.57	0.62
	Interest	0.86	0.74	0.8	0.34	0.47	0.39	0.86	0.82	0.84
Dataset 60	Confidence	0.67	0.51	0.58	0.33	0.23	0.27	0.63	0.66	0.64
	Excitement	0.51	0.62	0.56	0.29	0.56	0.38	0.57	0.58	0.57
	Frustration	0.63	0.52	0.57	0	0	0	0.49	0.5	0.5
	Interest	0.79	0.95	0.86	0.35	0.44	0.39	0.95	0.87	0.91

feature values that deviate significantly from the mean values of a given subject. These important findings imply that in designing an affective learning system, the system should try to predict academic emotion only at those instances when many of the EEG signals deviate significantly from the baseline values or when the mouse is being handled or clicked somewhat differently. Otherwise, prediction may not be dependable.

It can be imagined that in the future, affective tutoring systems would have physiological sensors (e.g. that monitor EEG, skin conductance, posture, heart rate), as well as tracking systems that monitor mouse usage, and other system-specific logs, so that when these sensors and tracking systems are picking up signals that are out of the ordinary, then the emotion prediction system can be launched in order to determine the academic emotion of the user. Depending on the predicted emotion, the appropriate learning modules are then offered to the user.

Moreover, the results clearly show that when combining the extracted features from EEG signals with mouse click behavior, the accuracy in predicting academic emotions is significantly better than when using only features extracted from EEG signals or just from mouse behavior alone. Future work would include the validation of the outlier detection approach on datasets with brainwaves features in the form

frequency waves (i.e. alpha, beta, gamma) and probably, with other features from system logs and user profile such as personality type, hand dominance and intelligence level.

REFERENCES

Arroyo, I., Cooper, D. G., Burleson, W., Woolf, B. P., Muldner, K., & Christopherson, R. M. (2009). Emotion sensors go to school. In V. Dimitrova, R. Mizoguchi, B. Du Boulay, & A. Graesser (Eds.), *Artificial intelligence in education* (Vol. 200, pp. 17–24). IOS Press.

Azcarraga, J., Ibañez, J. F., Jr., Lim, I. R., & Lumanas, N., Jr. (2011a, March). Predicting student affect based on brainwaves and mouse behavior. In *Proceedings of the 11th Philippine Computing Science Congress*, Naga City, Philippines.

Azcarraga, J., Ibañez, J. F., Jr., Lim, I. R., Lumanas, N., Jr., Trogo, R., & Suarez, M. T. (2011c). Predicting academic emotion based on brainwaves signals and mouse click behavior. In T. Hirashima et al., (Eds.), *Proceedings of the 19th International Conference on Computers in Education* (pp. 42-49). Chiang Mai, Thailand: Asia-Pacific for Computers in Education.

Azcarraga, J., Inventado, P. S., & Suarez, M. T. (2010). Predicting the difficulty level faced by academic achievers based on brainwaves analysis. In *the Proceedings of the 18th International Conference on Computers in Education* (pp. 107-109). Putrajaya, Malaysia: Asia-Pacific for Computers in Education.

Azcarraga, J. J., Ibañez, J. F., Jr., Lim, I. R., & Lumanas, N., Jr. (2011b). Use of personality profile in predicting academic emotion based on brainwaves signals and mouse behavior. In *the Proceedings of the 2011 Third International Conference on Knowledge and Systems Engineering* (pp. 239-244). Hanoi, Vietnam.

Burleson, W. (2006). *Affective learning companions: Strategies for empathetic agents with real-time multimodal affective sensing to foster meta-cognitive and meta-affective approaches to learning, motivation, and perseverance.* Unpublished Doctoral Dissertation, Massachusetts Institute of Technology.

Chanel, G. (2009). *Emotion assessment for affective computing based on brain and peripheral signals.* Unpublished Doctoral Dissertation. University of Geneva.

Cherkassky, V., & Mulier, F. (2007). *Learning from data: Concepts, theory, and methods* (2nd ed.). Hoboken, NJ: John Wiley & Sons, Inc. doi:10.1002/9780470140529.

D'Mello, S. K., & Graesser, A. (2009). Multimodal semi-automated affect detection from conversational cues, gross body language, and facial features. *User Modeling and User-Adapted Interaction, 20*(2), 147–187. doi:10.1007/s11257-010-9074-4.

Davidson, R. J., Ekman, P., Saron, C. D., Senulis, J. A., & Friesen, W. V. (1990). Approach-withdrawal and cerebral asymmetry: emotional expression and brain physiology. *Journal of Personality and Social Psychology, 58*(2), 330–341. doi:10.1037/0022-3514.58.2.330 PMID:2319445.

Ekman, P. (1984). Expression and the nature of emotion. In K. Scherer, & P. Ekman (Eds.), *Approaches to Emotion* (pp. 319–344). Hillsdale, NJ: Erlbaum.

Frantzidis, C. A., Bratsas, C., Klados, M. A., Konstantinidis, E., Lithari, C. D., & Vivas, A. B. et al. (2010). On the classification of emotional biosignals evoked while viewing affective pictures: An integrated data-mining-based approach for healthcare applications. *IEEE Transactions on Information Technology in Biomedicine, 14*(2), 309–318. doi:10.1109/TITB.2009.2038481 PMID:20064762.

Hall, M., Frank, E., Holmes, G., Pfahringer, B., Reutemann, P., & Witten, I. H. (2009). The WEKA data mining software: an update. *SIGKDD Explorations Newsletter, 11*(1), 10–18. doi:10.1145/1656274.1656278.

Haykin, S. (2008). *Neural networks and learning machines.* Upper Saddle River, NJ: Pearson Prentice Hall.

Heraz, A., Jraidi, I., Chaouachi, M., & Frasson, C. (2009). Predicting stress level variation from learner characteristics and brainwaves. In V. Dimitrova, R. Mizoguchi, B. Du Boulay, & A. C. Graesser (Eds.), *Artificial intelligence in education* (Vol. 200, pp. 722–724). Brighton, UK: IOS Press.

Heraz, A., Razaki, R., & Frasson, C. (2007). Using machine learning to predict learner emotional state from brainwaves. In *the Proceedings of the Seventh IEEE International Conference on Advanced Learning Technologies,* (pp. 853-857). IEEE Computer Society.

Hornik, K., Stinchcombe, M., & White, H. (1989). Multilayer feedforward networks are universal approximators. *Neural Networks, 2*(5), 359–366. doi:10.1016/0893-6080(89)90020-8.

Ibanez, J. F., Jr., Lim, I. R., & Lumanas, N., Jr. (2011). *Affect recognition using brainwaves and mouse behaviour for intelligent tutoring systems.* Unpublished Undergraduate Thesis. De La Salle University, Manila, Philippines.

Kaklauskas, A., Zavadskas, E. K., Seniut, M., Dzemyda, G., Stankevic, V., & Simkevicius, C. et al. (2011). Web-based biometric computer mouse advisory system to analyze a user's emotions and work productivity. *Engineering Applications of Artificial Intelligence, 24*(6), 928–945. doi:10.1016/j.engappai.2011.04.006.

Kapoor, A., Burleson, W., & Picard, R. (2007). Automatic prediction of frustration. *International Journal of Human-Computer Studies, 65*(8), 724–736. doi:10.1016/j.ijhcs.2007.02.003.

Nicaud, J.-F., Bouhineau, D., & Huguet, T. S. Cerri, G. Gouardères, & F. Paraguaçu (Eds.), Lecture notes in computer science: Vol. 2363. *(n.d.). The aplusix-editor: A new kind of software for the learning of algebra* (pp. 178–187). Berlin/Heidelberg, Germany: Springer.

Pekrun, R., Goetz, T., Titz, W., & Perry, R. P. (2002). Academic emotions in students' self-regulated learning and achievement: A program of qualitative and quantitative research. *Educational Psychologist, 37*(2), 91–105. doi:10.1207/S15326985EP3702_4.

Rumelhart, D. E., Hinton, G. E., & Williams, R. J. (1986). Learning internal representations by error propagation. In D. E. Rumelhart, & J. L. McClelland (Eds.), *Parallel distributed processing* (Vol. 1, pp. 318–362). MIT Press.

Sanei, S., & Chambers, J. A. (2007). EEG signal processing. West Sussex, UK: John Wiley & Sons, Ltd.

Scheirer, J., Fernandez, R., Klein, J., & Picard, R. W. (2001). Frustrating the user on purpose: A step toward building an affective computer. *Interacting with Computers*, *14*(2), 93–118. doi:10.1016/S0953-5438(01)00059-5

Stevens, R., Galloway, T., & Berka, C. (2007). EEG-related changes in cognitive workload, engagement and distraction as students acquire problem solving skills. In C. Conati, K. McCoy, & G. Paliouras (Eds.), User modeling 2007, 4511, 187–196. Springer.

Tomarken, A. J., Davidson, R. J., Wheeler, R. E., & Doss, R. C. (1992). Individual differences in anterior brain asymmetry and fundamental dimensions of emotion. *Journal of Personality and Social Psychology*, *62*(4), 676–687. doi:10.1037/0022-3514.62.4.676 PMID:1583591

Vapnik, V. N. (1995). *The nature of statistical learning theory*. New York, NY: Springer. doi:10.1007/978-1-4757-2440-0

Zimmermann, P., Guttormsen, S., Danuser, B., & Gomez, P. (2003). Affective computing--a rationale for measuring mood with mouse and keyboard. *International Journal of Occupational Safety and Ergonomics*, *9*(4), 539–551. PMID:14675525

Judith Azcarraga is studying towards a PhD in Computer Science student at the College of Computer Studies of De La Salle University (DLSU), in Manila, Philippines. Under a scholarship from the PCIEERD of the Department of Science and Technology, she is conducting her research at DLSU's Center for Empathic-Human Computer Interactions. Her doctoral thesis is on the recognition of academic emotions of intellectually-gifted students based on the pattern of their brainwaves, mouse behavior and their personality profile. She has been working on learning systems for children since her undergraduate thesis and Master's thesis. She has been an instructor at the College of Computer Studies of DLSU and a TAFE school in Singapore.

Merlin Teodosia Suarez is an Associate Professor of Computer Science at the College of Computer Studies of De La Salle University (DLSU), in Manila, Philippines. She heads the DLSU's Center for Empathic-Human Computer Interactions. She obtained her PhD from DLSU. Her dissertation investigated how a bug library for novice Java programmers can be built automatically using machine learning techniques. She serves as a member of the Department of Science and Technology's PCIEERD Technical Panel on Information and Communications Technology. She organized the 1st and 2nd International Workshop on Empathic Computing (IWEC-10 and IWEC-11) as their co-chairs. She is in the steering committee for the International Workshop on Empathic Computing (IWEC).

Towards Computational Fronesis:
Verifying Contextual Appropriateness of Emotions

Michal Ptaszynski, High-Tech Research Center, Hokkai-Gakuen University, Sapporo, Hokkaidō, Japan

Pawel Dybala, Department of Information and Management Science, Otaru University of Commerce, Sapporo, Hokkaidō, Japan

Michal Mazur, Graduate School of Information Science and Technology, Hokkaido University, Sapporo, Hokkaidō, Japan

Rafal Rzepka, Graduate School of Information Science and Technology, Hokkaido University, Sapporo, Hokkaidō, Japan

Kenji Araki, Graduate School of Information Science and Technology, Hokkaido University, Sapporo, Hokkaidō, Japan

Yoshio Momouchi, Department of Electronics and Information Engineering, Faculty of Engineering, Hokkai-Gakuen University, Sapporo, Hokkaidō, Japan

ABSTRACT

This paper presents research in Contextual Affect Analysis (CAA) for the need of future application in intelligent agents, such as conversational agents or artificial tutors. The authors propose a new term, Computational Fronesis (CF), to embrace the tasks included in CAA applied to development of conversational agents such as artificial tutors. In tutor-student discourse it is crucial that the artificial tutor was able not only to detect user/student emotions, but also to verify toward whom they were directed and whether they were appropriate for the context of the conversation. Therefore, as the first task in CF the authors focus on verification of contextual appropriateness of emotions. They performed some of the first experiments in this task for the Japanese language and discuss future directions in development and implications of Computational Fronesis.

Keywords: Affect Analysis, Applied E-Learning, Artificial Intelligence, Computational Fronesis (CF), Computational Linguistics, Contextual Affect Analysis (CAA)

DOI: 10.4018/jdet.2013040102

INTRODUCTION

In recent years there has been a major development in distant education technologies, such as E-learning, Online learning, Computer-based learning (CBL) or Technology-enhanced learning (TEL). In general E-learning aims at supporting or replacing usual classroom education with the use of modern information and communication technology. It is estimated that the E-learning industry has grown to be worth over 27 billion dollars (Ontario Media Development Corporation, 2010) and is estimated to exceed 100 billion in 2015 (Global Industry Analysts, 2010). It has also gained on popularity among students, who prefer E-learning courses to the usual courses in 25% of cases (Allen & Seaman, 2008).

One kind of E-learning is a virtual classroom lead either by a human teacher or, most recently, by an artificial tutor. These can be realized in Virtual Learning Environments (VLE), created on the basis of chat-rooms, either through text-based communication, or with the support of voice and online presentations. There have been also attempts to use virtual worlds, such as Second Life as a base for VLE (Redecker, 2009).

In such virtual classrooms a great role is assigned to knowledge acquisition through social interaction. Contrary to usual classroom scenario, where a teacher stands before students, gives a lecture and asks the students questions, VLE offer a kind of learning that is more interactive and emotionally engaging for students. Learning through conversation (Laurillard, 1993; Laurillard, 1999) with regards to students' emotional engagement (Baath, 1982) are thus two important issues in E-learning. These two issues have lead us in this research. We focused on supporting conversational artificial tutors with knowledge on user emotions. In particular we developed a method for context aware emotion recognition to be applied in such tutors. The method is responsible to verify whether emotions expressed by human users are appropriate to the context of conversation.

The outline of this paper is as follows. First we present the background for this research. We then describe the fields of Artificial Tutors (AT) development, and Contextual Affect Analysis (CAA). Afterwards, we also propose a novel term "Computational Fronesis" embracing the tasks of supporting AT with CAA. Followed by a section in which we describe previously developed tools applied in the research. Next we describe the method for verifying whether the emotions expressed in conversations are appropriate to the context of the situation. The two sections after contain descriptions of the design of evaluation experiment and its results, respectively. Then we present a discussion on further implication of context aware Affect Analysis. Finally, we conclude the paper and propose some ideas to improve the described method and point out some of the possible future applications.

BACKGROUND

Artificial Tutors

The research on artificial tutors is a relatively new field. Several artificial tutors have been developed in the form of non-task oriented conversational agents for second language acquisition (Jia, 2009); Tatai, Csordas, Kiss, Szalo, & Laufer, 2003; Stewart & File, 2007). In such research the pedagogical conversational agent/tutor assists students and provides a support to their learning efforts. In particular, Fryer et al. recently assessed the usefulness of chatterbots as language learning tools (Fryer & Carpenter, 2006).

There have been several VLE incorporating conversational agents to pedagogical tasks. CSIEC (Computer Simulation in Educational Communication) is an Artificial Intelligence (AI) framework developed at Peking University (Jia, 2009). It provides learners with a chatting partner for educational purposes. However, it deals with some problems regarding the ability to understand and generate natural language caused by textual ambiguity. *Let's Chat* is a prototype of a computer dialogue system allowing students to practice second language in social situations (Stewart & File, 2007). However, it uses only pre-stored utterances, so conversation topics in the dialogue system are significantly limited. A conversational language tutor in the form of an AI chatterbot CLIVE was presented by Zakos et al. (2008). CLIVE accepts input messages in two languages and thereby allows learning also for students with a limited knowledge of the second language.

Recently it has been noticed that equipping artificial tutors with knowledge on user/student emotions improves the overall impression of artificial tutors. Especially Florea (1999) and Florea and Kalisz (2005) proposed an artificial tutor integrated in an e-learning environment. The tutor develops lecture plans and tailors its behavior according to student's affective states. Vincente and Pain (2002) showed later that the recognition of emotions applied in artificial tutors can be useful in predicting students' motivation.

However, to guide the students appropriately, an artificial tutor, needs to have more than the ability to recognize emotions. For example, it needs to be able to detect toward whom an emotion is directed. The tutor also needs to have an ability to discriminate whether the expressed emotion is appropriate for the moment, or the context of conversation. In this paper we address this particular issue with regards to Japanese language speaking conversational agents.

Contextual Affect Analysis

Text based Affect Analysis (AA) has been defined as a field focused on developing natural language processing techniques for estimating the emotive aspect of text (Grefenstette, Qu, Shanahan, & Evans, 2004). For example, Elliott (1992) proposed a keyword-based Affect Analysis system applying an affect lexicon (including words like "happy", or "sad") with intensity modifiers (words like "extremely", "somewhat"). Liu et al. (2003) presented a model of text-based affect sensing based on

OMCS (Open-Mind Common Sense), a generic common sense database, with an application to e-mail interpretation. Alm et al. (2005) proposed a machine learning method for affect analysis of fairy tales. Aman and Szpakowicz also applied machine learning techniques to analyze emotions expressed on blogs (Aman & Szpakowicz, 2007).

There have also been several attempts to achieve this goal for the Japanese language. For example, Tsuchiya et al. (2007) tried to estimate emotive aspect of utterances with a use of an association mechanism. On the other hand, Tokuhisa et al. (2008) and Shi et al. (2008) used a large number of examples gathered from the Web to estimate user emotions. Furthermore, Ptaszynski et al. (2009a) proposed a Web-based supported affect analysis system for Japanese text-based utterances.

Research on emotions in the fields of Artificial Intelligence and Natural Language Processing, like the ones described above has flourished rapidly through several years. Unfortunately, in much of such research contextuality of emotions is disregarded. Based only on behavioral approaches, methods for emotion recognition ignore the context of emotional expression. Therefore, although achieving good results in laboratory conditions, such methods are often inapplicable in real world tasks. For example, a system for recognition of emotions from facial expressions, assigning "sadness" when user is crying would be critically mistaken if the user was, e.g., cutting an onion in the kitchen. Similarly in language, not including con text in the processing could lead to various processing errors. For example, one can consider a system detecting happiness when user uses a word "happy". The system would be critically mistaken if the user actually said: "I'm not happy at all!". This shows that not considering at least grammatical context in the processing causes erroneous detection of opposite emotion. However, a deeper problem appears when the user said something like "I would be so happy if that bastard was hit by a car!". Here a grammatical context does not suffice correct processing and deeper context is required in the processing. As the above examples show, recognizing emotions without recognizing their context is incomplete and cannot be sufficient for real-world applications.

Processing the context of emotions, or Contextual Affect Analysis (CAA) (Ptaszynski, Dybala, Shi, Rzepka, & Araki, 2009b; Ptaszynski, Dybala, Shi, Rzepka, & Araki, 2009c; Ptaszynski, Dybala, Shi, Rzepka, & Araki, 2009d; Ptaszynski, Dybala, Shi, Rzepka, & Araki, 2010; Zhang, 2010a; Zhang, 2010b; Zhang, 2011a; Zhang, 2011b; Zhang, 2011), is a newly recognized field. During its fifteen years of history, research on computer processing of emotions, or Affective Computing (Picard, 1997), was in great part focused on the recognition of expressions of user emotions. However, little research addressed the need for computing the context of the expressed emotions. In the age of information explosion, with an easy access to very large sources of data (such as the Internet), the time has come to finally address this burning need. Our research is focused on only one type of emotion processing, affect analysis of text. The future challenge will be to develop methods for processing the context in more general meaning, making the machines aware of the sophisticated environment humans live in. It has been shown that CAA is a feasible task, although much research in this matter needs to be done in the near future. In this paper, we focused in particular on applying context processing to text-based affect analysis. We did this in two ways.

Firstly, one of the common problems in the keyword-based systems for affect analysis is confusing the valence of emotion types, since the emotive expression keywords are extracted without their grammatical context. An idea aiming to solve this problem is the idea of Contextual Valence Shifters (CVS), words and phrases like "not", or "never", which change the valence of an emotion (positive/negative). As the first step towards contextual processing of emotions we applied CVS as a supporting procedure for affect analysis system for Japanese.

Secondly, we have developed a method making use of the wider context an emotion is expressed in. The method, using a Web mining technique, determines, whether the expressed emotion is appropriate for its context. It introduces an idea of Contextual Appropriateness of Emotions to the research on emotion processing. This idea adds a new dimension in emotion recognition, since it assumes that both positive and negative emotions can be appropriate, or inappropriate, depending on their contexts. The method is based on the assumption that the Internet can be considered as a database of experiences people describe on their homepages or weblogs. Since the context of emotions is formulated through collecting experiences, these experiences could be as well "borrowed" from the Internet (Rzepka & Araki, 2007).

In conclusions to this paper we present a discussion on future directions and applications of context processing within Affective Computing. We also propose a term, Computational Fronesis, to embrace the tasks related to Contextual Affect Analysis with regards to conversational artificial agents-companions, and artificial tutors in particular.

Computational Fronesis

Fronesis (often also spelled as *phronesis* or *phronēsis*), from Greek φρόνησις is a word originally used in Ancient Greek in the meaning of "practical wisdom" or "practical judgment" (sometimes also translated as "prudence"). The concept of fronesis is explained by Aristotle in *Nicomachean Ethics* (Aristotle, 1999). Aristotle defines it as practical judgment used to make good decisions according to a situation or context. He distinguishes *fronesis* from *techne*, which is a specific/expert knowledge and *sophia* ("theoretical wisdom"). Where *sophia* can be acquired by pure study/learning, and *techne* can be acquired by practice of some specific tasks, *fronesis* is a knowledge about everyday matters that can be acquired only by experience. This includes behaving appropriately to the occasion, although not always in a self-controlled and patient way. Rather the reaction, whether it is calm or explosive, respectful and modest or contemptuous and looking down on somebody, should be chosen according to the other person's behavior, their status and the overall situation. Solomon (1993) in his treaty on emotions and intelligence gives a number of examples for *fronesis*. For example, one could get angry at someone for making a fool of him in front of other people. However, if the person has significantly higher status (e.g., one's boss or supervisor), expressing the anger could end in losing a job. In such situation getting angry instead at ones children or pets is inappropriate. On the other hand, if the insult was said by a person of equal status (a colleague), the anger should be expressed reasonably. However, if the insulting person is of lower status (a subordinate), it is appropriate not only to react with great anger, but the anger should be expressed together with contempt and a lesson should be given to the person breaking the social rules. Moreover, if one does not react in this appropriate way, one could even be perceived as a fool (a person lacking *fronesis*). Therefore *fronesis* with regards to emotions is a kind of "good judgment", including knowledge on how to express ones emotions, towards whom they ought to be expressed, in which situations, and when it is appropriate to express them.

When it comes to artificial tutors interacting with human users, or conversational agents in general, it is often argued that these should be aware of their social role. Therefore, we find proposing a computational model of fronesis not only important, but crucial to the task of creating a fully socialized artificial tutor with human-like behavior. Therefore we propose a term "Computational Fronesis" (CF) as a general notion to deal with all kinds of contextual information in the research on Affect Analysis and computer processing of emotions in general. In particular, we propose an initial set of tasks in form of research questions below[1]:

1. Who expresses the emotion?
2. Why they express the emotion?

3. Is the expression of emotion appropriate to the situation/context?
4. Is the degree of expression appropriate to the situation/context?
5. If the expression is not appropriate, what would be the appropriate one?

These initial five questions can be put in a form of abilities or tasks, such as the ones below, respectively:

1. Determination of emotion subject;
2. Determination of emotion object;
3. Verification of contextual appropriateness of emotions;
4. Verification of appropriateness of the degree/intensity of the expressed emotion;
5. Emotion-related behavioral pattern modeling.

In this paper we focus on task III..We address task I. (Dokoshi, Oyama, Kurihara, Ptaszynski, Rzepka, & Araki, 2011) and II. (Ptaszynski, Dybala, Rzepka, Araki, & Momouchi, 2012; Ptaszynski, Rzepka, Araki, & Momouchi, 2012) in a different research. In the future we plan to address the two other tasks (verification of appropriateness of emotion intensity and behavioral pattern modeling) as well.

AFFECT ANALYSIS TOOLS

In this section we describe all tools and methods for basic AA used further in CAA tasks.

Emotive Expression Dictionary

Emotive Expression Dictionary (Nakamura, 1993) is a dictionary developed by Akira Nakamura in a period of over 20-year time. It is a collection of over two thousand expressions describing emotional states collected manually from a wide range of literature. It is not a tool per se, but was converted into an emotive expression database by Ptaszynski et al. (2009a; 2009) in their research on affect analysis of utterances in Japanese. In our task we needed to choose a lexicon proved to be the most appropriate for the Japanese language. Nakamura's dictionary is a state-of-the art example of a handcrafted lexicon of emotive expressions. It also proposes a classification of emotions that reflects the Japanese language and culture the most appropriately. In particular, Nakamura proposes ten emotion types: 喜 ki/yorokobi[2] (joy, delight; later referred to as *joy*), 怒 dō/ikari (anger), 哀 ai/aware (sorrow, sadness, gloom; later referred to as *sadness*), 怖 fu/kowagari (fear), 恥 chi/haji (shame, shyness, bashfulness; later referred to as *shame*), 好 kō/suki (liking, fondness; later referred to as *fondness*), 厭 en/iya (dislike, detestation; later referred to as *dislike*), 昂 kō/takaburi (excitement), 安 an/yasuragi (relief), and 驚 kyō/odoroki (surprise, amazement; later referred to as *surprize*). This classification is also applied in the lexicon itself. All expressions are classified as representing a specific emotion type, one or more if applicable. The distribution of separate expressions across all emotion classes is represented in Table 1.

A frequent manner in text-based Affect Analysis research is applying a list of emotion classes based on other modalities than linguistic, such as face recognition, or simply creating a new class list for the need of a particular research (see for example comparison of emotion class standards in Ptaszynski, Dybala, Rzepka, Araki, and Momouchi (2012)). In our research we aimed at contributing to the standardization of emotion class list in the language based research on emotions in Japanese. Therefore we selected

Nakamura's emotion type list, developed for over 20 years, as the most appropriate for our research.

ML-Ask

ML-Ask, or *eMotive eLement and expression Analysis system* is a keyword-based language-dependent system for automatic affect annotation on utterances in Japanese constructed by Ptaszynski et al. [24, 42]. It uses a two-step procedure:

1. Specifying whether an utterance is emotive; and
2. Recognizing the particular emotion types in utterances described as emotive.

ML-Ask is based on the idea of two-part classification of realizations of emotions in language into:

1. *Emotive elements* or *emotemes*, which indicate that a sentence is emotive, but do not detail what specific emotions have been expressed. For example, interjections such as "whoa!" or "Oh!" indicate that the speaker (producer of the utterance) have conveyed some emotions. However, it is not possible, basing only on the analysis of those words, to estimate precisely what kind of emotion the speaker conveyed. Ptaszynski et al. (2009) include in emotemes such groups as interjections, mimetic

Table 1. Distribution of emotive expressions across emotion classes in Nakamura's dictionary, ordered by the number of expressions per class

Emotion Class	Number of Expressions	Emotion Class	Nunber of Expressions
dislike	532	fondness	197
excitement	269	fear	147
sadness	232	surprise	129
joy	224	relief	106
anger	199	shame	65
		sum	**2100**

expressions, vulgar language and emotive markers. The examples in Japanese are respectively: *sugee* (great! - interjection), *wakuwaku* (heart pounding - mimetic), *-yagaru* (syntactic morpheme used in verb vulgarization) and '!', or '??' (sentence markers indicating emotiveness). Ptaszynski et al. collected and hand-crafted a database of 907 emotemes. A set of features similar to what is defined by Ptaszynski et al. as emotemes has been also applied in other research on discrimination between emotive (emotional/subjective) and non-emotive (neutral/objective) sentences (Wiebe, Wilson, & Cardie, 2005; Aman & Szpakowicz, 2007; Wilson & Wiebe, 2005);

2. Emotive expressions are words or phrases that directly describe emotional states, but could be used to both express one's emotions and describe the emotion without emotional engagement. This group could be realized by such words as *aijou* (love - noun), *kanashimu* (feel sad, grieve - verb), *ureshii* (happy - adjective), or phrases such as: *mushizu ga hashiru* (to give one the creeps [of hate]) or *ashi ga chi ni tsukanai* (walk on air [of happiness]). As the collection of emotive expressions ML-Ask uses a database created on the basis of Nakamura's *Emotive Expression Dictionary* (Nakamura, 1993).

With these settings ML-Ask was proved to distinguish emotive sentences from non-emotive with a very high accuracy (over 90%) and to annotate affective information on utterances with a sufficiently high Precision (85.7% compared to human annotators), and satisfying, although not ideal Recall (54.7%) (Ptaszynski, Dybala, Shi, Rzepka, & Araki, 2009;(Ptaszynski, Dybala, Rzepka, & Araki, 2009). To improve the system performance we also implemented Contextual Valence Shifters.

The idea of Contextual Valence Shifters (CVS) was first proposed by Polanyi and Zaenen (2006). They distinguished two kinds of CVS: negations and intensifiers. The group of negations contains words and phrases like "not", "never", and "not quite", which change the valence (also called polarity or the semantic orientation) of an evaluative word they refer to. The group of intensifiers contains words like "very", "very much", and "deeply", which intensify the semantic orientation of an evaluative word. ML-Ask fully incorporates the negation type of CVS with a 108 syntactic negation structures. Examples of CVS negations in Japanese are structures such as: *amari -nai* (not quite-), *-to wa ienai* (cannot say it is-), or *-te wa ikenai* (cannot [verb]-). In this paper we compared the performance of ML-Ask with and without (baseline) CVS improvement, within the evaluation of the procedure for verification of emotion appropriateness. As for intensifiers, although ML-Ask does not include them as a separate database, most Japanese intensifiers are included in the emoteme database. The system calculates emotive value, which is interpretable as emotional intensity of a sentence. It is calculated as the sum of emotemes in the sentence. The performance of setting the emotive value was evaluated on 84% comparing to human annotators (Ptaszynski, Dybala, Shi, Rzepka, & Araki, 2009). Finally, the last distinguishable feature of ML-Ask is implementation of Russell's two dimensional affect space (Russell, 1980). It assumes that all emotions can be represented in two dimensions: the emotion's valence (positive/negative) and activation (activated/deactivated). An example of negative-activated emotion could be "anger"; a positive-deactivated emotion is, e.g., "relief". The mapping of Nakamura's emotion types on Russell's two dimensions proposed by Ptaszynski et al. (2009) was proved reliable in several research (Ptaszynski, Dybala, Shi, Rzepka, & Araki, 2009b; Ptaszynski, Dybala, Rzepka, & Araki, 2009; Ptaszynski, Maciejewski, Dybala, Rzepka, & Araki, 2010). The mapping is represented in Figure 1. An example of ML-Ask output is represented in Figure 2.

Figure 1. Mapping of Nakamura's classification of emotions on Russell's 2D space

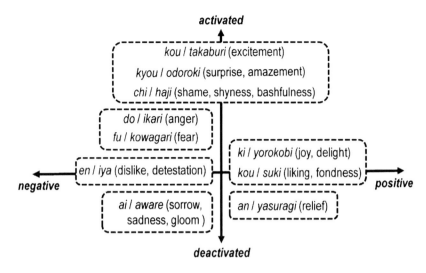

Figure 2. Output examples for ML-Ask and CAO

CAO

CAO, or *emotiCon Analysis and decOding of affective information system* is a system for estimation of emotions conveyed through emoticons[3] developed by Ptaszynski et al. (2010). Emoticons are sets of symbols widely used to convey emotions in text-based online communication, such as blogs. CAO extracts an emoticon from an input (a sentence) and determines specific emotion types expressed by it using a three-step procedure. Firstly, it matches the input to a predetermined raw emoticon database containing over ten thousand emoticons. The emoticons, which could not be estimated using only the database are automatically divided into semantic areas, such as representations of "mouth" or "eyes", basing on the idea of *kinemes*, or minimal meaningful body movements, from the theory of kinesics (Birdwhistell, 1952; Birdwhistell, 1970). The areas are automatically annotated according to their co-occurrence in the database. The annotation is firstly based on eye-mouth-eye triplet.

If no triplet was found, all semantic areas are estimated separately. This provides hints about potential groups of expressed emotions giving the system coverage of over 3 million possibilities. The performance of CAO was evaluated as close to 98% (Ptaszynski, Maciejewski, Dybala, Rzepka, & Araki, 2010) which proved CAO as a reliable tool for the analysis of Japanese emoticons. In the annotation process CAO was used as a supporting procedure in ML-Ask to improve the performance of the affect annotation system and add detailed information about emoticons appearing in the text. An example of CAO output is represented in Figure 2.

Web Mining Technique for Emotion Association Extraction

To verify the appropriateness of the speaker's affective states we applied Shi et al.'s (2008) Web mining technique for extracting emotive associations from the Web. Ptaszynski et al. (2009a) already showed that ML-Ask and Shi's technique are compatible and can be used as complementary means to improve the emotion recognition task. However, these two methods are based on different assumptions. ML-Ask is a language based affect analysis system and can recognize the particular emotion expression conveyed by a user. On the other hand, Shi's technique gathers from the Internet large number of examples and derives from this data an approximated reasoning about what emotion types usually associate with the input contents.

Therefore it is more reasonable to use the former system as emotion detector, and the latter one as a verifier of naturalness, or appropriateness of user emotions.

Shi's technique performs common-sense reasoning about which emotions are the most natural to appear in the context of an utterance, or in other words, which emotions should be associated with it. Emotions expressed, which are unnatural for the context (low or not on the list) are perceived as inappropriate. The technique is composed of three steps: 1) extracting context phrases from an utterance; 2) adding causality morphemes to the context phrases; 3) cross-referencing the modified phrases on the Web with emotive lexicon and extracting emotion associations for each context phrase.

Phrase Extraction Procedure

An utterance is first processed by MeCab, a tool for tokenization and part-of-speech analysis of Japanese (Kudo, 2001). Every element separated by MeCab is treated as a unigram. All unigrams are grouped into larger groups of n-grams preserving their word order in the utterance. The groups are arranged from the longest n-gram (the whole sentence) down to all groups of trigrams. N-grams ending with particles are excluded, since they gave too many ambiguous results in pre-test phase. An example of phrase extraction is presented in Table 2.

Table 2. Example of context n-gram phrases separation from an utterance. Grammar shortcuts: SUB = subject particle, GER = gerund, PRF = perfect form.

Original Utterance English Translation	Aa, pasokon ga kowarete shimatta... Darn, the PC has broken…					
Longest n-Gram	(1) *Aa*	*pasokon*	*ga*	*koware-*	*te*	*shimau*
(Here: Hexagram)	[interjection]	[noun]	[SUB]	[verb]	[GER]	[PRF]
Pentagram	(2) *pasokon ☐ga ☐koware ☐te ☐shimau*					
Tetragram	(3) *Aa, ☐pasokon ☐ga ☐kowareru*					
Trigrams	(4) *pasokon ☐ga ☐kowareru*			(5) *koware ☐te ☐ shimau*		

Morpheme Modification Procedure

On the list of n-gram phrases the ones ending with a verb or an adjective are then modified grammatically with causality morphemes. This is performed in line with linguistic argument that Japanese people tend to convey emotive meaning after causality morphemes (Yamashita, 1999). Shi et al. (2008) independently confirmed this argument experimentally. They distinguished eleven emotively stigmatized morphemes for the Japanese language using statistical analysis of Web contents and performed a cross reference of appearance of the eleven morphemes with the emotive expression database using the Google search engine. This provided the results (hit-rate) showing which of the eleven causality morphemes were the most frequently used to express emotions. For the five most frequent morphemes, the coverage of Web mining procedure still exceeded 90%. Therefore for the Web mining they decided to use those five ones, namely: -te, -to, -node, -kara and -tara (see Table 3). An example of morpheme modification is presented in Table 4.

Emotion Association Extraction Procedure

In this step the modified n-gram phrases are used as a query in Google search engine and 100 snippets for one morpheme modification per query phrase is extracted. This way a maximum of 500 snippets for each queried phrase is extracted. These are cross-referenced with emotive expression database (see Figure 3). The emotive expressions extracted from the snippets are collected, and the results for every emotion type are sorted in descending order. This way a list of emotions associated with the queried sentence is obtained. It is the approximated emotive commonsense used further as an appropriateness indicator. An example of emotive association extraction is shown in Table 5.

Blog Mining

The baseline of the Web mining method, using Google to search through the whole Web, was gathering a large amount of noise. To solve this problem we made two modifications. Firstly, we

Table 3. Hit-rate results for each of the eleven morphemes with the ones used in the web mining technique in bold font

Morpheme	-te	-node	-tara	-nara	-kotoga	-nowa
Result	41.97%	7.20%	5.94%	1.17%	0.35%	2.30%
Morpheme	-to	-kara	subtotal	-ba	-noga	-kotowa
Result	31.97%	6.32%	93.40%	3.19%	2.15%	0.30%

Table 4. Examples of n-gram modifications for web mining

Original n-Gram	pasokon ga koware te shimau	/causality morpheme/
n-gram phrase adjusting (morpheme modification)	*pasokon ga koware te shimat -te*	/ -te /
	pasokon ga koware te shimau -to	/ -to /
	pasokon ga koware te shimau -node	/ -node /
	pasokon ga koware te shimau -kara	/ -kara /
	...	...

Figure 3. Flow chart of the web mining technique

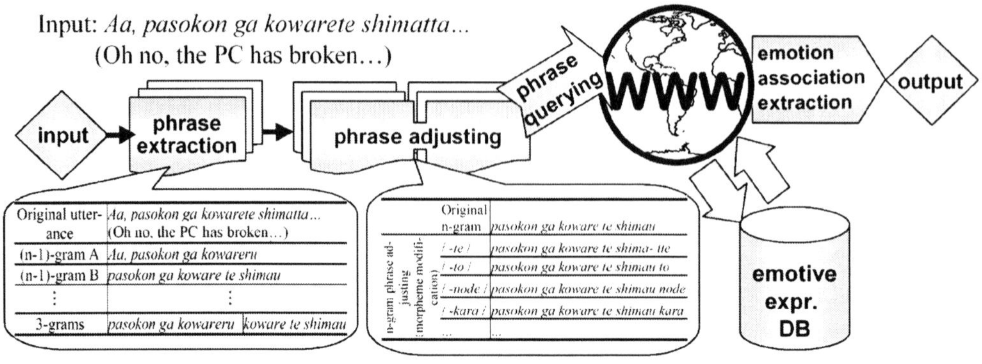

Table 5. Example of emotion association extraction from the web and its improvement by blog mining procedure

Sentence: *Konpyūta wa omoshiroi desu ne.* (Computers are so interesting.)				
Extracted Emotion Types	Baseline: Type Extracted / All Extracted Types (Ratio)	Extracted Emotion Types	Blogs: Type Extracted / All Extracted Types (Ratio)	
Fondness	79/284(0.287)	fondness	601/610(0.985)	
Surprise	30/284(0.105)	excitement	1/610(0.001)	[rejected
Excitement	30/284(0.105)	fear	1/610(0.001)	as
Fear	29/284(0.102)	relief	1/610(0.001)	noise]
...	...	...	...	

added a heuristic rule stopping the search if any emotions were found using the longer n-grams. This changed the method from Recall-oriented to Precision-oriented by assuring the extraction of only the closest emotive associations. It also speeds up the extraction process. Secondly, since, as mentioned before, people convey on blogs their opinions and emotions, we restricted the mining to blog contents to assure extraction of more accurate emotive associations. The blog mining procedure performs the query first on the public blogs from *Yahoo!Japan-Blogs[4]*. The paragraphs of each blog containing query phrases are co-referenced with emotive expression database to gather the emotive associations. If no information was gathered from the blog contents, the same search is performed with the baseline conditions - on the whole Web. An example of improvement is presented in Table 5.

METHOD FOR VERIFICATION OF CONTEXTUAL APPROPRIATENESS OF EMOTIONS

As one of the recent advances in affect analysis, it was shown that Web mining methods can improve the performance of language-based affect analysis systems (Tokuhisa, Inui, & Matsumoto, 2008; Shi, Rzepka, & Araki, 2008; Ptaszynski, Dybala, Shi, Rzepka, & Araki, 2008). However, in these methods, although the results of experiments appear to be positive, two extremely different approaches are mixed, the language/keyword based approach and the Web mining based approach. The former, in which the information provided by the user in input is matched to the existing lexicons and sets of rules, is responsible for recognizing the particular emotion expression conveyed by the user at a certain time. The latter one is based on gathering from the Internet large numbers of examples and derives from these an approximated reasoning about what emotions usually associate with certain contents. Using the Web simply as a complementary mean for the language based approach, although achieving reasonable results, does not fully exploit the potential lying in the Web (Rzepka & Araki, 2007).

Here we present a method utilizing these two approaches in a more effective way. The method is capable to analyze affect with regard to a context and estimate whether an emotion conveyed in a conversation is appropriate for the particular situation. In the method we used previously developed systems for affect analysis (ML-Ask and CAO described in the previous section). Next, we used a method for gathering emotive associations from the Web developed by Shi et al. (2008).

Furthermore, we checked several versions of the method to optimize its procedures. Firstly, we checked two versions of ML-Ask, with and without Contextual Valence Shifters. Secondly, we checked two versions of the Web mining technique, one performing the search on the whole Internet and the second one searching only through blogs.

Method Description

Affect Analysis

As the first step of the method for verification of contextual appropriateness of emotions, we used the two affect analysis systems described previously (ML-Ask and CAO). The affect analysis provides information on whether an utterance was emotive or not, and what type of emotion was expressed in the utterance. In a conversation between a user and an agent, the affect analysis is performed on each user utterance in user-agent conversation. For every emotive utterance with specified emotion type a Web mining technique is used as a verifier of emotion appropriateness.

Web Mining

In the second step a list of emotive associations is obtained from the Web. This is done with the use of the Web mining technique described previously. The list contains emotion types that associate with the sentence contents. The emotion types that correlate the most strongly appear on the top of the list. Emotion types with weaker correlations appear lower on the list. Emotion types that do not appear on the list at all are considered as the ones with no correlation with the sentence contents. As the rule of thumb we assumed that the emotion types appropriate for the sentence contents (or context in general) should appear in approximated 50% of all results. An example of such a list is represented in Table 5. It shows that when the Web mining is based on the whole Web, emotions considered as appropriate include fondness, and two more (surprise and excitement). However, when the Web mining is limited to blogs the emotion type extraction is more precise and the result (only fondness) is more accurate. Context phrases with less but frequent emotion types extracted are considered as more straightforward and unambiguous. Context phrases with numerous but less frequent emotion types are considered as more ambiguous.

Assessment and Verification of Contextual Appropriateness of Emotion

The final step is to use the two kinds of information (affect analysis and Web mining) in CAEV[5] procedure for assessing and verifying contextual appropriateness of the expressed emotions. The information obtained by affect analysis systems and the Web mining technique described above is combined as follows. When ML-Ask discovers an emotive utterance and the emotion types are successfully specified, the Web mining technique begins the process of verification of whether the expressed emotions are appropriate to be used in such context. The emotions commonly associated with the context of the utterance are extracted from the Web and the emotions reported by ML-Ask from the user utterances are compared to the Web mining results. If an emotion type detected by ML-Ask appears on the list of emotions frequently associated with the context (approx. 50% of the whole extracted list), the emotion expressed by the user is determined to be appropriate for the context. In such situations, a conversational agent equipped with this system could choose a dialog strategy that *sympathizes* with the user. Two hypothetical examples are presented below:

- Positive-appropriate emotion:
  - ◦ **User:** I'm so happy I passed the exam!
  - ◦ **ML-Ask:** joy; Web mining: joy, excitement
  - ◦ **Agent:** Yeah! That's great!
- Negative-appropriate emotion:
  - ◦ **User:** I hate him for making a fool of me in front of everyone.
  - ◦ **ML-Ask:** dislike; Web mining: anger, dislike
  - ◦ **Agent:** You have a reason to be angry.

However, if the verification procedure indicates that the expressed emotion is inappropriate for the context, the agent could undertake different measures, e.g., helping user manage his/her emotions, for example by changing the focus of the conversation from the object of emotion to the expressed emotion itself, or proposing an appropriate emotion. Two hypothetical examples are shown below:

- Positive-inappropriate emotion:
  - ◦ **User:** I'd be happy if that bastard was hit by a car!
  - ◦ **ML-Ask:** joy; Web mining: fear, sadness
  - ◦ **Agent:** Are you sure that is what you are really feeling?
- Negative-inappropriate emotion:
  - ◦ **User:** I won the prize, but I feel so bored.

- ◦ **ML-Ask:** dislike, depression; Web mining: excitement, joy
- ◦ **Agent:** You should be happy!

Two-Dimensional Model of Affect in CAEV Procedure

According to Solomon (1993), people sometimes misunderstand the specific emotion types, but they rarely misunderstand their generally perceived valence. One could, e.g., confuse anger with irritation, but not admiration with detestation. Therefore, we checked if at least the general features matched even when specific emotion types did not match perfectly with the emotive associations. By general features we refer to those proposed by Russell (1980) in the theory of the two-dimensional model of affect (valence and activation). Using the mapping of Nakamura's emotion types on Russell's model we checked whether the emotion types tagged by ML-Ask and CAO belonged to the same space, even if they did not perfectly match the emotive associations gathered from the Web.

EVALUATION EXPERIMENT

Initial Setting

To test the method, we performed an evaluation experiment on two non-task-oriented conversational agents. The first agent is a simple conversational agent which generates responses by 1) using Web-mining to gather associations to the content of user utterance; 2) making propositions by inputting the associations to the prepared templates; and 3) adding modality to the basic propositions to make the utterance more natural. The second agent, based on the first one, generates a humorous response to user utterance every third turn. The humorous response is a pun created by using user input as a seed to gather pun candidates from the Web and inputting the most frequent pun candidates into pun templates (for more detailed description of the agents see the sections below and the references). The choice of the agents was deliberate. They differed only in one feature - the humorous responses in the latter one. Humor processing is considered to be one of the most creative human activity and therefore difficult task in Artificial Intelligence (Boden, 1998). Therefore if appropriateness verification is done correctly, it should be easier to perform on the non-humor-equipped agent.

There were 13 participants in the experiment, 11 males and 2 females. All of them were university undergraduate students. The users were asked to perform a 10-turn conversation with both agents. No topic restrictions were made, so that the conversation could be as free and human-like as possible.

Two Conversational Agents: Short Description

Modalin is a non-task-oriented text-based conversational agent for Japanese. It automatically extracts from the Web sets of words related to a conversation topic set freely by a user in his utterance. The association words retrieved from the Web (with accuracy of over 80%) are then sorted by their co-occurrence on the Web, and the most frequent ones are selected to be used further in output generation. In the response generation, the extracted associations are put into one of the pre-prepared response templates. The choice of the template is random, but the agent keeps in its memory the last choice in order not to generate two similar sentence patterns in a row. Finally, the agent adds a modality pattern to the sentence and verifies its semantic reliability. The modality is added from a set of over 800 patterns extracted from chat-room logs. The naturalness of the final form of the response is then verified on the Web with a hit-rate threshold set arbitrary for 100 hits. The agent was developed by Higuchi and colleagues. For further details see Higuchi, Rzepka, and Araki (2008).

Pundalin is a non-task-oriented conversational agent for Japanese, created on the base of Modalin and combined with Dybala's Pun generating system PUNDA (Dybala,

Ptaszynski, Higuchi, Rzepka, & Araki, 2008). The system works as follows. From the user's utterance, a base word is extracted and transformed using Japanese phonetic pun generation patterns, to create a phonetic candidate list. The candidate with the highest hit-rate in the Japanese search engine Goo[6] is chosen as the most common word that sounds similar to the base word. Next, the base word and the candidate are integrated into a sentence. The integration is done in two steps, one for each part of the sentence including the base word and the pun candidate, respectively. Firstly, the base phrase is put into one of several pre-prepared templates making up the first half of the sentence. The second half of the sentence is extracted from KWIC on WEB - on-line Keyword-in-context sentence database (Yoshihira, Takeda, & Sekine, 2004) as the shortest latter half of an emotive sentence including the candidate. Every third turn of the conversation, Modalin's output was replaced by a joke-including sentence, generated by the pun generator. Pundalin therefore is a humor-equipped conversational agent using puns to enhance communication with the user. Pundalin was developed by Dybala and colleagues as a conversational agent for use in experiments on the influence of humor on human-agent interaction (Dybala, Ptaszynski, Higuchi, Rzepka, & Araki, 2008).

Overview of Conversations

As mentioned on the beginning of above sections, thirteen participants (11 males and 2 females) performed conversations with the agents. Each participant performed a 10 turn conversation with each of the two agents. Therefore each conversation consisted of 20 utterances. The order of which agent was the first to talk with the user was random. Since we assumed no topic restrictions, the conversations were usually small talks about weather, food or other casual topics. In the process of affect analysis only the utterances performed by human users were analyzed. In comparison with Pundalin, there were different emotional reactions to the presence of humorous responses. Some users actively engaged in the pun-generating game with the agent, which resulted in responses of positive emotional load. On the other hand, the users who did not find the jokes interesting tended to respond negatively. The emotion types that were expressed the most often across all conversations were: fondness, joy and dislike. Other emotions that appeared sporadically were sadness and fear. Positive emotions appeared more frequently in conversations with Pundalin than with Modalin. An example of conversation with one agent (Pundalin) is represented in Figure 4.

Experiment Design

In the experiment we used the chat logs of users with Modalin and Pundalin. All 26 conversations were analyzed by ML-Ask and CAO. Six out of all 26 conversations contained no specified emotional states and were excluded from further evaluation process. For the remaining conversations, among which 10 were with Modalin and 10 with Pundalin, the Web mining procedure was carried out to determine whether the emotions expressed by the user were contextually appropriate. We compared four versions of the method: 1) ML-Ask and Web mining baseline; 2) ML-Ask supported with CVS, Web mining baseline; 3) ML-Ask baseline and blog mining; 4) both improvements (affect analysis supported with CVS and blog mining). The difference in results appeared in 5 conversation sets (from the evaluated 20 sets). Then a questionnaire was designed to evaluate how close the results were to human thinking. One questionnaire set consisted of one conversation record and questions inquiring what were: 1) the valence (answer to the question: "Were the emotions expressed in this sentence positive or negative?" [choice of three: POS/NEG/Don't know]) and 2) the specific type of emotions conveyed in the conversation (answer to the question: "What was the specific emotion expressed in this sentence?" [free choice]), and 3) whether they were contextually appropriate (answer to the question: "Were the emotions

Figure 4. An example of conversation with one agent (Pundalin). Analyzed sentence underlined. Extracted emotive expression in bold type font. Grammatical errors translated to reflect errors in original conversation. Puns translated to represent puns in English as well.

Speaker	Utterance in Japanese	English Translation
User	*Iwate no jishin sugokatta mitai desu ne?*	The earthquake in Iwate was shocking, wasn't it?
Agent	*Iya, jishin ga sugoi desu kara*	Oh, earthquakes are shocking, you know
User	*Yamakuzure mo okite taihen sōdesu yo ne?*	It looks like there were landslides too, horrible isn't it?
Agent	*Iya, sore wa iyashii na*	Oh, its so mean
User	*Sodesu ka? Dono atari ga iyashii n desu ka?*	Really? Why do you think its mean?
Agent	*Kureyon wo ore ni katte kure yo n*	Don't cry on me, buy crayon for me
User	*Myakuraku ga nasasugi desu.*	That was just too silly.
Agent	*Sore wa omoshiroi tte*	But it was so funny
User	*Sore hodo **omoshiroku mo nakatta**desu yo.*	Well, it **wasn't** that **funny**.
Agent	*Kitai ga tsuyoidesu ka*	Maybe you had too strong expectations?
User	*Sore hodo tsuyoi sorehodo okina kitai wa motte inakatta n desu ga.*	I didn't have that strong that big expectations.
Agent	*Atama ga attamaru*	The head is heating up
User	*Tashika ni atama wa tsukau to omoimasu.*	Yes, I'm sure you use your head.
Agent	*Sore wa isogashii daro*	You must be busy
User	*Sorehodo demo nai desu yo.*	Not that much really.
Agent	*Sore wa takai to ka*	Is it high?
User	*Sonna koto nanno hanashi desu ka?*	What are you talking about?
Agent	*Idō ga ōi do*	It's your lot to move a lot!
User	*Yappari myakuraku naidesu.*	Yeah, you are silly.

appropriate for the context of the conversation? [choice of three: YES/NO/Don't know] If not, which emotion would be appropriate?" [free choice]). Every questionnaire set was filled by 10 people (undergraduate students, but different from the users who performed the conversations with the agents). This way we obtained 200 conversation sets as gold standard. The five conversation sets, where differences in results appeared for the different versions of the method, were compared to the gold standard separately. Therefore there were 20 questionnaire sets for the baseline method and additional 5 for the conversation sets in which results changed after improvements. With every questionnaire set filled by 10 human evaluators there were a total number of 250 different sets of results evaluated by different people.

For every conversation set we calculated how many of the human evaluators confirmed the system's results. The evaluated items were: A) specific emotion types determination; and B) general valence determination accuracies of affect analysis systems; and the accuracy of the method as a whole (affect analysis verified by Web mining) to determine the contextual appropriateness of C) specific emotion types and D) valence.

Evaluation Criteria

A common problem in emotion processing research is the number of evaluators employed in the evaluation process. In a third person evaluation, it is desirable to engage in the evaluation process as many evaluators as possible to get a wide view on the results, calculate an overall agreement and rectify potential errors. Unfortunately there has been no standard for a desirable number of evaluators. Often the evaluation is limited to, e.g., five people (Tsuchiya, Yoshimura, Watabe, & Kawaoka, 2007), three people (Endo, Saito, & Yamamoto, 2006) or even one (Tokuhisa, Inui, & Matsumoto, 2008). The evaluation with only one person, like in (Tokuhisa, Inui, & Matsumoto, 2008) assumes that if at least one person agrees with the system, the system has performed the evaluated

task on a human level. The evaluation criteria where three people are employed (Endo, Saito, & Yamamoto, 2006) usually assume that at least two people from the group of three must agree about the evaluated object. The problem becomes complicated with a larger number of evaluators. In the evaluation performed by Tsuchiya et al. (2007) there were five people employed in the evaluation. According to their explanations, a) if four or five people agreed with the system, the results were positive; b) if three or two people agreed with the system, the results were acceptable; c) if only one person or no person agreed with the system, the results were negative.

It can be easily noticed, that although the number of evaluators grows with the introduced approach, the general idea is that at least one person needs to agree with the system for the results to be positive (first approach), or the results are negative only in the case when one person or less from a larger group agree with the system (two latter approaches). These somewhat lenient conditions in evaluation of emotion processing-related systems comes from the fact that it is difficult to obtain a perfect agreement between people about emotion-related topics, since the cognition of emotions in people is highly subjective and context related.

Therefore we decided to look on the results from a more analytical point of view. In our research, apart from the 13 people who took part in conversations with the agents, we evaluated every questionnaire set 10 times. Then we checked how many people agreed with each other and with the results given by the system. Since every questionnaire set was evaluated 10 times, a number of agreements for each evaluated item (A-D) in all twenty evaluated cases could be from 0 (nobody agreed with the system) to 10 (all people agreed with the system). When comparing the four versions of the method described above, we assumed the better version of the system is the one which achieved more agreements with a larger number of evaluators. We took into the consideration all types of agreement conditions, from ideal (all

10 people agreed) to the smallest one (at least one person agreed with the system), similarly to the research described above. To visualize the results we named every level of agreement like in Table 6. Each level of agreement assumed that the results are positive if at least the specified number of evaluators agreed with the system. However, we focused the most on two of the ten agreement conditions. Firstly, since the idea of appropriateness is based on the rule of thumb, I checked how much of the cases could be considered as positive examples if at least half of the people (five) agreed. Secondly, as a more severe condition, I checked how much of the cases could be considered as correct examples if eight and more people (80%) agreed with the system. Moreover, to verify the strength of the agreements we independently calculated Fleiss' multi-rater kappa (Fleiss, 1971) between all human evaluators for all sets of the results.

RESULTS

We analyzed three aspects of the results. Firstly, we focused on evaluation of the affect analysis procedure. Although the two affect analysis systems were evaluated separately previously (Ptaszynski, Dybala, Shi, Rzepka, & Araki, 2009a; Ptaszynski, Dybala, Rzepka, & Araki, 2009; Ptaszynski, Maciejewski, Dybala, Rzepka, & Araki, 2010), there was no overall evaluation. This corresponds to items A) and B) investigated in the questionnaire. Secondly, we summarized the results of the CAEV procedure for all of the results considered together. This corresponds to items C) and D) investigated in the questionnaire. Finally, we analyzed the results separately for the two agents to check whether there were any differences between verifying the emotion appropriateness in a usual conversational agent (Modalin) and the joking agent (Pundalin).

Evaluation of Affect Analysis Procedure

The first part of the evaluation process consisted in evaluation of affect analysis procedure. The results were as follows. For all possible agreements of the system with the evaluators about the 20 evaluation sets (200 possible cases of agreement) baseline version of affect analysis obtained 110 (55%) agreements about determining emotion type and 126 (63%) agreements about determining valence. The strength of agreements in this setting was $\kappa=0.66$ and $\kappa=0.68$, respectively, which indicates substantial

Table 6. Criteria conditions and naming of the levels of agreements. Conditions of the highest interest are represented in bold type font.

Criteria Conditions	No. of People who had to Agree
ideal	all 10
rigorous	at least 9
grand majority	**at least 8**
fair	at least 7
weak majority	at least 6
medium	**at least 5**
optimistic	at least 4
easy	at least 3
lenient	at least 2
negligible	at least 1
no agreement	0

agreement for both sets according to Landis and Koch interpretation (Landis & Koch, 1977). As for the affect analysis procedure upgraded with CVS (ML-Ask last part of the procedure), there were 120 agreements (60%) for emotion types and 138 (68%) for valence determination. The strength of these sets of agreements was $\kappa=0.66$ and $\kappa=0.68$, respectively. As for the distribution of the agreements, most of the results for emotions types (over 50% of all actual agreements) were enclosed in a group where at least 8 people agreed with the system (grand majority conditions). Similarly, most of the results for valence were enclosed in a group where at least 9 people agreed with the system (nearly ideal, rigorous conditions). For the negligible condition ("at least one person"), often applied in other research, the results enclosed 100% of cases. However, ideal conditions (all agree) appeared from 18% to 29% of cases,

which shows that the negligible condition is far from objectivity. However, the grand majority of the results (over 80%) were enclosed in a group where at least 6 people agreed with the system. The conditions including medium (at least 5 people) and more relaxed conditions enclosed from nearly 90% and above. The results are represented in Table 7. Visualization of the distribution of agreements for both versions of affect analysis procedure is represented on Figure 5 (for emotion type determination) and Figure 6 (for valence determination).

Evaluation of CAEV Procedure: General

Secondly we checked the results for the determination of emotion appropriateness by the CAEV procedure. The results were as follows. For all possible agreements of the system with

Table 7. Results for evaluation of affect analysis procedure. Upper part of the table: results for specifying emotion types; Lower part: results for specifying valence. The table represents numbers of people who agreed with the system. Distribution of numbers shows how many there were agreements with how many people;%of all: shows percentage of this group of agreements within all agreements;%sums: shows percentage of results applicable when the condition for agreement was set as "at least this group of agreements (or higher)"; agr.ratio: overall number of agreements divided by ideal number of agreements and ratio; kappa: multi-rater kappa, or inter-rater agreement coefficient, representing the strength of agreements in this setting.

A) TYPES	Number of people who agreed with the system											agr.ratio (kappa)
	10	9	8	7	6	5	4	3	2	1	0	
baseline	2	0	5	2	3	1	2	1	0	2	2	110/200
% of all	18%	0%	36%	13%	16%	5%	7%	3%	0%	2%	0%	55%
% sums	18%	18%	55%	67%	84%	88%	95%	98%	98%	100%	100%	(κ= 0.66)
cvs	3	0	5	2	3	1	2	1	0	2	1	120/200
% of all	25%	0%	33%	12%	15%	4%	7%	3%	0%	2%	0%	60%
% sums	25%	25%	58%	70%	85%	89%	96%	98%	98%	100%	100%	(κ= 0.66)

B) VALENCE	Number of people who agreed with the system											agr.ratio (kappa)
	10	9	8	7	6	5	4	3	2	1	0	
baseline	3	4	2	1	2	3	0	2	2	0	1	126/200
% of all	24%	29%	13%	6%	10%	12%	0%	5%	3%	0%	0%	63%
% sums	24%	52%	65%	71%	80%	92%	92%	97%	100%	100%	100%	(κ= 0.68)
cvs	4	4	2	1	2	3	0	2	2	0	0	136/200
% of all	29%	26%	12%	5%	9%	11%	0%	4%	3%	0%	0%	68%
% sums	29%	56%	68%	73%	82%	93%	93%	97%	100%	100%	100%	(κ= 0.68)

Figure 5. Visualization of the distribution of agreements for both versions of affect analysis procedure in determining about emotion types. Figure corresponds to the upper part of Table 7.

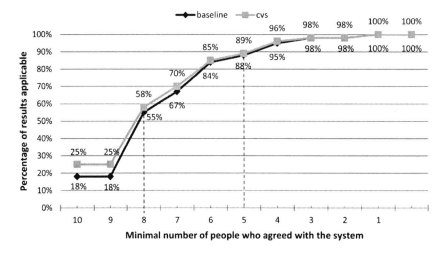

Figure 6. Visualization of the distribution of agreements for both versions of affect analysis procedure in determining about emotion valence. Figure corresponds to the lower part of Table 7.

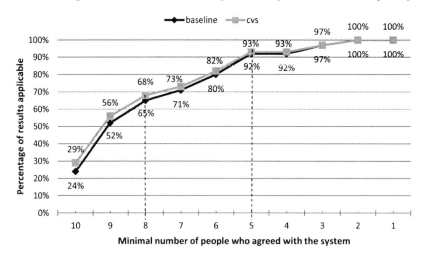

the evaluators about the 20 evaluation sets (200 possible cases of agreement) baseline version of CAEV procedure obtained 69 (35%) agreements about determining the appropriateness of emotion type and 85 (43%) agreements about determining the appropriateness of valence. The strength of agreements in this setting was $\kappa=0.652$ and $\kappa=0.677$, respectively, which indicates substantial agreements. As for the version of CAEV procedure with affect analysis

upgraded with CVS, there were 78 agreements (39%) for emotion type- and 94 (47%) for valence based appropriateness determination. The strength of these sets of agreements was $\kappa=0.642$ and $\kappa=0.667$, respectively. As for the version of CAEV procedure with Web mining restricted to blogs, there were 81 agreements (41%) for emotion type and 95 (48%) for valence-based appropriateness determination. The strength of these sets of agreements was $\kappa=0.667$ and

κ=0.643, respectively. Finally, for the version of CAEV procedure with both improvements (ML-Ask upgraded with CVS and Web mining restricted to blogs), there were 90 agreements (45%) for emotion type- and 104 (52%) for valence-based determination. The strength of these sets of agreements was κ=0.643 and κ=0.633, respectively.

As for the distribution of the agreements, the majority of the results (over 50% of all actual agreements) for determining about appropriateness of emotion types were enclosed in a group where at least 5 people agreed with the system (medium conditions). For determining about valence appropriateness, most of the results were enclosed in a group where at least 8 people agreed (grand majority conditions). The results which enclosed at least 80% of agreements oscillated for emotion types verification around groups where at least three (easy) to four (optimistic) people agreed. For valence verification the groups enclosing at least 80% of agreements oscillated from optimistic (at least 4) to medium (at least 5) condition group. Although there were no cases with ideal conditions, the best version of the system (both improvements) encapsulated with the use of grand majority condition (at least 8 people) 48% of results for emotion types and 64% for valence.

The results are represented in Table 8. Visualization of the distribution of agreements for all four versions of CAEV procedure is represented on Figure 8 (for emotion type determination) and Figure 10 (for valence determination). The visualization of percentage of results encapsulated for each condition (from "at least 9" to "at least 1") is presented on Figure 7 (for emotion type determination) and Figure 9 (for valence determination). Some of the successful examples are represented in Table 12.

Evaluation of CAEV Procedure: Agents Separately

Finally, we checked the results for the verification of emotion appropriateness by the CAEV procedure separately for each agent, Modalin and Pundalin. This was done to find out whether

verification of emotion appropriateness differs for different types of conversations. Modalin, designed by Higuchi et al. (2008), is a non-task oriented keyword-based conversational agent, which uses modality to enhance dialog propositions extracted from the Web. Apart from this, the agent has no distinctive features. Pundalin is also a non-task oriented conversational agent. It was created by adding to Modalin a pun generating system developed by Dybala et al. (2008). Therefore the only distinctive feature of Pundalin with comparison to Modalin was using puns. We compared the results achieved by the agents separately to check whether the presence of jokes (puns) helps or interrupts the process of verification of emotion appropriateness.

The results were as follows. The overall number of agreements with human evaluators about verification of contextual appropriateness was higher for Modalin (from 41% to 55%) than for Pundalin (from 28% to 49%). This was true for both, emotion types and valence. Also the number of agreements encapsulated for different conditions showed similar tendency. The conditions which encapsulated at least 50% of agreements were, for Pundalin/ emotion types, from medium (at least 5 people agreed) to rigorous (at least 9 people agreed). For Pundalin/valence, the results were from medium to grand majority (at least 8 people agreed). The same results for Modalin were approximately higher. For emotion types the condition that encapsulated most of the agreements (over 70%) was a stable medium condition, and for valence it was a stable condition of grand majority (at least 8 people agreed). The conditions that enclosed over 80% of the results oscillated around optimistic and medium conditions. The strength of agreements was considerably high with kappa oscillating from 0.573 to 0.697 across all separate results. The results are summarized for Modalin in Table 9 and for Pundalin in Table 10.

Both improvements, the one with CVS procedure and the one limiting the query scope in the Web mining procedure to search only through blog contents, positively influenced the

Table 8. Results for evaluation of Contextual Appropriateness of Emotion Verification (CAEV) Procedure. Upper part of the table: results for specifying emotion types; Lower part: results for specifying valence. The Table presents numbers of people who agreed with the system. Distribution of numbers shows how many there were agreements with how many people; % of all: shows percentage of this group of agreements within all agreements; %sums: shows percentage of results considered when the condition for agreement was set as "at least this group of agreements (or higher)"; agr.ratio: overall number of agreements divided by ideal number of agreements and ratio; kappa: strength of agreements in this setting.

C) TYPES	Number of people who agreed with the system										agr.ratio (kappa)
	9	8	7	6	5	4	3	2	1	0	
BASELINE	1	2	0	0	4	2	2	4	2	3	69/200
% of all	13%	23%	0%	0%	29%	12%	9%	12%	3%	0%	35%
% sums	13%	36%	36%	36%	65%	77%	86%	97%	100%	100%	(κ= 0.652)
CVS	2	2	0	0	4	2	2	4	2	2	78/200
% of all	23%	21%	0%	0%	26%	10%	8%	10%	3%	0%	39%
% sums	23%	44%	44%	44%	69%	79%	87%	97%	100%	100%	(κ= 0.642)
BLOGS	2	2	0%	0%	4	3	2	4	1	2	81/200
% of all	22%	20%	0%	0%	25%	15%	7%	10%	1%	0%	41%
% sums	22%	42%	42%	42%	67%	81%	89%	99%	100%	100%	(κ= 0.667)
CVS+BLOGS	3	2	0%	0%	4	3	2	4	1	1	90/200
% of all	30%	18%	0%	0%	22%	13%	7%	9%	1%	0%	45%
% sums	30%	48%	48%	48%	70%	83%	90%	99%	100%	100%	(κ= 0.643)

D) VALENCE	Number of people who agreed with the system										agr.ratio (kappa)
	9	8	7	6	5	4	3	2	1	0	
BASELINE	2	4	0	0	4	0	4	1	1	4	85/200
% of all	21%	38%	0%	0%	24%	0%	14%	2%	1%	0%	43%
% sums	21%	59%	59%	59%	82%	82%	96%	99%	100%	100%	(κ= 0.677)
CVS	3	4	0	0	4	0	4	1	1	3	94/200
% of all	29%	34%	0%	0%	21%	0%	13%	2%	1%	0%	47%
% sums	29%	63%	63%	63%	84%	84%	97%	99%	100%	100%	(κ= 0.667)
BLOGS	2	5	0	1	2	1	4	2	1	2	95/200
% of all	19%	42%	0%	6%	11%	4%	13%	4%	1%	0%	48%
% sums	19%	61%	61%	67%	78%	82%	95%	99%	100%	100%	(κ= 0.643)
CVS+BLOGS	3	5	0	1	2	1	4	2	1	1	104/200
% of all	26%	38%	0%	6%	10%	4%	12%	4%	1%	0%	52%
% sums	26%	64%	64%	70%	80%	84%	95%	99%	100%	100%	(κ= 0.633)

performance of the Contextual Appropriateness of Emotion Verification procedure, in all of the cases for both of the agents. The improvement was noticeable both on the level of specific emotion types and of valence, and also for the result of both agents taken together as well as separately.

The most effective version of the method was the one with both improvements applied, by which the system's performance (number of agreements with evaluators) was generally improved for all considered cases. For example, for the grand majority condition (at least 8 people agreed) the results were improved from 36% to 48% (emotion types) and from 59% to 64% (valence), with the highest score achieved in conversations with Modalin (75% under the "grand majority" condition).

The results were generally better in Modalin. This confirms the assumption we made on the beginning of the previous section. We assumed that since humor is one of the most

Figure 7. Visualization of percentage of results encapsulated for each condition, from "at least 9" to "at least 1" (for emotion type determination)

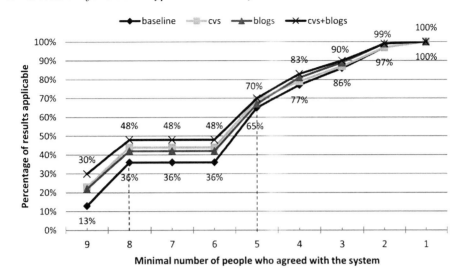

Figure 8. Visualization of the distribution of agreements for all four versions of CAEV procedure (for emotion type determination)

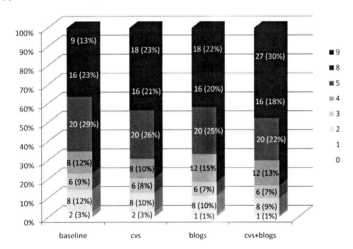

creative human activities, the appropriateness verification should be more difficult to perform in humorous conversations and easier in non-humorous conversations.

In almost all cases the results which changed after the improvements were statistically significant on a 5% level (see Table 11). The only version in which the change of the results was not significant was the baseline method compared to only CVS improvement (P value = 0.1599). Improving the system with blog mining, when compared to both - baseline version of the method and with CVS, were statistically significant (P value = 0.0274) and, what is the most important, the results of the version fully improved were the most significant of all (P value = 0.0119).

Figure 9. Visualization of percentage of results encapsulated for each condition, from "at least 9" to "at least 1" (for valence determination)

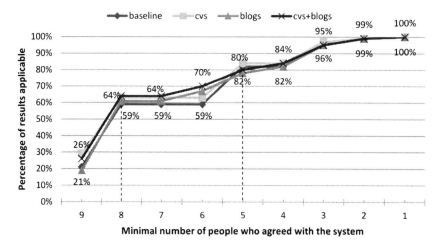

Figure 10. Visualization of the distribution of agreements for all four versions of CAEV procedure (for valence determination)

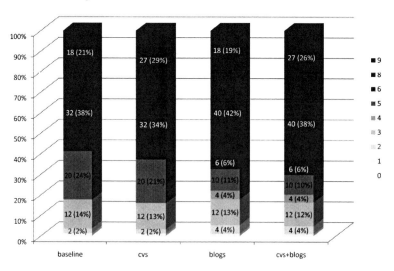

Although the method for verification of contextual appropriateness of emotion presented here is still not ideal, the increase in results after implementation of different improvements to the intermediary systems (ML-Ask in affect analysis procedure and Web mining) indicate the method is easily improvable. Considering the further enhancements that are already in plans, We are expecting a high improvement of this method in the near future.

Table 9. Results for evaluation of Contextual Appropriateness of Emotion Verification (CAEV) procedure for Modalin. Description of table contents like in Table 8.

MODALIN								
C) **TYPES**	**Number of people who agreed with the system**							**agr.ratio** **(kappa)**
	8	5	4	3	2	1	0	
BASELINE	2	3	1	1	1	1	1	41/100
% of all	39%	37%	10%	7%	5%	2%	0%	41%
% sums	39%	76%	85%	93%	98%	100%	100%	(κ= 0.606666)
CVS	2	3	1	1	1	1	1	41/100
% of all	39%	37%	10%	7%	5%	2%	0%	41%
% sums	39%	76%	85%	93%	98%	100%	100%	(κ= 0.606666)
BLOGS	2	3	2	1	1	0	1	44/100
% of all	36%	34%	18%	7%	5%	0%	0%	44%
% sums	36%	70%	89%	95%	100%	100%	100%	(κ= 0.573333)
CVS+BLOGS	2	3	2	1	1	0	1	44/100
% of all	36%	34%	18%	7%	5%	0%	0%	44%
% sums	36%	70%	89%	95%	100%	100%	100%	(κ= 0.573333)

D) **VALENCE**	**Number of people who agreed with the system**							**agr.ratio** **(kappa)**
	9	8	5	4	3	2	0	
BASELINE	1	4	1	0	2	0	2	52/100
% of all	17%	62%	10%	0%	12%	0%	0%	52%
% sums	17%	79%	88%	88%	100%	100%	100%	(κ= 0.688888)
CVS	1	4	1	0	2	0	2	52/100
% of all	17%	62%	10%	0%	12%	0%	0%	52%
% sums	17%	79%	88%	88%	100%	100%	100%	(κ= 0.688888)
BLOGS	1	4	1	0	3	0%	1	55/100
% of all	16%	58%	9%	0%	16%	0%	0%	55%
% sums	16%	75%	84%	84%	100%	100%	100%	(κ= 0.642222)
CVS+BLOGS	1	4	1	0	3	0%	1	55/100
% of all	16%	58%	9%	0%	16%	0%	0%	55%
% sums	16%	75%	84%	84%	100%	100%	100%	(κ= 0.642222)

DISCUSSION

Implications Towards Computational Conscience

Public opinion is a second conscience. -William R. Alger

Conscience is, in most men, an anticipation of the opinions of others. - Henry Taylor

As mentioned above, expressing and understanding emotions is one of the most important cognitive human behaviors present in everyday communication. In particular, Salovey and Mayer (1990) showed that emotions are a vital part of human intelligence, and Schwarz (2000) showed, that emotional states influence the decision making process in humans. If the process of decision making is defined as distinguishing between good and bad, or appropriate and inappropriate, the emotions appear as an influential part of human conscience. The thesis that emotions strongly influence the development of human conscience was proved by Thompson and colleagues (Thompson, Laible, & Ontai, 2003) who showed, that children acquire the conscience by learning the emotional patterns from other people. The significance of the society was pointed out also by Rzepka et al. (2006), who defined the Internet, being a collection of other people's ideas and experiences, as an approximation of general human common sense. Since conscience can be also defined as

Table 10. Results for evaluation of Contextual Appropriateness of Emotion Verification (CAEV) procedure for Pundalin. Description of table contents like in Table 8.

PUNDALIN										
C) TYPES	**Number of people who agreed with the system**									**agr.ratio (kappa)**
	9	8	6	5	4	3	2	1	0	
BASELINE	1	0	0	1	1	1	3	1	2	28/100
% of all	32%	32%	32%	18%	14%	11%	21%	4%	0%	28%
% sums	32%	32%	32%	50%	64%	75%	96%	100%	100%	(κ= 0.698)
CVS	2	0	0	1	1	1	3	1	1	37/100
% of all	49%	49%	49%	14%	11%	8%	16%	3%	0%	37%
% sums	49%	49%	49%	62%	73%	81%	97%	100%	100%	(κ= 0.678)
BLOGS	2	0	0	1	1	1	3	1	1	37/100
% of all	49%	49%	49%	14%	11%	8%	16%	3%	0%	37%
% sums	49%	49%	49%	62%	73%	81%	97%	100%	100%	(κ= 0.678)
CVS+BLOGS	3	0	0	1	1	1	3	1	0	46/100
% of all	59%	59%	59%	11%	9%	7%	13%	2%	0%	46%
% sums	59%	59%	59%	70%	78%	85%	98%	100%	100%	(κ= 0.658)
D) VALENCE	**Number of people who agreed with the system**									**agr.ratio (kappa)**
	9	8	6	5	4	3	2	1	0	
BASELINE	1	0	0	3	0	2	1	1	2	33/100
% of all	27%	0%	0%	45%	0%	18%	6%	3%	0%	33%
% sums	27%	27%	27%	73%	73%	91%	97%	100%	100%	(κ= 0.664)
CVS	2	0	0	3	0	2	1	1	1	42/100
% of all	43%	0%	0%	36%	0%	14%	5%	2%	0%	42%
% sums	43%	43%	43%	79%	79%	93%	98%	100%	100%	(κ= 0.644)
BLOGS	1	1	1	1	1	1	2	1	1	40/100
% of all	23%	20%	15%	13%	10%	8%	10%	3%	0%	40%
% sums	23%	43%	58%	70%	80%	88%	98%	100%	100%	(κ= 0.644)
CVS+BLOGS	2	1	1	1	1	1	2	1	0	49/100
% of all	37%	16%	12%	10%	8%	6%	8%	2%	0%	49%
% sums	37%	53%	65%	76%	84%	90%	98%	100%	100%	(κ= 0.624)

Table 11. Statistical significance of differences between the results for different versions of the system. The highest significance in bold font.

Versions of the System	Baseline vs CVS	Baseline vs Blogs	CVS vs CVS+Blogs	Baseline vs CVS+Blogs
Statistical Significance (p Value)	0.1599 ($p>5\%$)	0.0274 ($p<5\%$)	0.0274 ($p<5\%$)	**0.0119 ($p<5\%$)**

a part of common sense (moral common sense in particular), this statement can be expanded further to saying that the Web can also be used to determine human conscience. The need for research in this matter, was pointed out *inter alia* by Rzepka et al. (2008), who raised the matter not of creating an artificial human being, as it is popularly ventured in Artificial Intelligence research, but rather an intelligent agent in the form of a toy or a companion, designed to support humans in everyday life. To perform that, the agent needs to be equipped, not only in procedures for recognizing phenomena concerning the user, in which emotions play a great role, but it also needs to be equipped with evaluative procedures distinguishing about whether the phenomena are appropriate or not for a situation the user is in. This is an up to date matter in fields such as Roboethics (Veruggio & Operto, 2006), Human Aspects in Ambient Intelligence (Treur, 2007), and in Artificial Intelligence in general. In our research we

Table 12. Three examples of the results provided by the emotion appropriateness verification procedure (CAVP) with a separate display of the examples showing the improvement of the procedure after applying CVS

Part of Conversation in Japanese (English Translation)	ML-Ask Output		Web Mining	CAEV
USER: *Konpyūta wa omoshiroi desu ne.* (Computers are so interesting!)	positive [joy]		positive [joy]	appropriate
SYSTEM: *Sore wa oishii desu ka.* (Is it tasty?) [about instant noodles]	x		x	x
USER: *Oishii kedo, ore wa akita kana.* (Its tasty, but I've grown tired of it.)	negative [dislike]		negative [dislike]	appropriate
Part of conversation in Japanese (English translation)	**ML-Ask baseline**	**ML-Ask +CVS**	**Web Mining**	**CAEV**
SYSTEM: *Sore wa omoshiroi tte* (It's so funny!) [about conversation]	x	x	x	X
USER: *Sore hodo omoshiroku mo nakatta yo.* (It wasn't that funny.)	positive [joy]	negative [dislike]	negative [fear], [sad]	appropriate

performed that by verifying emotions expressed by the user with a Web mining technique for gathering an emotional common sense, which could be also defined as an approximated vector of conscience. We understand, that the idea of conscience is far more sophisticated, however, when defined narrowly as the ability to distinguish between what is appropriate and what is inappropriate, our method for verifying contextual appropriateness of emotions could be applied to obtain simplified conscience calculus for machines. We plan to develop further this idea and introduce it as a complementary algorithm for the novel research on discovering morality level in text utterances presented by Rzepka and colleagues (Rzepka, Masui, & Araki, 2009; Komuda, Ptaszynski, Momouchi, Rzepka, & Araki, 2010).

CONCLUSION AND FUTURE WORK

In this paper we presented our work on Contextual Affect Analysis (CAA) with a future goal of its application in conversational agents such as agent companions or artificial tutors. We applied two systems for affect analysis and a Web mining technique to develop a method for enhancement of human-computer interaction in human-agent based dialogs.

The first system for affect analysis we applied was ML-Ask, a system for affect analysis of textual input utterances in Japanese. The system firstly determines whether an utterance is emotive or not and in emotive utterances determines specific emotion types expressed by the user. The second system for affect analysis we applied was CAO, a prototype system for automatic affect analysis of Eastern type emoticons (*kaomoji*). The system was created using a database of over ten thousand of unique emoticons automatically extracted from the Internet and expanded to over three million emoticon combinations.

The above two systems are used in an affect analysis procedure applied in a method for estimating contextual appropriateness of emotions. The method is composed of two parts, a language based affect analysis procedure utilizing the two affect analysis systems (used as an emotion detector), and a Web mining technique for extracting from the Internet lists of emotional associations considered as a generalized emotive common sense (used as an emotion verifier). We checked the performance of four versions of the method. The affect analysis procedure is compared with and without Contextual Valence Shifters. As for the Web mining technique, two versions are compared: one, using all of the Internet resources and the second one improved by restricting the search scope to the contents of blog documents. The improvements positively influenced the results and were statistically significant. We also observed that emotion appropriateness was more difficult to determine in conversations containing humorous responses (puns).

The method provides the conversational agent with computable means to determine whether emotions expressed by a user are appropriate for the context they appear in. A conversational agent equipped with this method could be provided with hints about what communication strategy would be the most desirable at a certain moment. For example, a conversational agent could choose to either sympathize with the user or take precautions and help the user manage his/her emotions.

By proposing computational means for verification of contextual appropriateness of emotional states in conversation, this research defines a new set of goals for Affective Computing. In particular we proposed a set of tasks to be addressed with regards to broadening the scope of Affect Analysis. The tasks, which we include under a general term Computational Fronesis (CF), include: determination of emotion subject, object, verification of contextual appropriateness of emotional expression and its degree, and modeling of behavior appropriate for the situation or context.

We showed that computing emotions in context is a feasible task. Although the methods are still not ideal and its components (ML-Ask, CAO, the Web mining technique) need further improvement, there have been seen a significant improvement, e.g., by restricting Web mining to the contents of *Yahoo!Japan-Blogs*. As for the future work, we plan to focus on deepening the understanding of emotions by bootstrapping the context phrases. For example, in a sentence "I'm so depressed since my girlfriend left me..."

the context phrase would be "my girlfriend left me". The Web mining procedure provides for such phrases a list of appropriate emotions. However, using similar Web mining procedure we plan to go further and find out the reason for an emotion object to happen. For example, to find out "why girls leave their boyfriends?". An answer for this question, found in the Internet, could be, e.g., "because boys are not sporty enough", or "because boys have no money". Next asked question could be, e.g., "why boys have no money?", etc. Sufficient accuracy in such bootstrapping method would provide a deeper knowledge about the causality of experiences. When applied in artificial tutor, or a companion agent in general, this would help providing hints about predictable undesirable consequences of user activities.

ACKNOWLEDGMENT

This research was supported by (JSPS) KAK-ENHI Grant-in-Aid for JSPS Fellows (Project Number: 22-00358).

REFERENCES

Allen, I. E., & Seaman, J. (2008). *Staying the course: Online education in the United States*. Needham, MA: Sloan Consortium.

Alm, C. O., Roth, D., & Sproat, R. (2005). Emotions from text: Machine learning for text based emotion prediction. In *Proceedings of HLT/EMNLP* (pp. 579-586).

Aman, S., & Szpakowicz, S. (2007). Identifying expressions of emotion in text. In *Proceedings of the 10th International Conference on Text, Speech, and Dialogue (TSD-2007), LNCS 4629* (pp. 196-205), Berlin/Heidelberg, Germany: Springer-Verlag.

Aristotle. (1999). Nicomachean ethics (transl. Terence Irwin, 2nd ed.). Indianapolis, IN: Hackett Publishing.

Baath, J. A. (1982). Distance students' learning - empirical findings and theoretical deliberations. *Distance Education*, 3(1), 6–27. doi:10.1080/0158791820030102.

Birdwhistell, R. L. (1952). *Introduction to kinesics: An annotation system for analysis of body motion and gesture.* Louisville, KY: University of Louisville.

Birdwhistell, R. L. (1970). *Kinesics and context.* Philadelphia, PA: University of Pennsylvania Press.

Boden, M. A. (1998). Creativity and artificial intelligence. *Artificial Intelligence, 103*(1-2), 347–356. doi:10.1016/S0004-3702(98)00055-1.

de Vicente, A., & Pain, H. (2002). Informing the detection of the students' motivational state: An empirical study. In *Proceedings of the Sixth International Conference on Intelligent Tutoring Systems* (LNCS 2363, pp. 933-943). Berlin/Heidelberg, Germany: Springer-Verlag.

Dokoshi, H., Oyama, S., Kurihara, M., Ptaszynski, M., Rzepka, R., & Araki, K. (2011). Emotion estimation of actors and non-actors in text using web mining [in Japanese]. In *Proceedings of the Hokkaido Symposium on Information Processing,* (pp. 223-224).

Dybala, P., Ptaszynski, M., Higuchi, S., Rzepka, R., & Araki, K. (2008a). Humor prevails! -Implementing a joke generator into a conversational system. In *Proceedings of the 21st Australasian Joint Conference on Artificial Intelligence (LNAI 5360,* pp. 214-225).

Dybala, P., Ptaszynski, M., Higuchi, S., Rzepka, R., & Araki, K. (2008b). Extracting DajareCandidates from the web - Japanese puns generating system as a part of humor processing research. In *The Proceedings of the First International Workshop on Laughter in Interaction and Body Movement (LIBM'08)* (pp. 46-51).

Elliott, C. (1992). *The affective reasoner: A process model of emotions in a multi-agent system.* Unpublished doctoral dissertation, Northwestern University Institute for the Learning Sciences, Chicago, IL.

Endo, D., Saito, M., & Yamamoto, K. (2006). *Kakariuke kankei wo riyo shita kanjoseiki hyogen no chushutsu* (Extracting expressions evoking emotions using dependency structure). In *Proceedings of The Twelve Annual Meeting of The Association for Natural Language Processing (NLP2006)* (pp. 947-950).

Fleiss, J. L. (1971). Measuring nominal scale agreement among many raters. *Psychological Bulletin, 76*(5), 378–382. doi:10.1037/h0031619.

Florea, A. M. (1999). An agent-based collaborative learning system. In *Proceedings of The 7th International Conference on Computers in Education (ICCE99),* Chiba, Japan (pp. 4-7).

Florea, A. M., & Kalisz, E. (2005). Embedding emotions in an artificial tutor. In *Proceedings of The Seventh International Symposium on Symbolic and Numeric Algorithms for Scientific Computing (SYNASC '05)* (pp. 223-228). Washington, DC: IEEE Computer Society Press.

Fryer, L., & Carpenter, R. (2006). Emerging technologies: Bots as language learning tools. *Language Learning & Technology, 10*(3), 8–14.

Global Industry Analysts. (2010). Global elearning market to reach 107.3 billion by 2015, according to new report by global industry analysis. *PRWeb.* Retrieved from http://www.prweb.com/releases/elearning/corporate_elearning/prweb4531974.htm

Grefenstette, G., Qu, Y., Shanahan, J. G., & Evans, D. A. (2004). Coupling niche browsers and affect analysis for an opinion mining. *Proceedings of, RIAO-04,* 186–194.

Higuchi, S., Rzepka, R., & Araki, K. (2008). A casual conversation system using modality and word associations. *Proceedings of the EMNLP, 2008,* 382–390. doi:10.3115/1613715.1613765.

Jia, J. (2009). CSIEC: A computer assisted English learning chatbot based on textual knowledge and reasoning. *Knowledge-Based Systems, 22*(4), 249–255. doi:10.1016/j.knosys.2008.09.001.

Komuda, R., Ptaszynski, M., Momouchi, Y., Rzepka, R., & Araki, K. (2010). Machine moral development: Moral reasoning agent based on wisdom of web-crowd and emotions. *International Journal of Computational Linguistics Research, 1*(3), 155–163.

Kudo, T. (2001). MeCab: Yet another part-of-speech and morphological analyzer. Retrieved from http://mecab.sourceforge.net/

Landis, J. R., & Koch, G. G. (1977). The measurement of observer agreement for categorical data. *Biometrics, 33,* 159–174. doi:10.2307/2529310 PMID:843571.

Laurillard, D. (1993). *Rethinking university teaching: A conversational framework for the effective use of learning.* New York, NY: Routledge.

Laurillard, D. (1999). A conversational framework for individual learning applied to the 'learning organisation' and the 'learning society'. *Systems Research and Behavioral Science, 16*(2), 113–122. doi:10.1002/(SICI)1099-1743(199903/04)16:2<113::AID-SRES279>3.0.CO;2-C.

Liu, H., Lieberman, H., & Selker, T. (2003). A model of textual affect sensing using real-world knowledge. In *Proceedings of IUI 2003* (pp. 125-132).

Nakamura, A. (1993). *Kanjō hyōgen jiten* [Dictionary of emotive expressions]. Tokyo, Japan: Tokyodo Publishing. (in Japanese).

Ontario Media Development Corporation. (2010). eLearning industry snapshot. Ontario Media Development Corporation.

Picard, R. W. (1997). *Affective computing.* Cambridge, MA: The MIT Press.

Ptaszynski, M., Dybala, P., Rzepka, R., & Araki, K. (2009). Affecting corpora: Experiments with automatic affect annotation system - a case study of the 2channel forum. In *Proceedings of the Conference of the Pacific Association for Computational Linguistics 2009 (PACLING-09)* (pp. 223-228).

Ptaszynski, M., Dybala, P., Rzepka, R., Araki, K., & Momouchi, Y. (2012). Annotating affective information on 5.5 billion word corpus of Japanese blogs. In *Proceedings of The Eighteenth Annual Meeting of The Association for Natural Language Processing (NLP-2012)* (pp. 405-408).

Ptaszynski, M., Dybala, P., Shi, W., Rzepka, R., & Araki, K. (2008). Disentangling emotions from the Web: Internet in the service of affect analysis. *Proceedings of KEAS, 08*, 51–56.

Ptaszynski, M., Dybala, P., Shi, W., Rzepka, R., & Araki, K. (2009a). A System for Affect Analysis of Utterances in Japanese Supported with Web Mining. *Journal of Japan Society for Fuzzy Theory and Intelligent Informatics, 21*(2), 30–49. doi:10.3156/jsoft.21.194.

Ptaszynski, M., Dybala, P., Shi, W., Rzepka, R., & Araki, K. (2009b). Towards context aware emotional intelligence in machines: Computing contextual appropriateness of affective states'. In *Proceedings of Twenty-First International Joint Conference on Artificial Intelligence (IJCAI-09)* (pp. 1469-1474).

Ptaszynski, M., Dybala, P., Shi, W., Rzepka, R., & Araki, K. (2009c). Shifting valence helps verify contextual appropriateness of emotions. In *Working Notes of Twenty-first International Joint Conference on Artificial Intelligence (IJCAI-09)*, (pp. 19-21).

Ptaszynski, M., Dybala, P., Shi, W., Rzepka, R., & Araki, K. (2009d). Conscience of blogs: Verifying contextual appropriateness of emotions basing on blog contents. In *Proceedings of the Fourth International Conference on Computational Intelligence (CI 2009)* (pp. 1-6).

Ptaszynski, M., Dybala, P., Shi, W., Rzepka, R., & Araki, K. (2009e). A system for affect analysis of utterances in Japanese supported with web mining. *Journal of Japan Society for Fuzzy Theory and Intelligent Informatics, 21*(2), 30–49. doi:10.3156/jsoft.21.194.

Ptaszynski, M., Dybala, P., Shi, W., Rzepka, R., & Araki, K. (2010). Contextual affect analysis: A system for verification of emotion appropriateness supported with contextual valence shifters. *International Journal of Biometrics, 2*(2), 134–154. doi:10.1504/IJBM.2010.031793.

Ptaszynski, M., Maciejewski, J., Dybala, P., Rzepka, R., & Araki, K. (2010). CAO: Fully automatic emoticon analysis system. In *Proceedings of the 24th AAAI Conference on Artificial Intelligence (AAAI-10)* (pp. 1026-1032).

Ptaszynski, M., Rzepka, R., Araki, K., & Momouchi, Y. (2012). A robust ontology of emotion objects. In *Proceedings of The Eighteenth Annual Meeting of The Association for Natural Language Processing (NLP-2012)* (pp. 719-722).

Redecker, C. (2009). Review of learning 2.0 practices: Study on the impact of web 2.0 innovations on education and training in Europe. *JRC Scientific and technical report. EUR, 23664*, EN-2009.

Russell, J. A. (1980). A circumplex model of affect. *Journal of Personality and Social Psychology, 39*(6), 1161–1178. doi:10.1037/h0077714.

Rzepka, R., & Araki, K. (2007). Consciousness of crowds - The internet as a knowledge source of human's conscious behavior and machine self-understanding. In *Proceedings of AAAI Fall Symposium on AI and Consciousness: Theoretical Foundations and Current Approaches* (pp. 127-128).

Rzepka, R., Ge, Y., & Araki, K. (2006). Common Sense from the Web? Naturalness of Everyday Knowledge Retrieved from WWW. *Journal of Advanced Computational Intelligence and Intelligent Informatics*, *10*(6), 868–875.

Rzepka, R., Higuchi, S., Ptaszynski, M., & Araki, K. (2008). Straight thinking straight from the net - on the web-based intelligent talking toy development. In *Proceedings of SMC-08*.

Rzepka, R., Masui, F., & Araki, K. (2009). The first challenge to discover morality level in text utterances by using web resources. In *Proceedings of the 23rd Annual Conference of the Japanese Society for Artificial Intelligence*.

Salovey, P., & Mayer, J. D. (1990). Emotional intelligence. *Imagination, Cognition and Personality*, *9*, 185–211. doi:10.2190/DUGG-P24E-52WK-6CDG.

Schwarz, N. (2000). Emotion, cognition, and decision making. *Cognition and Emotion*, *14*(4), 433–440. doi:10.1080/026999300402745.

Shi, W., Rzepka, R., & Araki, K. (2008). Emotive information discovery from user textual input using causal associations from the internet [In Japanese]. *Proceedings of, FIT2008*, 267–268.

Solomon, R. C. (1993). *The passions: Emotions and the meaning of life*. Indianapolis, IN: Hackett.

Stewart, I., & File, P. (2007). Let's chat: A conversational dialogue system for second language practice. *Computer Assisted Language Learning*, *20*(2), 97–116. doi:10.1080/09588220701331386.

Tatai, G., Csordas, A., Kiss, A., Szalo, A., & Laufer, L. (2003). Happy chatbot, happy user. In *Proceedings of 4th International Workshop on Intelligent Virtual Agents (IVA 2003)*, (LNCS 2792, pp. 5-12). Berlin/Heidelberg, Germany: Springer-Verlag.

Thompson, R. A., Laible, D. J., & Ontai, L. L. (2003). Early understandings of emotion, morality and self: Developing a working model. *Advances in Child Development and Behavior*, *31*, 137–171. doi:10.1016/S0065-2407(03)31004-3 PMID:14528661.

Tokuhisa, R., Inui, K., & Matsumoto, Y. (2008). Emotion classification using massive examples extracted from the web. *Proceedings of Coling, 2008*, 881–888. doi:10.3115/1599081.1599192.

Treur, J. (2007). On human aspects in ambient intelligence. In *Proceedings of the First International Workshop on Human Aspects in Ambient Intelligence*, (pp. 5-10).

Tsuchiya, S., Yoshimura, E., Watabe, H., & Kawaoka, T. (2007). The method of the emotion judgment based on an association mechanism. *Journal of Natural Language Processing*, *14*(3), 219–238. doi:10.5715/jnlp.14.3_219.

Veruggio, G., & Operto, F. (2006). Roboethics: A bottom-up interdisciplinary discourse in the field of applied ethics in robotics. *International Review of Information Ethics. Ethics in Robotics*, *6*(12), 2–8.

Wiebe, J., Wilson, T., & Cardie, C. (2005). Annotating expressions of opinions and emotions in language. *Language Resources and Evaluation*, *39*(2-3), 165–210. doi:10.1007/s10579-005-7880-9.

Wilson, T., & Wiebe, J. (2005). Annotating attributions and private states. In *Proceedings of the ACL Workshop on Frontiers in Corpus Annotation II* (pp. 53-60).

Yamashita, Y. (1999). Kara, node, te-conjunctions which express cause or reason in Japanese. *Journal of the International Student Center*, *3*, 1–14.

Yoshihira, K., Takeda, Y., & Sekine, S. (2004). KWIC system for web documents (in Japanese). In *Proceedings of the 10th Annual Meeting of the Japanese Association for NLP* (pp. 137-139).

Zaenen, A., & Polanyi, L. (2006). Contextual valence shifters. In J. G. Shanahan, Y. Qu, & J. Wiebe (Eds.), *Computing attitude and affect in text* (pp. 1–10). Dordrecht, The Netherlands: Springer Verlag.

Zakos, J., & Capper, L. (2008). CLIVE - An artificially intelligent chat robot for conversational language practice. In *Proceedings of the 5th Hellenic Conference on Artificial Intelligence (SETN 2008) (LNAI 5138*, pp. 437-442). Berlin/Heidelberg, Germany: Springer-Verlag.

Zhang, L. (2010a). Exploration of metaphorical and contextual affect sensing in a virtual improvisational drama. Transactions on Edutainment IV, LNCS 6250, 105-116, Berlin/Heidelberg, Germany: Springer-Verlag.

Zhang, L. (2010b). Exploitation of contextual affect-sensing and dynamic relationship interpretation. *ACM Computers in Entertainment, 8*(3).

Zhang, L. (2011). Affect sensing in metaphorical phenomena and dramatic interaction context. In *Proceedings of the Twenty-second International Joint Conference on Artificial Intelligence (IJCAI)* (pp. 1903-1908).

Zhang, L. (2011a). Affect Sensing and Contextual Affect Modeling from Improvisational Interaction. *International Journal of Computational Linguistics, 1*(4), 45–60.

Zhang, L. (2011b). Exploitation in context-sensitive affect sensing from improvisational interaction. *Transactions on Edutainment, 8. LNCS, 6872*, 12–23.

ENDNOTES

1. We understand that the notion of fronesis is far more sophisticated than the one explained here, but for practical reasons we generalize the term and limit its scope to emotion-related processing.
2. Separation by "/" represents two possible readings of the character.
3. In particular Japanese emoticons called *kaomoji*.
4. blogs.yahoo.co.jp
5. Abbreviation from Contextual Appropriateness of Emotions Verification
6. http://search.goo.ne.jp/

Michal Ptaszynski was born in Wroclaw, Poland in 1981. He received the MA degree from the University of Adam Mickiewicz, Poznan, Poland, in 2006, and PhD in Information Science and Technology from Hokkaido University, Japan in 2011. At the moment he is a JSPS Post-doctoral Research Fellow at the High-Tech research Center, Hokkai-Gakuen University, Japan. His research interests include natural language processing, dialogue processing, affect analysis, sentiment analysis, HCI, and information retrieval. He is a member of the ACL, the AAAI, the IEEE, the HUMAINE, the AAR, the SOFT, the JSAI, and the ANLP.

Pawel Dybala was born in Ostrow Wielkopolski, Poland in 1981. He received his MA in Japanese Studies from the Jagiellonian University in Krakow, Poland in 2006, and PhD in Information Science and Technology from Hokkaido University, Japan in 2011. Currently he is a director and general project manager at Kotoken Language Laboratory in Krakow. His research interests include natural language processing, dialogue processing, humor processing, HCI, and information retrieval.

Michal Mazur was born in Krakow, Poland in 1981. He received his MA in Language Education from the Pedagogical University in Krakow, Poland in 2005. He is studying towards his PhD at Graduate School of Information Science and Technology, Hokkaido University. His research interests include e-learning, artificial tutoring systems, natural language processing, dialogue processing, HCI, and information retrieval.

Rafal Rzepka received the MA degree from the University of Adam Mickiewicz, Poznan, Poland, in 1999, and the PhD degree from Hokkaido University, Japan, in 2004. Currently, he is an assistant professor in the Graduate School of Information Science and Technology at Hokkaido University. His research interests include natural language processing, Web mining, common sense retrieval, dialogue processing, language acquisition, affect analysis, and sentiment analysis. He is a member of the AAAI, the ACL, the JSAI, the IPSJ, the IEICE, the JCSS, and the ANLP

Kenji Araki received the BE, ME, and PhD degrees in electronics engineering from Hokkaido University, Sapporo, Japan, in 1982, 1985, and 1988, respectively. In April 1988, he joined Hokkai-Gakuen University, Sapporo, Japan, where he was a professor. He joined Hokkaido University in 1998 as an associate professor in the Division of Electronics and Information Engineering and became a professor in 2002. Presently, he is a professor in the Division of Media and Network Technologies at Hokkaido University. His research interests include natural language processing, spoken dialogue processing, machine translation, and language acquisition. He is a member of the AAAI, the IEEE, the JSAI, the IPSJ, the IEICE, and the JCSS.

Yoshio Momouchi was born in 1942 in Hokkaido, Japan. He obtained a master's degree and a doctorate in engineering from Hokkaido University. He was a member of the Division of Information Engineering in Graduate School at Hokkaido University from 1973 to 1988. Since 1988 he has been a professor in the faculty of engineering at Hokkai-Gakuen University. He fulfilled duties of Dean of Graduate School of Engineering at Hokkai-Gakuen University in years 2005-2008. He specializes in intelligent information processing, computational linguistics and machine translation. He is a member of the IPSJ, the ANLP, the ACL, the MLSJ, the JCSS, and the JSAI.

Towards a Semantic-Based Approach for Affect and Metaphor Detection

Li Zhang, School of Computing, Engineering and Information Sciences, Northumbria University, Newcastle, UK

John Barnden, School of Computer Science, University of Birmingham, Birmingham, UK

ABSTRACT

Affect detection from open-ended virtual improvisational contexts is a challenging task. To achieve this research goal, the authors developed an intelligent agent which was able to engage in virtual improvisation and perform sentence-level affect detection from user inputs. This affect detection development was efficient for the improvisational inputs with strong emotional indicators. However, it can also be fooled by the diversity of emotional expressions such as expressions with weak or no affect indicators or metaphorical affective inputs. Moreover, since the improvisation often involves multi-party conversations with several threads of discussions happening simultaneously, the previous development was unable to identify the different discussion contexts and the most intended audiences to inform affect detection. Therefore, in this paper, the authors employ latent semantic analysis to find the underlying semantic structures of the emotional expressions and identify topic themes and target audiences especially for those inputs without strong affect indicators to improve affect detection performance. They also discuss how such semantic interpretation of dialog contexts is used to identify metaphorical phenomena. Initial exploration on affect detection from gestures is also discussed to interpret users' experience of using the system and provide an extra channel to detect affect embedded in the virtual improvisation. Their work contributes to the journal themes on affect sensing from text, semantic-based dialogue processing and emotional gesture recognition.

Keywords: Affect Detection, Dialogue Contexts, Metaphor, Semantic Interpretation and Gesture, Virtual Improvisation

INTRODUCTION

Human behaviour in social interaction has been intensively studied. Intelligent agents are used as an effective channel to validate such studies. For example, mimicry agents are built to employ mimicry social behaviour to improve human

DOI: 10.4018/jdet.2013040103

agent communication (Sun et al., 211). Intelligent conversational agents are also equipped to conduct personalised tutoring and generate small talk behaviours to enhance users' experience. However, the Turing test introduced in 1950 (Turing, 1950) still poses big challenges to our intelligent agent development. Especially, the proposed question, "can machines think?", makes many of our developments shallow.

We believe it will make intelligent agents possess human-like behaviour and narrow the communicative gap between machines and human-beings if they are equipped to interpret human emotions during the interaction. Thus in our research, we equip our AI agent with emotion and social intelligence as the potential attempts to answer the above Turing question. According to Kappas (2010), human emotions are psychological constructs with notoriously noisy, murky, and fuzzy boundaries that are compounded with contextual influences in experience and expression and individual differences. These natural features of emotion also make it difficult for a single modal recognition, such as via acoustic-prosodic features of speech or facial expressions. Since human being's reasoning process has taken related context into consideration, in our research, we intend to make our agent take multi-channels of subtle emotional expressions embedded in social interaction contexts into consideration to draw reliable affect interpretation. The research presented here focuses on the production of intelligent agents with the abilities of interpreting dialogue contexts semantically to support affect detection as the first step of building a 'thinking' machine. Emotional gesture recognition is also briefly discussed to provide a potential extra channel to interpret affect implied in the improvisation and detect users' experience unintrusively.

Our research is conducted within a previously developed online multi-user role-play virtual drama framework, which allows school children aged 14 – 16 to talk about emotionally difficult issues and perform drama performance training. In this platform young people could interact online in a 3D virtual drama stage with others under the guidance of a human director. In one session, up to five virtual characters are controlled on a virtual stage by human users ("actors"), with characters' (textual) "speeches" typed by the actors operating the characters. The actors are given a loose scenario around which to improvise, but are at liberty to be creative. An intelligent agent is also involved in improvisation. It included an affect detection component, which detected affect from human characters' each individual turn-taking input (an input contributed by an individual character at one time).

This previous affect detection component[1] was able to detect 25 emotions including basic and complex emotions and value judgments, but the detection processing has not taken any context into consideration. The basic emotions used referred to Ekman's six cross-cultural universally accepted emotions (Ekman, 1999) including anger, disgust, fear, happiness, sadness and surprise. The complex emotions were taken from the global structure of emotion types, which is also known as the OCC model (Ortony, Clore, & Collins, 1988). In this model, emotions were regarded as the results of appraising events, agents, and objects. The previous development borrowed emotion categories such as approval/disapproval and gloating to annotate emotions embedded in the users' inputs. Other emotions we used included meta-emotions (emotions about emotions) such as desiring to overcome anxiety; moods such as hostility; and value judgments (judgments of goodness, importance, etc.). The intelligent agent also made attempts to produce appropriate responses to help stimulate the improvisation based on the detected affect. The detected emotions were also used to drive the animations of the avatars so that they reacted bodily in ways that was consistent with the affect that they were expressing (Zhang et al., 2009; Zhang, 2010). Although merely detecting affect is limited compared to extracting the full meaning of characters' utterances, we have found that in many cases this was sufficient for the purposes of stimulating the improvisation.

The previous affect detection processing was mainly based on pattern-matching rules that looked for simple grammatical patterns or templates partially involving specific words or sets of specific alternative words. A rule-based Java framework called Jess (http://www.jessrules.com/) was used to implement the pattern/template-matching rules in the AI agent allowing the system to cope with more general wording and ungrammatical fragmented sentences. From the analysis of the previously collected transcripts, the original affect interpretation based on the analysis of individual turn-taking input itself without any contextual inference is proved to be effective enough for those inputs containing strong clear emotional indictors such as 'yes/no', 'haha', 'thanks' etc. There are also situations that users' inputs do not have any obvious emotional indicators or contain very weak affect signals, thus contextual inference is needed to further derive the affect conveyed in such user inputs.

The inspection of the collected transcripts also indicates that the improvisational dialogues are often multi-threaded. This refers to the situation that social conversational responses of different discussion themes to previous several speakers are mixed up due to the nature of the online chat setting. Therefore the detection of the most related discussion theme context using semantic analysis is very crucial for the accurate interpretation of the emotions implied in those inputs with ambiguous target audiences and weak affect indicators.

Moreover, in our previous study, we mainly focused on affect expressed by the human-controlled characters in their virtual improvisation and have not made attempts to find out users' experience by detecting users' emotions expressed in real world via body language and facial expressions while they were operating their characters in front of their computers. During the previous user testing, we also realized that although emotions expressed during their role-play in the virtual world may not be the same emotions experienced at that moment in the real world, the users' improvisation sometimes still reveals hints about their user experience of using the system. And vice versa, the gestures showed in the real world also sometimes indicate users' feelings and emotions embedded in the virtual improvisation, such as boredom (typing in "I'm getting bored about this" in the meantime showing a gesture such as checking time on their watches), disagreement (saying "I don't like his attitude" and showing an arm-cross gesture) and confusion (typing in "who is the bully? Aren't you the bully?" then showing a scratching head gesture). Thus

emotional gesture recognition provides a non-intrusive channel to identify users' experience and also shows the potential to provide an extra source of information to contribute to the interpretations of affect implied in the virtual improvisation. Therefore, it is also explored and discussed in this paper.

RELATED WORK

There is much well-known research that has been done on affect detection and creating affective virtual characters in interactive systems. Endrass, Rehm, and André (2011) carried out study on the culture-related differences in the domain of small talk behaviour. Their agents were equipped with the capabilities of generating culture specific dialogues. There is much other work in a similar vein. Recently textual affect sensing has also drawn researchers' attention. Neviarouskaya et al. (2010) provided sentence-level textual affect sensing to recognize judgments, appreciation and different affective states. They adopted a rule-based domain-independent approach with semantic analysis of verbs. Although some linguistic contexts introduced by conjunctions such as 'but' were considered, the detection task setup was still limited to the analysis of individual input. Ptaszynski et al. (2009) employed context-sensitive affect detection with the integration of a web-mining technique to detect affect from users' input and verify the contextual appropriateness of the detected emotions. The detected results made an AI agent either sympathize with the player or disapprove the user's expression by the provision of persuasion. However, their system targeted interaction only between an AI agent and one human user in non-role-playing situations, which greatly reduced the complexity of the modelling of the interaction context.

Moreover metaphorical language has been used in literature to convey emotions, which also inspires cognitive semanticists (Kövecses, 1998). Indeed, the metaphorical description of emotional states is common and has been extensively studied (Fainsilber & Ortony,

1987; Zhang & Barnden, 2010), for example, "he nearly exploded" and "joy ran through me," where anger and joy are being viewed in vivid physical terms. Such examples describe emotional states in a relatively explicit way. But affect is also often conveyed more implicitly via metaphor, as in "his room is a cess-pit"; affect (such as 'disgust') associated with a source item (cess-pit) gets carried over to the corresponding target item (the room). There is also other work focusing on metaphors in affective expressions (Craggs & Wood, 2004; Barnden, 2007) useful to our application.

Scherer (2003) explored a boarder category of affect concepts including emotion, mood, attitudes, personality traits and interpersonal stances (affective stance showed in a specific interaction). Mower et al. (2009) argued that it was very unlikely that each spoken utterance during natural human robot/computer interaction contained clear emotional content. Thus, dialog modeling techniques, such as emotional interpolation, emotional profiling, and utterance-level hard labelling, have been developed in their work to interpret these emotionally ambiguous or non-prototypical utterances. Such development would benefit classification of emotions expressed within the context of a dialog. Batliner et al. (2008) focused on the modeling of the frequently used seven emotional states in their study such as reprimanding, motherese, angry etc, into two dimensions: Valence and Interaction. They stated that "typical emotions are to a large extent rather private". Such emotions may not be observed very often in public settings. Their research thus focused on social interaction modeling dimension.

Moreover, as discussed earlier, naturalistic emotion expressions usually consist of a complex and continuously changed symphony of multimodal expressions, rather than rarely unimodal expressions. However, most existing systems consider these expressions in isolation. This limitation may cause inaccuracy or even lead to a contrary result in practice. For instance, currently many systems can accurately recognize smile from facial expressions, but it is inappropriate to conclude a smiling user is really happy (Kappas, 2010). In fact, the same expression can be interpreted completely differently depending on the context that is given (Russell, 2003). It also motivates us to use semantic interpretation of social contexts to inform affect detection and employ initial developments of emotional gesture recognition as a potential channel to inform users' experience and affect detection in virtual improvisation.

THE PREVIOUS AFFECT DETECTION PROCESSING

The language created during the improvisation severely challenges existing language-analysis tools if accurate semantic information is sought, even in the limited domain of restricted affect-detection. Previously we implemented pre-processing components to deal with misspellings, abbreviations, slang etc in order to recover the standard user inputs and adopted robust parsing using Rasp, a syntactical parser (Briscoe & Carroll, 2002), rule-based reasoning, pattern matching, semantic and sentimental profiles for affect detection analysis.

Especially the pattern/template-matching rules in the AI agent allowed the system to cope with more general syntax and wording. In detail, the rules conjectured the character's emotions, evaluation dimension (negative or positive), politeness (rude or polite) and what response the automated actor should make. However, it lacked other types of generality and can be fooled when the phrases were suitably embedded as subcomponents of other grammatical structures. In order to go beyond certain such limitations, sentence type information obtained from the Rasp parser has also been adopted in the pattern-matching rules. This information not only helped the AI agent to detect affective states in the user's input (such as the detection of imperatives), and to decide if the detected affective states should be counted (e.g. affects detected in conditional sentences will not be valued), but also contributed to proposing appropriate responses.

We have also developed responding regimes for AI agent development. Previously we made the AI actor respond every three utterances in order to simulate human-like conversational behaviour. However, it also responded whenever the AI agent's character's name was mentioned, and made no response if it cannot detect anything useful in the utterance it was responding to. The AI agent generally was able to respond according to how confident it was about what it has discerned in the utterance at hand. It made a random response from several stored response candidates that were suitable for the affective quality it discerned in the utterance it was responding to. The previous user testing results also indicated that comparing with a human actor who played the same role as the AI agent, the AI agent's performance was as good as that of the human actor with no statistically significant differences on the measurement of their usefulness in drama improvisation and influences to other users' engagement and enjoyment (Zhang et al., 2009).

SEMANTIC INTERPRETATION OF INTERACTION CONTEXTS AND METAPHORICAL PHENOMENA

As mentioned above, we noticed that the language used in our previously collected transcripts is often complex, idiosyncratic and invariably ungrammatical. Most importantly, the language also contains a large number of weak cues to the affect that is being expressed. These cues may be contradictory or they may work together to enable a stronger interpretation of the affective state. In order to build a reliable and robust analyser of affect it is necessary to undertake several diverse forms of analysis and to enable these to work together to build stronger interpretations. It thus guides not only our previous research but also our current developments. For example, in our previous work, we undertook several analyses of any given utterance. These would each build representations which may be used by other components (e.g.

syntactic structure) and would construct (possibly weak) hypotheses about the affective state conveyed in the input. In our current study, we also integrate contextual information to further derive the affect embedded in the interaction contexts and to provide metaphor identification.

Since our previous affect detection was performed solely based on the analysis of individual input, the context information was ignored. In order to detect affect accurately from inputs without strong affect indicators and clear target audiences, we employ semantic interpretation of social interaction contexts to inform affect analysis. In this section, we discuss our approaches of using latent semantic analysis (LSA) (Landauer & Dumais, 2008) for terms and documents comparison to recover the most related discussion themes and potential target audiences for those without strong affect signals.

As mentioned earlier, in our previous rule-based driven affect detection implementation, we mainly relied on keywords and partial phrases matching with simple semantic analysis using WordNet (Fellbaum, 1998). However, we notice many terms, concepts and emotional expressions can be described in various ways. Especially if the inputs contain no strong affect indicators, other approaches focusing on underlying semantic structures in the data should be considered. Thus latent semantic analysis is employed to calculate semantic similarities between sentences to derive discussion themes for such inputs.

Latent semantic analysis generally identifies relationships between a set of documents and the terms they contain by producing a set of concepts related to the documents and terms. In order to compare the meanings or concepts behind the words, LSA maps both words and documents into a 'concept' space and performs comparison in this space. In detail, LSA assumed that there is some underlying latent semantic structure in the data which is partially obscured by the randomness of the word choice. This random choice of words also introduces noise into the word-concept relationship. LSA aims to find the smallest set of concepts that spans all the documents. It uses a statistical technique, called singular value decomposition (Klema & Laub, 1980), to estimate the hidden concept space and to remove the noise. This concept space associates syntactically different but semantically similar terms and documents. We use these transformed terms and documents in the concept space for retrieval rather than the original terms and documents.

In our work, we employ the semantic vectors package (Widdows & Cohen, 2010) to perform LSA, analyze underlying relationships between documents and calculate their similarities. This package provides APIs for concept space creation. It applies concept mapping algorithms to term-document matrices using Apache Lucene, a high-performance, full-featured text search engine library implemented in Java (Widdows & Cohen, 2010). We integrate this package with our AI agent's affect detection component to calculate the semantic similarities between improvisational inputs without strong affect signals and training documents with clear discussion themes. In this paper, we target the transcripts of the Crohn's disease[2] scenario used in previous testing for context-based affect analysis.

In order to compare the improvisational inputs with documents belonging to different topic categories, we have to collect some sample training documents with strong topic themes. Personal articles from the Experience project (www.experienceproject.com) are borrowed to construct training documents. These articles belong to 12 discussion categories including Education, Family & Friends, Health & Wellness, Lifestyle & Style, Pets & Animals etc. Since we intend to perform discussion theme detection for the transcripts of the scenarios used in the user testing including the School bullying and Crohn's disease scenarios, we have extracted sample articles close enough to these scenarios including articles of Crohn's disease (five articles), school bullying (five articles), family care for children (five articles), food choice (three articles), school life including school uniform (10 short articles) and school lunch (10 short articles). Phrase and sentence

level expressions implying 'disagreement' and 'suggestion' have also been gathered from several other articles published on the Experience website. Thus we have training documents with eight discussion themes including 'Crohn's disease', 'bullying', 'family care', 'food choice', 'school lunch', 'school uniform', 'suggestions' and 'disagreement'. The first six themes are sensitive and crucial discussion topics to the above scenario, while the last two themes are intended to capture arguments expressed in multiple ways.

Affect detection from metaphorical expressions often poses great challenges to automatic linguistic processing systems. In order to detect a few frequently used basic metaphorical phenomena, we include four types of metaphorical examples published on the following website: http://knowgramming.com, in our training corpus. These include cooking, family, weather, and farm metaphors. We have also borrowed a group of 'Ideas as External Entities' metaphor examples from the ATT-Meta project databank (http://www.cs.bham.ac.uk/~jab/ATT-Meta/ Databank/) to enrich the metaphor categories. Individual files are used to store each type of the metaphorical expressions, such as cooking_metaphor.txt, family_metaphor.txt and ideas_metaphor.txt etc). All the sample documents of the above 13 categories are regarded as training files and have been put under one directory for further analysis.

Especially, the example training documents with the themes of bullying and school uniform are included mainly to support the semantic interpretation of the transcripts of the school bullying scenario used for the user testing. For example, the bully tends to pick the bullied victim on his/her appearance including hair styles and clothes wearing. These topics are also closely related the Crohn's disease scenario since the sick leading character sometimes has been bullied because of the side effects of the operation, e.g. wearing a special bag around the stomach or a special underwear. Similarly, although metaphorical example training files, such as cooking, family and ideas metaphors are more frequently used in the discussions of the two chosen scenarios, another two metaphorical phenomena, weather and farm metaphors, are also included in order to justify the semantic-based interpretation (e.g. producing a higher similarity value for a semantically much closer metaphor category and vice versa) and detect much wider and broader metaphorical expressions.

The training corpus overall contains 38 full articles from the Experience website with an average length of 585 words per article. Another 20 articles from the same website are employed as sources to extract phrases and sentences indicating 'disagreement' and 'suggestions' in order to gather the diversity of such expressions. The average length of these two training files is 350 words. Each metaphor sample training file contains sentence-level metaphor examples belonging to one specific type. These metaphorical samples are extracted from dedicated metaphor resources as mentioned above (the ATT-Meta databank and a metaphor example website: http://knowgramming.com). The average length of the metaphor training files is 1223 words per file. When handling semantic processing, command line parameters are used to remove stemming and stop words from the corpus. With default settings, the semantic vector API generates a LSA concept space with 200 dimensions.

We have used one example interaction of the Crohn's disease scenario produced by testing subjects during our previous user testing in the following to demonstrate how we detect the discussion themes for those inputs with weak or no affect indicators and ambiguous target audiences:

1. **Peter:** im going to *have an ileostomy* [sad];
2. **Peter:** *im scared* [scared];
3. **Dave:** *i'm ur friend* peter and *i'll stand by you* [caring];
4. **Peter:** yeah i know, but *the disease stuff sucks* [sad];

5. **Dave:** if it's what u want, you should *go for it* though [caring];
6. **Janet:** peter you must go throu with this operation. *Its for the best* [caring];
7. **Peter:** but *no one else can do* nethin [disapproval];
8. **Arnold:** *take it easy*, consider all your options peter [caring];
9. **Matthew:** u have had operations b4 I'm sure *u'll be ok* [caring];
10. **Dave:** what are your other options peter [*A question sentence; neutral*];
11. **Peter:** im trying very hard but there is too much stuff blocking my head up [*Topics: family care, ideas metaphor, bullied; Target audience: Dave; Emotion: negative*];
12. **Peter:** my plate is already too full.... there aint otha options dave [*Topics: food, cooking metaphor, bullied; Target audience: Dave; Emotion: stressful*].

Affect implied by the inputs with strong affect indicators in the above interaction is detected by the previous affect detection processing. The emotion indicators are also illustrated in italics in the above examples. The inputs without an affect label followed straightaway are those with weak or no strong affect indicators (10th, 11th & 12th inputs). Therefore further processing is needed to recover their most related discussion themes and identify their most likely target audiences in order to identify implied emotions more accurately. Our general regime for the detection of discussion themes is to create the 'concept' space by generating term and document vectors for all the training corpus and a test input. Then we use these transformed terms and documents in the concept space for retrieval and comparison. For example, we use the generated concept space to calculate semantic similarities between user inputs without strong affect indicators and training files with clear topic themes and search for documents including the user input closest to the vector for a specific topic theme. We start with the 11th input from Peter to demonstrate the topic theme detection. First of all, this input is stored as a separate individual test file (test_corpus1. txt) under the same folder containing all the training sample documents of the 13 categories.

In the topic theme detection processing, first of all, the corresponding semantic vector APIs are used to create a Lucene index for all the training samples and the test file, i.e. the 11th input. This generated index is also used to create term and document vectors, i.e. the concept space. In this application context, there are 45 vectors of dimension 200 generated for the document vectors and 5383 vectors of dimension 200 generated for the term vectors. Various search options could be used to test the generated concept model. In order to find out the most effective approach to extract the topic theme of the test inputs, we, first of all, provide rankings for all the training documents and the test sentence based on their semantic distances to a topic theme. We achieve this by searching for document vectors closest to the vector for a specific topic term (e.g. 'bullying', 'disease' or 'family care'). We have tested the 11th input using the vectors of all 13 topic terms mentioned above. The input from Peter obtains the highest ranking for the following topic themes, 'ideas

metaphor' (ranking top 2), 'cooking metaphor' (top 3), and 'bullied' (top 5), among all the rankings for the 13 topics. Partial output is listed in Figure 1 for the rankings of some of the training documents and the 11th input based on their semantic distances to the topic theme, 'ideas metaphor', as mentioned above to which the 11th input achieves the best semantic similarity among all of the 13 topic terms.

Semantic similarities between documents are also produced in order to further inform topic theme detection. All the training sample documents are taken either from articles under clear discussion themes within the 12 categories of the Experience project or the metaphor websites with clear metaphor classifications. The file titles used indicate the corresponding discussion or metaphor themes. If the semantic distances between files, esp. between training files and the test file, are calculated, then it provides another source of information for the topic theme detection. Therefore we use the CompareTerms semantic vector API to find out semantic similarities between all the training corpus and the test document. We provide the top five rankings for semantic similarities between the training documents and the 11th input in Figure 2.

Figure 1. Partial output for searching for document vectors closest to the vector of 'ideas metaphor' (test_corpus1.txt containing the 11th input, ranking the top 2)

```
Found vector for 'ideas metaphor'
Search output follows ...
0.9687636802981049:F:\ideas_metaphor.txt
0.6109025620852475:F:\test_corpus1.txt
0.468855438977363:F:\family_care5.txt
0.4384741083934003:F:\family_care2.txt
0.4371725898952773 5:F:\suggestion1.txt
0.4348188427608230 5:F:\bullied1.txt
0.4251612046490438 3:F:\bullied2.txt
0.4205562139818102 6:F:\crohn2.txt
```

Figure 2. Part of the output for semantic similarities between training documents and the test file, i.e. the 11th input

Similarity of "family_care3.txt" with
"test_corpus1.txt": 0.7437130626759305

Similarity of "ideas_metaphor.txt" with
"test_corpus1.txt": 0.7344774236952176

Similarity of "crohn3.txt" with
"test_corpus1.txt": 0.7149712240914611

Similarity of "bullied1.txt" with
"test_corpus1.txt": 0.689368455185548

Similarity of "family_care2.txt" with
"test_corpus1.txt": 0.6773127042549564

The semantic similarity test in Figure 2 indicates that the 11th input is more closely related to topics of 'family care (family_care3. txt)' and 'ideas metaphor (ideas_metaphor. txt)' although it is also closely related to negative topic themes such as 'disease' and 'being bullied'. In order to identify the 11th input's potential target audiences, we have to conduct topic theme detection starting from the 10th input and retrieving backwards until we find the input with a similar topic theme or with a posed question for Peter. As mentioned earlier, the pre-processing of the previous rule-based affect detection includes a syntactical parsing using a Rasp parser and it identifies the 10th input from Dave is a question sentence with the mentioning of Peter's name. Thus the syntactical processing regards the 10th input from Dave posed a question toward the target audience, Peter. We also derive its most likely topic themes for the 10th input to provide further confirmation. Using the processing discussed earlier, the topic theme detection identifies the following semantically most similar training documents to the 10th input: disagree1.txt, family_care5.txt and suggestion1.txt. They respectively recommend the discussion themes: 'disagreement', 'family care' and 'suggestion'.

We also noticed that in English, the expression of question sentences is so diverse. Most of them will require confirmation or replies from other characters, while there is a small group of question sentences that do not really require any replies, i.e. rhetorical questions. Such questions (e.g. "What the hell are you thinking?", "Who do you think you are?", "How many times do I need to tell you?", "Are you crazy?") encourage the listener to think about what the (often obvious) answer to the question must be. They tend to be used to express dissatisfaction. In this application domain, we especially detect such rhetorical questions using latent semantic analysis after Rasp's initial analysis of the sentence type information. We construct two training documents for questions sentences: one with normal questions and the other with rhetorical questions. We use the semantic vector API to perform semantic similarity comparison between the two training document vectors and the 10th input from Dave.

The result shown in Figure 3 indicates that the input from Dave is more likely to be a normal question sentence rather than a rhetorical expression. Thus it is more inclined to imply a normal discussion theme such as 'family care' than to express 'disagreement' or 'suggestion' comparing with a rhetorical question. Thus the 10th input from Dave has the same discussion theme to one of the themes implied by the 11th input from Peter. Thus the target audience of the 11th input is Dave, who has asked Peter a question in the first place. Since the 11th input is also regarded as an 'ideas metaphor' with a high confidence score, the following processing

Figure 3. Output for semantic similarities between rhetorical and normal question training documents and the test file, test_corpus2.txt, i.e. the10^{th} input

Similarity of "rhetorical1.txt" with "test_corpus2.txt": 0.41996908397317273

Similarity of "question1.txt" with "test_corpus2.txt": 0.4886129715563037

using Rasp and WordNet is applied to the partial input "there is too much stuff blocking my head up" to recognize the metaphor phenomenon:

1. Rasp: 'EX (there) + VBZ (is) + RG (too) + DA1 (much) + NN1 (stuff) + VVG (blocking) + APP$ (my) + NN1 (head) + RP(up)';
2. WordNet: 'stuff' -> hypernym: information abstract entity, since 'stuff' has been described by a singular after-determiner ('much'). 'Head' -> hypernym: a body part physical entity. 'Block'-> hypernyms: PREVENT, KEEP;
3. The input implies -> 'an abstract subject entity (stuff) + an action (block) + a physical object entity' (head) -> showing semantic preference violation (an abstract entity performs an action towards a physical object) -> recognised as a metaphor.

In this example, ideas are viewed in terms of external entities. They are often cast as concrete physical objects. They can move around, or be active in other ways. The above processing recognises that this 'ideas as external entities' metaphorical example shows semantic preference violation, i.e. an information abstract subject performs physical actions. Since the 11th input is also semantically close to 'disease' and 'bullied' topics derived from the above topic theme detection processing, this metaphorical input implies a 'negative' emotion.

Previously the intelligent agent has also been equipped with the capabilities of interpretation of a few metaphorical language phenomena, including affect as external enti-ties metaphor ("Joy ran through me"), the food metaphor ("Lisa has a pizza face (insulting)"), and the cooking metaphor ("She knew she was fried when the teacher handed back her paper") (Zhang & Barnden, 2010). Especially a rule-based approach is used to recognize the semantic preference violations embedded in the above mentioned several types of metaphorical expressions. Another semantic labeling tool (Rayson, 2003) and WordNet-affect (Strapparava & Valitutti, 2004) were also used in order to derive the syntactical and semantic interpretation of the inputs.

In a similar way, the 12th input from Peter also does not contain strong affect indicators. Thus the conversation theme detection has identified its input vector is semantically most closely related to the vector of the topic term, 'food' (ranking top 5) and 'cooking metaphor' (top 6). In other words, although this input only achieves top 5 and 6 rankings when calculating its semantic distances to these two discussion themes, it shows the highest semantic closeness to the above two themes among all the 13 topics.

The topic theme detection also identifies the 12th input shows high semantic similarities with training corpus under the themes of 'cooking metaphor (cooking_metaphor.txt: 0.563)' and 'being bullied (bullied3.txt: 0.513)'. Since Dave's name is mentioned in this input, our processing automatically classifies Dave as the target audience. Thus the 12th input is regarded as a potential cooking metaphor related to a negative bullying theme. The above syntactic and semantic processing using Rasp and Wordnet is also applied to this input. The first part of the 12th input closely related to cooking and food themes is interpreted as 'a physical tableware-object subject followed by a copular form and a quantitative adjective'. However it does not show any semantic preference violation as the 11th input did and the only cooking related term is 'plate'. Context information is also retrieved for the recognition of this cooking metaphorical phenomenon.

We start from the 11th input to find out the topic themes of those inputs most similar to the topics of the 12th input. As discussed earlier, the 11th input is contributed by Peter as well with embedded 'family care' and 'bullied' themes, but not related to 'food'. The 10th input is a question sentence from Dave with a 'family care' theme. The 8th and 9th inputs contain strong affect indicators (see italics) implying 'family care' themes as well. The backward retrieval stops at the 7th input, the last round input contributed by Peter. Thus the 11th input shares the same 'bullied' topic with the 12th input and the 12th input contributed by the same speaker is regarded as a further answer to the previous question raised by Dave. Moreover the 11th input is recognized as an 'ideas as external entities' metaphor with a negative indication. Thus the 12th input is not really 'food' related but an extension of the ideas metaphor and more likely to indicate a physical tableware object entity, plate, is a flat, limited space for solid ideas. Its most recent interaction context (8th – 11th) also shares a consistent positive theme of 'family care', but not a bullying context. Therefore the processing is inclined to recognize it as a cooking metaphor due to Peter's previous negative ideas metaphor input and the 'family care' positive theme of the most recent context. Incorporation of Peter's profile, a sick character, Peter is thus more likely to indicate a 'stressful' emotion caused by the disease in the 12th input. Rule sets are generated for such metaphorical and affect reasoning with the support of the semantic interpretation of the interaction contexts.

Especially, the rule set now accepts the recognized sentence or metaphor type of the current input, the averaged relationship between the speaking character and the target audiences (ranging from one to four in an improvisation with five characters), most recent emotions of the target audiences indicated by their discussion themes and the speaking character profile (such as a bullying, bullied, or sick character). Thus for the 12th input, the pseudo-code of the affect detection rule activated is presented in the following:

```
(defrule example_affect_detection_rule
(sentence type 'a cooking metaphor' and the
character is 'a sick leading character' and
shares positive relationships with target
audiences, who show a positive emotion
context indicated by the discussion
theme 'family care')
=>
(obtain affect and response from the
knowledge database))
```

Topic theme detection using semantic analysis and Rasp are able to recognize different types of metaphors, rhetorical questions and other sentence types. The conversation theme detection using semantic vectors is also able to detect the most related discussion themes and therefore to identify the target audiences of user inputs. We believe these are important aspects for the accurate interpretation of the emotion context. Relationships between characters are also derived from the characters' profiles although relationships could also be dynamically developed and changed during the improvisation. Three values are used to describe relationships between characters: -1, 0, and 1 used to respectively represent negative, neutral and positive relationships. For example, Arnold has a positive relationship with Janet, a neutral relationship with Matthew, and a negative relationship with Peter. If an input has more than one target audience, then an average relationship value is calculated. Therefore the rule set is able to detect emotions embedded in the interaction contexts.

As mentioned above, the previous rule-based affect detection was inspired by the previous testing transcripts of the chosen scenarios including the school bullying and Crohn's disease. Most of the rules related to the bullying topic were developed to deal with aggressive and rude behaviours of the human characters. Since in this disease scenario, there were recorded inputs mainly describing the attack of the diseases, such as "can your body cope with the side effects?", "the disease turns my life upside down", and "lead me down this slippery path to death", another set of rules associated with the aggressive behaviour of diseases was also developed. For example, the above discussed example rule to detect affect from contexts is one example rule extended from the previous disease-related rule set. The 12th input is thus regarded as an extension of the attack of disease related discussions.

We envisage the conversational theme detection would also be useful to distinguish task un-related small talk and task-driven behaviours during human agent interaction. The summarization of the algorithms used for topic theme detection, target audience identification and rhetorical question detection is provided in Table 1.

INITIAL DEVELOPMENTS ON EMOTIONAL GESTURE RECOGNITION

As discussed earlier, since human emotions are psychological constructs with notoriously noisy and vague boundaries, affect detection from a single isolated channel sometimes may not be sufficient enough. Thus our long term research goal is to combine the affect detection results obtained respectively from the above semantic interpretation of the dialogue contexts and emotional body language recognition in order to draw a stronger conclusion on affect detection. As mentioned earlier, the gestures showed in the real world also sometimes indicate users' feelings and emotions embedded in the virtual improvisation.

Such emotional gesture study and developments may also help to identify ironic social interactions in daily life situations, such as showing an arm-cross gesture indicating potential disagreement and in the meantime saying "oh, this is great!". Or someone may applause and in the meantime saying "this is simply waste of time". In the long term research goal, we also

Table 1. Summarization of algorithms used for topic theme detection, target audience identification and rhetorical question detection

Functions	Algorithms
Semantic similarity calculation between a file and a topic term	To use BuildIndex Java API to produce both term and document vectors and use semanticvectors.Search API to search for document vectors closest to the vector for a topic theme using cosine similarity.
Semantic similarity calculation between any two files	To use the Java API for the CompareTerms tool to compare two file vectors.
Target audience identification	To find out if two inputs from two individual speakers sharing at least one of the same discussion topics. Or to check if target audiences' names are mentioned in the input.
Rhetorical question detection	To recognize an input as a question sentence type by Rasp and then calculate semantic distances between this input and the two training question files (one containing normal questions and the other file containing rhetorical questions).

aim to extend our application to a broader daily life context to identify such complex phenomena of human behaviors during social interactions and to help users better in learning situations.

In this initial gesture study and recognition, we focus on several universally accepted emotional gestures such as the following. Pease (1984) claimed that standard arm-cross is a universal gesture signifying defensive or negative attitude. Hands-on-hips pose especially when standing is regarded as one of the common gestures used to communicate an aggressive attitude. He also pointed out that when two men are standing in this pose, then a fight is about to occur. Scratching one's head is normally seen during exams and tends to indicate confusion. If someone is spotting with both hands holding forehead, it probably indicates frustration or a disaster situation. If a person shows one hand holding one elbow, it probably indicates shyness. Therefore, we make initial exploration to recognize the above gestures including: folded arms (aggressive), one hand on elbow (shy), one hand scratching head (confused), both hands holding hips (angry) and both hands holding forehead (frustrated). These gestures mainly refer to upper body language in order to represent typical emotional behaviors expressed while the users are in a sitting position such as in this application.

In order to recognize the target emotional gestures, Kinect (http://www.microsoft.com/en-us/kinectforwindows), a motion sensing device produced by Microsoft, is used. It provides skeleton tracking APIs and is capable of establishing positions of 20 skeleton joints. We have developed an algorithm in C++ based on these standard APIs to especially identify the positions of seven joints (e.g. head, hand right, hand left, elbow left, elbow right, hip left and hip right) in real-time interactions. The Kinect sensor's skeleton tracking engine is also able to perform well on a partially occluded body (such as when a person is sitting near a table).

An unsupervised learning neural network algorithm, Adaptive Resonance Theory (ART-2), is employed to perform emotional gesture recognition. Initial recognition results indicate that all the emotional gestures are well recognized with averaged 0.80+ precision and recall scores. We also aim to incorporate affect detection from verbal communication mentioned above with the emotional gesture recognition presented here in order to draw a more reliable conclusion on affect detection in social contexts in future work.

EVALUATION

The context-based affect detection will only be activated if the user inputs contain weak or no obvious strong affect indicators. Then the semantic vector APIs are activated to detect their topic themes and identify their potential target audiences. Finally, the rule-based affect detection implemented in Jess is used to detect affect for these inputs with the consideration of character profiles, interpersonal relationships between the speakers and target audiences, the inputs' discussion themes and sentence types, and the target audiences' most recent emotions.

We have taken previously collected transcripts recorded during our user testing with 180 school children to evaluate the efficiency of the updated affect detection component with contextual inference. In order to evaluate the performances of the topic theme detection and the rule based affect detection in the social context, three transcripts of the Crohn's disease scenario are used. Two human judges are employed to annotate the topic themes of the extracted 300 user inputs from the test three transcripts using the previously mentioned 13 topic categories. Cohen's Kappa is a statistical measurement of inter-annotator agreement. It provides robust measurement by taking the agreement occurring by chance into consideration. We used it to measure the inter-agreement between human judges for the topic theme annotation and obtained 0.83. Then the 265 example inputs with agreed topic theme annotations are used as the gold standard to test the performance of the topic theme detection. A keyword pattern matching baseline system has been used to compare the performance with that of the LSA. The results are provided in Table 2.

The detailed results indicated that discussion themes of 'bullying', 'disease' and 'food choices' have been very well detected by the semantic-based analysis. The discussions on 'family care' and 'suggestion' topics posed most of the challenges. For example, the following input is from Peter classified as a 'suggestion' topic by the human annotators, "This is so hard and I need your support". The semantic analysis has given the highest similarity score (0.905) to one of the 'bullying' theme training documents and the 2nd highest score (0.901) to the training document with the 'suggestion' theme. Although the topic detection using LSA made errors like the above sometimes, the similarity scores for the ideal classifications became very close to the top score for another topic category. We also notice that sometimes without many contexts, the test inputs showed ambiguity for the topic detection task even for human judges. Generally the semantic-based interpretation achieves promising results.

The two human judges have also annotated these 265 example inputs with the 15 frequently used emotions including 'neutral', 'approval', 'disapproval', 'angry', 'grateful', 'regretful', 'happy', 'sad', 'worried', 'stressful', 'sympathetic', 'embarrassed', 'praising', 'threatening' and 'caring'. They are chosen simply because of their high occurrences in the recorded transcripts of this Crohn's disease scenario than the occurrences of other emotions such as 'gloating', which is more frequently used in another testing scenario, the school bullying scenario.

Cohen's Kappa is used again to as an effective channel to measure our system's performance. In our application, since 15 emotions

were used for annotation and the annotators may not experience the exact emotions as the test subjects did, it led to the low inter-agreement between human judges. The inter-agreement between human judge A/B is 0.63. While the previous version of the affect detection without any contextual inference achieves 0.46 in good cases, the new version achieves inter-agreements with human judge A/B respectively 0.56 and 0.58. Although the inter-agreement improvements are comparatively small due to using a large category of emotions, many expressions regarded as 'neutral' by the previous version have been annotated appropriately as emotional expressions.

As mentioned earlier, since concepts, terms and emotional expressions can be expressed in multiple ways, the semantic interpretation of the interaction contexts can go beyond linguistic syntactical features and focuses on the underlying semantic structures of the inputs. It can associate syntactically different but semantically similar terms and documents to detect topic themes. The topic theme detection is able to identify sudden topic changes to benefit rule-based affect detection from improvisational contexts. Example inputs from the school bullying scenario and articles from the Experience website are also used to further prove the robustness of the semantic-based analysis and rule-based affect detection.

120 inputs have been taken from the transcripts of the school bullying scenario. Human judges also provide topic theme annotations using the 13 categories of topic themes. Comparing with the annotations provided by one human judge, the semantic-based topic theme detection achieves an 83% accuracy rate shown in Table 3. The latent semantic analysis implemented using the semantic vector pack-

Table 2. The averaged precision and recall scores for the 13 topic theme detection using the LSA-based approach comparing with a baseline system

	The Average Precision	The Averaged Recall
LSA-based topic detection	0.736	0.733
The baseline system	0.603	0.583

age proves to perform well for the topic theme detection using sample inputs from another scenario. Another 26 articles taken from the Experience website (16 articles) and the ATT-Meta databank (10 files) are also used to further evaluate the performance of LSA-based topic theme detection. The test articles borrowed from the Experience website belong to the following themes: 'Crohn's disease', 'bullying', 'family care', 'food choice', 'school lunch', 'school uniform', 'suggestions' and 'disagreement'. Two articles with six sentences on average per article for each of the above themes are included in the test documents. Metaphorical examples are borrowed from the ATT-Meta databank targeting the following phenomena: cooking, family, weather, farm and ideas metaphors. Each metaphorical input consists of one test document. Two metaphorical documents are included in the test files. Thus 26 files in total are used to further evaluate the robustness and generalization abilities of the topic theme detection. As shown in Table 3, the LSA-based topic detection achieves an 86% accuracy rate for the topic classification for the 16 test articles borrowed from the Experience website and an accuracy rate of 82% for the recognition of the 10 metaphorical expressions.

Moreover, the 120 example inputs from the bullying scenario are also annotated by the human judges using three labels of positive, negative and neutral. The 120 inputs contain 33% negative, 32% positive and 35% neutral expressions. The outputs of the rule-based affect detection are also converted into binary values. Comparing with the annotation provided by one human annotator, the rule-based affect detection achieves a 68% accuracy rate for the negative emotions, a 63% accuracy rate for the positive

emotions and 60% for the neutral expressions. The above evaluation results indicate that the system can perform reasonably stably for comparatively new application contexts. In future work, a bigger sample size will be used to further evaluate the system's efficiency and generalization abilities.

CONCLUSION

Although there is related work to detect emotions from sentence-level inputs, the use of contexts to inform affect detection is very rarely addressed. Especially, our application focuses on multi-party dialog contexts and this makes the interpretation of social contexts even more challenging. The work presented here focuses on the affect detection from interaction contexts using latent semantic analysis and rule-based reasoning. Especially, the semantic-based analysis is able to identify the discussion themes and target audiences of the current input to inform affect detection. The evaluation results also indicate the semantic analysis and rule-based affect reasoning performed reasonably stably in comparatively new application domains.

Moreover, in this research, we also made initial exploration to recognize several universally accepted emotional gestures. Such multi-modal affect detection shows great potential in interpreting affect embedded in complex social interactions. It also provides a non-intrusive channel to identify users' experience on a moment-by-moment basis.

In future work, we are interested in using topic extraction to inform affect detection directly, e.g. the suggestion of a topic change indicating potential indifference to or un-interest

Table 3. Further evaluation of topic theme detection using transcripts of the bullying scenario, articles extracted from the experience website and other metaphorical examples

	120 Inputs from the Bullying Scenario	26 Articles from the Experience Website	10 Metaphorical Examples
Accuracy rate for topic theme detection	83%	86%	82%

in the current discussion theme. It will also ease the interaction if our agent is equipped with culturally related small talk behavior. We also aim to incorporate each weak affect indicator embedded in semantic analysis and emotional gesture recognition to draw more reliable affect interpretation in improvisational contexts. We believe these are crucial aspects for the development of personalized intelligent agents with social and emotion intelligence.

REFERENCES

Barnden, J. A. (2007). Metaphor, semantic preferences and context-sensitivity. In K. Ahmad, C. Brewster, & M. Stevenson (Eds.), *Words and intelligence II: Essays in honor of Yorick Wilks* (pp. 39–62). Dordrecht, Netherlands: Springer. doi:10.1007/1-4020-5833-0_2.

Batliner, A., Steidl, S., Hacker, C., & Nöth, E. (2008). Private emotions vs. social interaction — A data-driven approach towards analysing emotions in speech. *User Modeling and User-Adapted Interaction, 18*, 175–206. doi:10.1007/s11257-007-9039-4.

Briscoe, E., & Carroll, J. (2002). Robust accurate statistical annotation of general text. In *Proceedings of the 3rd International Conference on Language Resources and Evaluation* (pp. 1499-1504), Las Palmas de Gran Canaria, Canary Islands.

Craggs, R., & Wood, M. (2004). A two dimensional annotation scheme for emotion in dialogue. In *Proceedings of AAAI Spring Symposium: Exploring Attitude and Affect in Text* (pp. 44-49).

Ekman, P. (1999). Basic emotions. In T. Dalgleish, & M. Power (Eds.), *Handbook of cognition and emotion*. Sussex, UK: John Wiley & Sons.

Endrass, B., Rehm, M., & André, E. (2011). Planning small talk behavior with cultural influences for multiagent systems. *Computer Speech & Language, 25*(2), 158–174. doi:10.1016/j.csl.2010.04.001.

Fainsilber, L., & Ortony, A. (1987). Metaphorical uses of language in the expression of emotions. *Metaphor and Symbolic Activity, 2*(4), 239–250. doi:10.1207/s15327868ms0204_2.

Fellbaum, C. (1998). *WordNet: An electronic lexical database*. Cambridge, MA: MIT Press.

Kappas, A. (2010). Smile when you read this, whether you like it or not: Conceptual challenges to affect detection. *IEEE Transactions on Affective Computing, 1*(1), 38–41. doi:10.1109/T-AFFC.2010.6.

Klema, V., & Laub, A. (1980). The singular value decomposition: Its computation and some applications. *IEEE Transactions on Automatic Control, 25*(2), 164–176. doi:10.1109/TAC.1980.1102314.

Kövecses, Z. (1998). Are there any emotion-specific metaphors? In A. Athanasiadou, & E. Tabakowska (Eds.), *Speaking of emotions: Conceptualization and expression* (pp. 127–151). Berlin, Germany: Mouton de Gruyter. doi:10.1515/9783110806007.127.

Landauer, T. K., & Dumais, S. (2008). Latent semantic analysis. *Scholarpedia, 3*(11), 4356. doi:10.4249/scholarpedia.4356.

Mower, E., Metallinou, A., Lee, C., Kazemzadeh, A., Busso, C., Lee, S., & Narayanan, S. S. (2009). Interpreting ambiguous emotional expressions. In *Proceedings of International Conference on Affective Computing and Intelligent Interaction* (pp. 662-669). Amsterdam, The Netherlands.

Neviarouskaya, A., Prendinger, H., & Ishizuka, M. (2010). Recognition of affect, judgment, and appreciation in text. In *Proceedings of the 23rd International Conference on Computational Linguistics* (pp. 806-814), Beijing, China.

Ortony, A., Clore, G. L., & Collins, A. (1988). *The cognitive structure of emotions*. Cambridge, UK: Cambridge University Press. doi:10.1017/CBO9780511571299.

Pease, A. (1984). *Body language – How to read others' thoughts by their gestures*. London, UK: Sheldon Press.

Ptaszynski, M., Dybala, P., Shi, W., Rzepka, R., & Araki, K. (2009). Towards context aware emotional intelligence in machines: Computing contextual appropriateness of affective states. In *Proceedings of Twenty-First International Joint Conference on Artificial Intelligence* (pp. 1469-1474), Pasadena, CA.

Rayson, P. (2003). Matrix: A statistical method and software tool for linguistic analysis through corpus comparison. Unpublished doctoral dissertation, Lancaster University, Lancaster, UK.

Russell, J. A., Bachorowski, J.-A., & Fernández-Dols, J. M. (2003). Facial and vocal expressions of emotion. *Annual Review of Psychology, 54*, 329–349. doi:10.1146/annurev.psych.54.101601.145102 PMID:12415074.

Scherer, K. R. (2003). Vocal communication of emotion: A review of research paradigms. *Speech Communication, 40*, 227–256. doi:10.1016/S0167-6393(02)00084-5.

Strapparava, C., & Valitutti, A. (2004). WordNet-affect: An affective extension of WordNet. In *Proceedings of the 4th International Conference on Language Resources and Evaluation*, Lisbon, Portugal (pp. 1083-1086).

Sun, X., Lichtenauer, J., Valstar, M. F., Nijholt, A., & Pantic, M. (2011). A multimodal database for mimicry analysis. In Proceedings of Affective Computing and Intelligent Interaction (pp. 367-376), Memphis, TN.

Turing, A. M. (1950). Computing machinery and intelligence. *Mind, 59*, 433–460. doi:10.1093/mind/LIX.236.433.

Widdows, D., & Cohen, T. (2010). The semantic vectors package: New algorithms and public tools for distributional semantics. In *Proceedings of IEEE International Conference on Semantic Computing*, Pittsburgh, PA (pp. 9-15).

Zhang, L. (2010). Exploitation on contextual affect sensing and dynamic relationship interpretation. *ACM Computers in Entertainment, 8*(3).

Zhang, L., & Barnden, J. A. (2010). Affect and metaphor sensing in virtual drama. *International Journal of Computer Games Technology*. doi:10.1155/2010/512563.

Zhang, L., Gillies, M., Dhaliwal, K., Gower, A., Robertson, D., & Crabtree, B. (2009). E-drama: Facilitating online role-play using an AI actor and emotionally expressive characters. *International Journal of Artificial Intelligence in Education, 19*(1), 5–38.

ENDNOTES

[1] The previous work was supported by grant RES-328-25-0009 from the ESRC under the ESRC/EPSRC/DTI 'PACCIT' programme. It was also partially supported by EPSRC grant EP/C538943/1.

[2] Peter has Crohn's disease and has the option to undergo a life-changing but dangerous surgery. He needs to discuss the pros and cons with friends and family. Janet (Mum) wants Peter to have the operation. Matthew (Peter's brother) is against it. Arnold (Dad) is not able to face the situation. Dave (the best friend) mediates the discussion.

Li Zhang is a Senior Lecturer in the School of Computing, Engineering and Information Sciences, Northumbria University since Sept 2011. She is also a member of Computational Intelligence Research Group. Currently, Dr. Zhang is also an Honorary Research Fellow in the School of Computer Science, University of Birmingham. Before joining Northumbria, Dr. Zhang worked in Teesside University as a Senior Lecturer since Oct 2007. Moreover, she holds a PhD degree awarded by the School of Computer Science, University of Birmingham and also gained Research Fellow experience in the University of Birmingham collaborated with partners from academia and industry. Dr. Zhang holds expertise in the field of artificial intelligence and affective computing and has been involved in a number of EPSRC, ESRC and EU funded projects. She has collaborated with national and international industrial and academic partners for research work development, funding application and research visiting.

John A. Barnden is a Professor in Artificial Intelligence in the School of Computer Science, University of Birmingham. He has led several EPSRC/ESRC funded projects in the past. He is currently working on a project in figurative language area funded by the Leverhulme Trust. His research interests mainly include Natural language Processing and Artificial Intelligence. He was a co-proposer of a series of EURESCO conferences focusing on metaphor. Previously he joined the organizational board of the RAAM (Researching and Applying Metaphor) series of international conferences. He co-organized workshops on figurative language at the Corpus'01 and Corpus'03 conferences (Lancaster Univ.) and at ACL 2003 (Sapporo). He was an invited contributor to the Handbook on Metaphor *edited by Ray Gibbs for Cambridge University Press. Currently Prof. Barnden is also a Programme chair for AISB/IACAP World Congress 2012.*

Using Emotional Intelligence in Training Crisis Managers:
The Pandora Approach

Lachlan Mackinnon, School of Computing & Mathematical Sciences, Old Royal Naval College, University of Greenwich, London, UK

Liz Bacon, School of Computing & Mathematical Sciences, Old Royal Naval College, University of Greenwich, London, UK

Gabriella Cortellessa, Consiglio Nazionale delle Ricerche-Istituto di Scienze e Tecnologie della Cognizione, Rome, Italy

Amedeo Cesta, Consiglio Nazionale delle Ricerche-Istituto di Scienze e Tecnologie della Cognizione, Rome, Italy

ABSTRACT

Multi-agency crisis management represents one of the most complex of real-world situations, requiring rapid negotiation and decision-making under extreme pressure. However, the training offered to strategic planners, called Gold Commanders, does not place them under any such pressure. It takes the form of paper-based, table-top exercises, or expensive, real-world, limited-scope simulations. The Pandora project has developed a rich multimedia training environment for Gold Commanders, based on a crisis scenario, timeline-based, event network, with which the trainees and their trainer interact dynamically. Pandora uses the emotional intelligence of the trainees, through a behavioural modelling component, to support group dynamic and decision-making. It applies systemic emotional intelligence, based on inferred user state and rule-based affective inputs, to impact the stress levels of the trainees. Pandora can impose variable stress on trainees, to impact their decision-making, and model their behaviour and performance under stress, potentially resulting in more effective and realisable strategies.

Keywords: Affective Markup, Affective State Manipulation, Behavioural Modelling, Crisis Management Training Environment, Crisis Scenario Planning, Emotional Intelligence, Gold Commanders, Timeline-Based Event Network

DOI: 10.4018/jdet.2013040104

1. INTRODUCTION

When a crisis occurs, the resources to control and manage all the services and functions necessary to enable an effective response have to be released, coordinated and targeted, within the shortest possible time, to minimise the impact of that crisis on civil society. To achieve this, strategic plans are in place to mobilise and divert resources and personnel, under emergency measures, to deal with local, national and international level incidents. These strategic plans provide a general infrastructure in which specific strategic decisions, relative to the particular crisis, can be taken and then tactically and operationally enacted. The individuals responsible for developing the general strategic plans and then making the crisis-specific strategic decisions are entitled Gold Commanders, in the UK and a number of other countries. Those individuals who operate at Gold Commander level will usually be senior managers or executives within the services engaged in crisis management or control, or senior local authority or local government executives with direct responsibility for protecting the functions of civil society. As such, one can anticipate that these individuals will bring a wealth of knowledge and experience in their particular fields to the process of crisis management strategic planning, but the coordination, negotiation and pragmatic trade-offs necessary to deal with a real-world major crisis scenario still have to be learnt.

Recent developments in rich multimedia environments, in particular in computer games and serious games technologies, offer the opportunity for the development of realistic computer-based simulations of complex real-world crisis scenarios. This in turn offers the opportunity to develop training environments, utilising such technologies, in which Gold Commanders can hone and develop their strategic planning and decision-making skills, in multi-agency negotiation situations, set against timeline-based unfolding crisis scenarios. Techniques taken from the games industry in the creation of effective simulation of real world scenarios are already well understood in the creation of learning environments (Atkin, 2004; Graven & MacKinnon, 2006), and much of the serious games industry has grown up around the concept of "Serious Games for Serious Training" (Chan, 2007) with applications being developed for a range of situations from military and security, through health and education (Graven & MacKinnon, 2008), all the way to politics (Ochalla, 2007). However, creating realistic representations of real-world situations requires more than just the provision of information in multimodal forms, the stresses associated with decision-making in a constrained time frame, with conflicting requirements for different services that have to be negotiated and prioritised, also need to be replicated.

The context for this work, therefore, is very specifically related to the requirements for the training of Gold Commanders, and all design decisions taken in the development of the work are motivated by that consideration. In this context, we can consider issues of emotional intelligence from two perspectives. Firstly, the development of a systemic capability to engage with the emotions and behaviours of trainees, to replicate the stresses and emotional affects of a real world situation. Realistically, the provision of systemic emotional intelligence can be considered, as it is in the affective computing community, as an application of artificial intelligence (AI). This would involve the use of inferencing mechanisms and rule-based consequences and actions, which are invoked at appropriate points during the training session to increase or decrease the stress of an individual trainee or group of trainees. Secondly, to consider the group dynamics of an on-line training situation, from the perspective of individual trainees utilising emotional intelligence to achieve consensus or personal goals. In this situation, the application of emotional intelligence is entirely human in its form, but the use of that intelligence to negotiate and manipulate on-line activities and decisions is embedded in, and supported by, the training system.

In order to support both perspectives of emotional intelligence, a key consideration for the development of a simulation environment for crisis management strategic planning therefore needs to be the provision of affective inputs. Such inputs will create a highly stressed and time-constrained ambience, resulting in more realistic decision-making under pressure, pragmatic strategic negotiation and planning, and, as a result, more accurate trainee performance measures. However, the existing demographic of Gold Commanders precludes providing training through a fully virtual immersive serious game environment (evidenced from a detailed user requirements exercise), and requires an evolutionary development from existing fully physical environments through a rich multimedia, augmented reality environment. As a result, the consideration of the development of affective management of the environment, including affect detection, will require techniques that work within both the physical and digital elements of that environment. The Pandora project is seeking to address just these issues, in developing a training environment for Gold Commanders that captures behavioural and emotional information about the trainees prior to the commencement of training, physiological and personally reported information on behavioural and emotional state during training, decision-making monitoring information during training, trainer observation information during training, and provides detail of all that information as part of performance assessment and feedback. The Pandora system also provides the facility to create affective ambience to impact the stress levels, and hence the emotional and behavioural performance of the trainees, through the use of information management and manipulation techniques, rule-based multimedia mashups and emotive character representations through non-playing characters.

The rest of this paper sets out the details of the Pandora project and the tools and facilities it provides. This is followed by a detailed description of the Behavioural Framework, providing the emotion and behaviour capture facilities described above, providing support for the emotional intelligence of the trainees in addressing the tasks within the training scenario. We then describe the Emotion Engine, in which the systemic emotional intelligence of Pandora is utilised to manage information within the training environment, providing the mechanisms to create affective ambience. Finally, we briefly discuss system testing and the analysis of the user experiments. A short conclusion then identifies the contributions to date, and the future work and expansive potential of the Pandora outcomes.

2. THE PANDORA PROJECT

As described above, the Pandora system is designed to enhance and expand training exercises for Gold Commanders in crisis management, who are specifically engaged in the development of strategic plans to deal with a wide range of potential crisis situations that can arise in civil society. These crisis situations typically require a multi-agency response and could be caused by:

- **Natural events:** extreme weather, earthquake, landslides, storms, wind, heat wave etc.;
- **Transport events:** plane, train or vehicle crashes;
- **Service failures:** electrical power plant failure, water supply failure, etc.;
- **Health crises:** pandemics, epidemics, containment conditions, disease (including animal disease), toxic chemical release impacting the environment etc.;
- **Technology failures:** breakdown of automated control systems, central services;
- **Policing and terrorism events:** fire or explosions;
- **Some combination of some or all of the above:** which has the potential to risk human health and life and / or impact the supply of essential services.

In order to develop strategic plans to deal with such situations, individuals who carry executive responsibility for the services and facilities identified as strategically critical within these situations e.g. Police, Fire, Ambulance Service, Local Authorities, Health Service, are expected to work together. These individuals are identified as Gold Commanders, and their role is explicitly strategic. They are in overall control of the emergency however, they will not generally be at the site of the emergency, but typically co-located in a control room. They will set the direction and propose solutions for the tactical (Silver) commanders to implement who will also typically not be physically present at the site of the emergency. Silver commanders give direction to operational commanders (Bronze) who are responsible for organising resources on the ground. In practice some Gold Commanders may also have tactical or operational responsibility. Their objectives are to: save and protect life; relieve suffering; contain the emergency; provide the public with information; protect the health and safety of staff; safeguard the environment; protect property; maintain/restore critical services; maintain normal services appropriately; promote and facilitate self-help; facilitate the investigation/inquiry; facilitate community recovery and to evaluate and identify lessons learned.

The training of Gold Commanders to prepare them to manage a crisis is very important and is currently typically undertaken in two ways:

- **Through the use of table-top exercises:** these are low cost, paper-based exercises, with some limited audio-visual input, undertaken by groups of Gold Commanders representing different emergency services etc. led by an expert trainer. These events take place in a dedicated training environment or in a standard meeting room at a Gold Commander venue, as required. The expert trainer provides guidance to the Gold Commanders on the case study being used, tries to provide an intensive time constrained activity to simulate the pressure of a real crisis and provides feedback to the Gold Commanders after the event. This type of training exercise can be easily organised and is cheap to run however it lacks the authentic feel of a real crisis which would place the Gold Commanders under extreme pressure to make rapid and effective decisions. Immersion in the scenario is heavily reliant on the ability of the trainer to enthuse and engage the students;

- **Real-world simulations:** these train Gold Commanders in the field through the use of simulation exercises. These are very effective, however they are also extremely expensive, time consuming to set up, require specialist equipment and can generally only simulate a small part of a potential scenario, and a limited number of outcomes.

As discussed earlier, all Gold Commanders will have pre-prepared plans ready for an emergency however, each emergency will present unique challenges and plans will inevitably have to be adapted on-the-fly to each emergency situation. It is therefore important that during a training session, Gold Commanders are presented with situations that force them to move away from their pre-prepared plans and out of their comfort zone, to see how they cope with previously unforeseen problems, what stress this causes them, and how they work with other Gold Commanders to resolve a crisis in a collaborative way. In summary, the purpose of these types of training events is to:

- Develop the collaborative skills of the trainees in formulating strategic responses across a number of organisations and events;
- Develop the strategic thinking of the trainees in considering the implications of their decisions and the effects on other services;
- Develop the responsive skills of trainees in formulating alternative strategies and remediating actions in the event of the failure of a strategic response;
- Determine the strategic planning ability, decision-making capability, flexibility and capability under pressure of the trainees;

- Develop skills to deal with the media, which are inevitably required in the event of a crisis.

However, as outlined above, the typical table-top training model that is used has severe limitations in achieving these goals, and is almost entirely dependent on the ability of the trainer to engage and motivate the trainees, and to assess their performance subjectively in the training event. When a crisis occurs, human behaviour and preparedness is critical to the delivery of an effective solution and therefore training needs to be as realistic as possible. It is important to be able to simulate the information overload and related stress, together with the pressure in making decisions. Pandora therefore aims to bridge the gap between the low cost, table-top exercises and the expensive real world simulations by providing an on-line e-learning environment in which the group and the trainer can participate in a realistic, dynamically changing, time sensitive, immersive crisis simulation exercise, that allows trainees to practice their decision making and negotiation skills within a realistic, stress-controlled environment (Bacon et al., 2011).

2.1. Pandora Modes of Delivery

The Pandora crisis training room, which is where training is conducted, is designed to work in three different modes. These are:

1. **Single site training:** in this mode, the training takes place in a physical room where the trainees and the trainer are co-located. The trainees work independently within the room and regularly meet collectively around the table in the same way, as they would have done for the paper-based table-top exercise. However, with Pandora, a range of consoles are used to provide multimedia information using sound, pictures, maps, animations, videos etc. for example, to simulate receiving information about the crisis such as a news broadcast. Biometric sensors are also used to gather physiological information about the trainees to assist in an analysis of their stress levels etc. The trainer is able to configure the scenario to e.g. set up non-playing characters (NPC) to play the role of an emergency service not represented within the group of trainees; subject matter experts; represent higher control (HICON) such as Government ministers - these individuals would be above the level of Gold Commanders and have the authority to demand actions or constrain resources, and can impose their decisions on the crisis team and the scenario; lower control (LOCON) such as Silver Commanders (tactical) or Bronze Commanders (operational) - these represent the lower levels of command within the crisis team, and can provide valuable feedback on the tactical level realisation of the strategy being developed by the Gold Commanders. (N.B. A non-playing character, in the context of Pandora, is a computer based actor within the scenario that either provides an automated, fixed, pre-scripted representation of one of the above roles, or can be taken over by the trainer to provide a dynamic capability);
2. **Deployed training:** this is essentially the same as for the single site training however it is not delivered in a dedicated room, but elsewhere, for example at the site of one of the Gold Commanders taking part in the training. The Pandora system, equipment and setup must therefore be portable to enable this delivery mode to be realised;
3. **Distributed training:** the standard Pandora model described in modes 1 & 2 can be accessed through a web browser for trainees who are geographically distributed, and the training then run remotely. Alternatively, as shown in Figure 1 and Figure 2, the physical room is replaced by a virtual room and trainees participate through a web-based interface. The 3D virtual room contains non-playing characters, as with the other two modes these fulfil any key emergency service roles that are missing from the group of trainees. Each trainee is represented

Copyright © 2013, IGI Global. Copying or distributing in print or electronic forms without written permission of IGI Global is prohibited.

Figure 1. In-world slide-show and streaming video

Figure 2. In-world map application

by their own avatar. It provides the same multimedia channels as the physical room to provide the trainees with information on the unfolding crisis with which they have to deal (Liu et al., 2011).

2.2. Pandora Architecture

The underpinning architecture of the system is the same for all three deployment modes and is made up of several key components which are described below:

- **The Crisis Module Framework:** This provides an event network to model a crisis scenario against a timeline, supporting the management of the training process including the introduction of decision points for trainees incorporated into events within the crisis scenario. Event network planning and mapping to timelines is managed through a knowledge-based approach, utilising rules stored in the Crisis Knowledge Base;
- **The Behavioural Framework:** This considers the behaviour of trainees, based on a

pre-determined user model, and feedback from biometric sensors and the trainer during the training session. This component shows how a complete loop crisis-stimuli/ trainee-reaction/Pandora-behaviour-analysis can be implemented and shown to work in a training environment;

- **The Trainer Support Framework:** This allows the trainer to carry out four key functions:
  - The setup of a scenario for use with a particular group of trainees e.g. configuring an avatar to represent a missing trainee from one of the emergency services;
  - Customise a training session and dynamically update a scenario whilst it is being executed e.g. by compressing the timeline in which events occur and / or to interject additional events, in order to increase or decrease the stress levels of one of more of the trainees;
  - Rollback a scenario to a previous decision point, if a decision taken by the trainees resulted in an inappropriate or disastrous outcome, the trainer could offer them the opportunity to rerun that part of the scenario. This also offers the facility to model various choices and outcomes for the trainees, to aid in developing trainee understanding of the full range of outcomes;
  - Record each run of the scenario, keeping a note of every event and communication in sequence, so that the trainer can review the training session after it has been completed with one or more trainees to reflect on the rationale for the decisions made and the alternative choices that could have been chosen during the simulation;
- **The Emotion Engine:** This is a middleware component within the Pandora system, providing facilities for the development, configuration and introduction of non-playing characters (NPC) into the crisis scenario to interact with the trainees, and multimedia information assets, tagged for

emotional affect. The NPC framework also permits the trainer to take control of an NPC to provide direct inputs, in specific events, to the trainees. The Affective Framework, which is a sub-component of the emotion engine, manages a repository of affectively tagged multimedia assets. It uses inputs from the behavioural framework and local mashup rules to produce combinations of those assets to provide emotionally and behaviourally affective information to the trainees. This facility represents the emotional intelligence of the system, as it uses the inferred emotional state of the trainee from the behavioural framework together with AI rule combinations to develop an emotional trajectory to move the trainee to a desired state. The trajectory is realised through the output of the Emotion Engine, generated through the Environment Framework Builder, which is a rendering specification describing the environmental conditions, multimedia information assets and NPCs to be represented in the training environment;

- **The Emulated Crisis Room:** in essence this is the trainee environment, since the rendering of the information generated from the other components is realised within this component. The virtual representation of the room is shown in Figure 1 and Figure 2;
- **Integration of the above components:** managed through a middleware model that has been developed for the project, and various test beds and test harnesses are also being constructed specifically to meet the needs of the Pandora system.

3. BEHAVIORAL CLASSIFICATION AND CAPTURE

Emotions, and emotional intelligence, play a key role in adaptive behaviour. Research in neuroscience and psychology has shown the strong connection between cognition and emotion. In particular, cognition plays an important role in creating emotions through cognitive processes involved in the cognitive appraisal. Emotions, in turn, cause a wide range of effects on attention, perception and cognitive processes involved in decision making, problem solving and learning. Recently, researchers have broadened the spectrum of elements of interest and used the word "affect" to consider other variables besides emotions.

A seminal issue on "Affective modelling and adaptation" that appeared in User Modelling and User-Adapted Interaction Journal (Springer Netherlands) introduces some issues that are particularly relevant to frame the purpose of our study. In an introduction to the special issue (Carberry & De Rosis, 2008), affective computing is described through four areas of interest. The first area is on the analysis of affective states as well as the analysis of the relationship between affection and cognition, such as learning. The second area of interest is the automatic recognition of affective states. Examples of research in this direction concern the analysis of facial expressions, linguistic expressions, acoustic signals such as prosody, posture, or physiological signals such as heart rate. The third issue concerns the adaptation of a system to a particular affective state of a person while the last dimension of affective computing concerns the design of avatars able to exhibit affective states, with the objective of ensuring a more effective interaction.

Such distinction is useful to introduce the work done in Pandora. We have worked at integrating features of the second, third and fourth areas of interest in a uniform framework devoted to train "Gold Commanders". More precisely we aim at:

1. Detecting affective states that influence crisis decision-making. With respect to the analysis provided by (Calvo & D'Mello, 2010), it is worth noting our use of a combination of psychological self-assessment with physiological measures to detect changes of monitored user states. An original point stems also from the use of

timeline-based techniques for modelling user features as described later in the paper;

2. Personalising stimuli to the trainee (both individuals and the whole class) starting from the specific trainee's affective state. It is worth observing how personalization techniques have been previously used, for example, to influence the student learning curves (e.g., Shute & Psotka, 1996; Baffes & Mooney, 1996; Conati et al., 2002; Conati & Maclaren, 2009). The Pandora engine plans personalised stimuli with the aim of maximising training effectiveness, in particular this is obtained through a combination of causal rules, enacted by an adaptation feature of the Crisis Planner;

3. Producing engaging and emotionally affective interactions. As identified in the Introduction, the environment developed for Pandora needs to provide a rich multimedia, augmented reality experience for the trainees. Within that environment, prior to, and during, training, a combination of techniques will be used to detect and monitor trainee emotion, predominantly through stress levels. Since this environment includes both physical and digital interactive elements, it is not feasible to consider the use of purely digital affective techniques in this case. Pandora has, therefore, looked to develop techniques based on existing games technologies, particularly those which have a group physical interaction component. For example, Yannakakis et al. (2008) consider interaction with a game, Playtime, as a tool to study how fun can be recognised from the integration of physiological data with data from self-assessment. The ultimate objective of this research is to estimate the level of engagement in games in order to adjust the virtual environment to the preferences of children. In Pandora, we are using the capture of behavioural and emotional information about the trainees prior to the commencement of training, physiological and personally reported information on behavioural and emotional state during

training, decision-making monitoring information during training, and trainer observation information during training to support affect detection and management. Based on this information, we then use dynamic adaptation of multi-media assets to produce realistic, contextualised and engaging crisis situations, targeted to provide appropriate levels of affective ambience to impact the stress levels of the trainees. The process is described later in this paper, in Section 4.1.

Of critical importance in considering the effectiveness of the training offered through the Pandora system is the application and use of emotional intelligence by the trainees, in managing and in particular leading, the activities within the training (Goleman et al., 2002). The use of emotional intelligence in interactions with the other trainees, with a view to achieving consensus, or advancing personal goals, is also captured to support analysis of trainee performance within the system.

3.1. Relevant Factors for Modelling Trainees

A preliminary analysis of the literature referring to the variables that have an influence on decision-making has been performed as a specific task of the project. Different variables have been considered, but the final choice has been deeply influenced also by frequent interviews with expert trainers, as well as participation in simulated training exercises as both trainees and observers in order to better understand and capture the specifics of Gold Commander training requirements. Specifically the analysis of the state-of-the-art has been particularly useful in identifying the main "affective factors" that have been already demonstrated as playing a crucial role in the training for decision-making in a crisis situation, while the last two sources have contributed to grounding the choice on a solid, and somehow pragmatic basis, considering the particular domain of application of the Pandora system. The variables eventually taken

into account were *personality traits*, *leadership style*, *background experience*, *self-efficacy*, *stress* and *anxiety*:

*   **Personality Traits:** According to Funder (2007), *personality* refers to an "individuals characteristic patterns of thought, emotion, and behaviour, together with the psychological mechanisms, hidden or not, behind those patterns." Several models are available in the literature, which classify the personality traits according to specific dimensions. Within Pandora we chose the Big Five model according to which of the personality traits can be modelled through five major dimensions: (1) neuroticism vs. emotional stability; (2) extraversion vs. introversion; (3) openness to experience vs. not open to experience; (4) agreeableness vs. antagonism; (5) conscientiousness vs. un-directedness. The Revised NEO Personality Inventory, or NEO-FFI (Five Factors Inventory) (Costa & McCrae, 1992), was therefore selected. The NEO has been widely used to correlate behaviour and internal personality traits and each of the "big five" has been associated with specific behaviours and/or predicted significantly differing job performances by managers. For example The Impact of Emotional Stability/Neuroticism appears to be related to the ability to form and maintain positive relationships in their work environment. Van Vianen and De Dreu (2001) found that high levels of emotional stability contribute to social cohesion in team work, in contrast high levels of Neuroticism may be predictive of anger and abandonment in relationships (Barta & Kiene, 2005). Moreover, this factor appears to be negatively correlated with leadership skills.

Judge and Ilies (2002) also found that conscientiousness is a strong predictor of motivation for good performance. People with high conscientiousness are more likely to be ordered, determined, and autonomous in defining their goals; they also demonstrate a greater capacity to address issues related to time management and stress, and are generally interested in continuous improvement of their performance (Judge & Ilies, 2002; Thoreson et al., 2004). Considering the Openness to experience, it seems that employees who are intellectual, curious and imaginative, are more likely to benefit from training (Barrick & Mount, 1991; Salgado, 1997). These people are generally more willing to be involved in learning experiences:

- **Leadership Style:** In Northouse, (2007) leadership is defined as a "process whereby an individual influences a group of individuals to achieve a common goal". Different classifications exist related to the leadership style. In particular Bales 91958) distinguishes between *socio-emotional* and *task oriented* leadership. The "socio-emotional leader" takes into account feelings and moods of individuals, pays attention to the emotional aspects of interpersonal relationships. A leader focused on the task has as his constant concern the attainment by the group of its purposes. In order for a group to be "successful", both a socio-emotional leadership and a "task leadership centred style" are necessary.

The leadership style can obviously not be changed with a short term training, but the training can be personalised in order to help the trainee understand the consequences of their leadership style in making certain decisions and to encourage them to learn accordingly. This is of particular importance in developing the emotional intelligence of the trainees, both in terms of their understanding of their own emotional makeup, and in consideration of the emotions of their fellow trainees. Developing skills in using their own emotions effectively, and in managing the emotions of others, will enable them to be more effective leaders, in particular when seeking to achieve consensus or to advance their own personal goals (Palmer et al., 2001):

- **Background Experience:** Among the defining characteristics of leaders is their ability to develop and implement appropriate responses to a variety of problem situations (Mumford et al., 2000). These problems include resource allocation, interdepartmental coordination, interpersonal conflict and so on. Traditionally, scholars have tried to understand and explain this ability either in terms of personality traits or in terms of leaders' behaviours. A more recent explanation views effective leadership as a form of developed expertise, requiring a wide range of responses on which to rely, as well as the ability to use that knowledge. Thus, knowledge as a manifestation of intelligence and experience may be seen as a relevant factor in understanding leadership effectiveness.

As a matter of fact, in order to successfully solve the problems they encounter, leaders must make use of a body of knowledge gained from formal education, advice from other leaders and personal experience. It has been pointed out that through experience one may acquire knowledge about how to act in specific situations, although it is not openly expressed. This type of knowledge has been called "tacit" and it is often associated with successful performance, as pointed out by research on expertise in a variety of domains (Hedlund et al., 2003). In other words, experience enables the acquisition of knowledge. This applies equally when we consider emotional intelligence, as this leads to both self-knowledge and knowledge of the emotions and behaviours of others, but this may be tacit in the sense that it is experientially gained and not overtly expressed or recognised by the individual:

- **Self-efficacy:** Bandura (1986) defines Self-Efficacy (SE) as individual belief in the capability to perform a certain task successfully. This belief is likely to differ depending on the activity to which it is related. Accordingly, evidence suggests that self-efficacy is not stable over time, but may vary throughout a training or a learning episode (McQuiggan et al., 2008). For example, in the educational context it has been found that self-efficacy may predict which problems and sub-problems a student will select to solve, how long s/he will persist and how much effort will be expended.

As regards leaders, their level of self-efficacy may be a relevant factor in predicting their performance in crisis situations. Leadership efficacy has been defined as "a specific form of efficacy associated with the level of confidence in the knowledge, skills and abilities associated with leading others" (Hanna et al., 2008). Moreover, leaders must be able to recognise the strengths and weaknesses of their group and possibly make changes that improve the work of the group. They must also be able to gain the trust of the group, to form a relationship with its members in order to have a basis to address their work and motivate them to overcome obstacles and get them committed to work hard. This is clearly an area where individuals with strong emotional intelligence will be successful, and indeed their performance may be improved by explicit understanding of the concepts of emotional intelligence. From this perspective, it follows the definition of leadership self-efficacy as "a person's judgment that s/he can successfully exerts leadership by setting a direction for the work group, building relationships with followers in order to gain their commitment to change goals and working with them to overcome obstacles to change" (Paglis & Green, 2002).

Previous studies (Bandura, 1986) indicate that individuals, who believe they are not capable of handling difficult situations, are more likely to experience stress and anxiety, compared to those who believe they are able to do it. Accordingly, we expect that the lower the level of self-efficacy (SE), the higher the stress and anxiety experienced by leaders. In addition, self-efficacy has the advantage of being open to influence (e.g. training) rather than a trait-like quality, which will remain fixed

(Stajkovic & Luthans, 1998). As a consequence, SE is especially useful not only for assessing the quality of leadership in crisis, but also for improving it:

- **Stress & Anxiety:** For a long time the "ideal decision maker" was seen as rational and behaving with a "cool head", although early studies (Keinan, 1987) have underlined the role played by specific internal states, like stress and anxiety. Stress is defined as "a process by which certain work demands evoke an appraisal process in which perceived demands exceed resources and result in undesirable physiological, emotional, cognitive and social changes" (Salas et al., 1996). This definition is considered particularly relevant, since in an emergency situation, a key factor is that demands often exceed resources, both in the management of an emergency and in response options. Evidences suggest that individuals under stress and anxiety often fail to adopt rational-choice models. In other words, they do not often base their decisions on the utilities and probabilities associated with all available courses of actions. Rather, they:
  - Devote insufficient time to the consideration of available alternatives;
  - Make decisions before considering all potential information;
  - Consider alternatives in a disorganised manner.

It should be noted, however, that scholars have made a distinction between "state anxiety", which reflects a "transitory emotional state or condition of the human organism that is characterised by subjective, consciously perceived feelings of tension and apprehension, and heightened autonomic nervous system activity" and "trait anxiety" that denotes "relatively stable individual differences in anxiety proneness and refers to a general tendency to respond with anxiety to perceived threats in the environment".

This distinction is very important in the context of leading a crisis because it has significant implications for leaders' behaviours. While trait anxiety implies that a leader who has this trait will be constantly anxious across situations, state anxiety implies variability in the emotional state of leaders depending on the characteristic of the situations and their belief in their own ability to cope with a crisis condition. Obviously, the level of emotional intelligence exhibited by the leader in this situation will determine how realistic their response is to the anxiety they are feeling (Spielberger, 2010). Particularly in situations of trait anxiety, one would anticipate that an emotionally intelligent and aware individual would recognise this condition in themselves and be able to distinguish a standard threshold level of anxiety from an increased level representing state anxiety. We should also identify that an individual undertaking a leadership role should be in a position to recognise anxiety within others within the group, and should have the emotional intelligence to understand the nature and strength of that anxiety. Using emotional intelligence wisely in such situations can make a leader more effective.

Negative affective state, such as anxiety, may alter the process through which people make decisions. It is widely recognised that anxiety interferes with the ability of individuals to process information (Eysenck, 1982), more specifically they process information less systematically in judgment and decision-making processes (Conway & Giannopoulos, 1993). In addition, anxiety may influence decisions by shaping decision-makers' motivations, by reducing their belief in their capability to control negative events and outcomes in general. This occurs mainly because anxiety is generally experienced in response to situations where the person is uncertain about an impending outcome that may be relevant either for the person or the community, especially when the outcome is potentially harmful and the person feels unable to alter the course of an event (Raghunathan & Pham, 1999). From an affect–as–information perspective (Schwarz, 1990), individuals who are experiencing anxiety are likely to interpret their feelings as signalling high uncertainty and a lack of control.

All the above mentioned variables are subdivided between (a) *static* features that do not change during training episodes, being mainly related to individual personality and (b) *dynamic* features, which can be on the contrary related to both the context and the time, so they may vary during the training. Both dynamic and static variables are used to create the initial trainee profile, while the dynamic ones are also used to update the model. An additional variable that could be added in future is the *individual* and *group performance*, so that the training stimuli can also be adjusted according to this variable.

The following section is focused on how to measure such characteristics in order to investigate their relation to the performance of crisis decision makers. It is evident that it is important to get a good understanding of how leaders respond effectively to a crisis situation and how their personal characteristics can be evaluated in advance of a crisis occurring, in order to facilitate the development of capability-building interventions before crisis events occur and, in this way, try to prevent their negative consequences.

3.2. Assessing Behavioural Aspects in Pandora

In order to maintain an updated model of the Pandora trainees, based on the selection of relevant variables presented in the previous subsection, we designed a framework able to capture different information from trainees both static and dynamic. Figure 3 shows the three main sources of feedback that are considered in assessing trainee behavioural aspects:

- **Interaction Analysis:** This includes all the interactions of the trainees in terms of actions, decisions, amount of information shared with other members of the group and so on. Specifically, some information is automatically gathered by the Pandora system (e.g., trainee decisions), while additional information is also recorded by the system based on the personal annotations of the trainer who observes the training sessions and can annotate the executed plans with respect to the observed trainee behaviours. This additional information can contribute to gathering useful feedback on trainee interaction with the system that can be presented to the trainer both during the exercise as an immediate feedback and at the end of the session to support the debriefing phase;

- **Psychological Self-Assessment:** A set of standardised questionnaires are used to assess the level of the psychological variables used in the system. For example, Crisis Leader Efficacy is assessed by the Assessing and Deciding (C-Lead) Scale (Hadley et al., 2009), which is used to measure self-efficacy within the Pandora Advanced Training Environment (PATE). The Scale consists of 9 items; leaders are classified according to 2 levels of self-efficacy (low: -1 SD and high: + 1 SD), based on their responses on a scale ranging from 1 (Strongly Disagree) to 7 (Strongly Agree).

Anxiety is assessed using the Spielberg's state-trait anxiety inventory, STAI (Spielberger, 2010), which consists of 40 items: 20 are designed to assess state anxiety (S-anxiety scale) and the other 20 are aimed at evaluating trait anxiety (T-anxiety scale). The first one assesses how respondents feel "right now, at this moment". The second one evaluates how people "generally feel". Leader anxiety is compared with a reference sample before the start of the training in order to establish a baseline level. Subsequently this measure will serve as a personal control for the rest of their training. Because we want to know whether the training will have any effect on the leader anxiety level, we assess their anxiety before and after their training and verify any variations in the relationship between the self-efficacy level and anxiety level. Leonard (2004) claimed that the difficulty or confidence, and related anxiety that leaders experience while assessing information and making crisis decisions, can be considered as potentially important indicators of their performance. Accordingly, during the training process (e.g. after a decision has been taken) the trainees are ask dynamically to assess their level

Figure 3. Behavioural framework architecture: Main components to capture trainee behavioural feedback

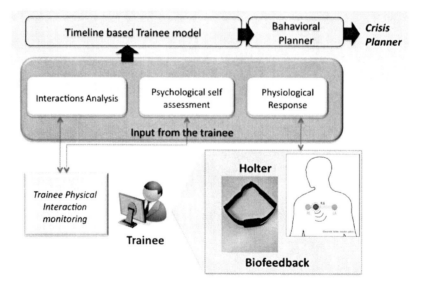

of perceived anxiety and their judgment is then compared with their physiological response:

- **Physiological response:** In order to enrich the trainee model within Pandora as well as to adopt an orthogonal approach for the assessment of some trainee variables, we also use neurophysiologic measures to measure stress and anxiety. A Holter Monitor is part of the Pandora system and is responsible for recording parasympathetic activity (i.e., Heart Rate, HR and Heart Rate Variability, HRV). The physiological measures have been used both during the training to dynamically update the trainee model and after the training to correlate personality traits to physiological responses, as well as to compare this response with the trainee self-assessment. All these variables are mapped onto the timeline base model, which provides input to the Planner to personalise the training stimuli, both in terms of content and in mode of presentation (Cortellessa et al., 2011). Figure 4 shows a screenshot of the Heart Activity monitor of a participant in a training session. Starting from this observation, we can analyse the Heart Rate Variability

that gives us an indication of the emotional involvement of the trainees. In Figure 4, the decision points are indicated by icons, and demonstrate clearly increased heart rate at two of the three decision points. Based on this indication the trainer could propose an interactive intervention to personalise the stimuli. Overall the Heart Activity and Heart Rate variability are stored for post analysis and experimental purposes also with respect to the correlation of selected variables of the user model and trainee emotional response.

3.3. Behavioural Modelling through Timelines

In Pandora we use a timeline-based approach for both the behavioural and crisis planner. In general terms, a *timeline* can be seen as a stepwise constant function of time. Specifically it can be seen as an ordered sequence of values associated with subsequent temporal intervals. Different kinds of values can be used with timelines but, for the current purposes, we will consider only predicate values.

A *predicate* is a statement $P(x, y, ...)$ that depends on one or more arguments $x, y, ...$ each

Figure 4. Physiological feedback trace during training exercise

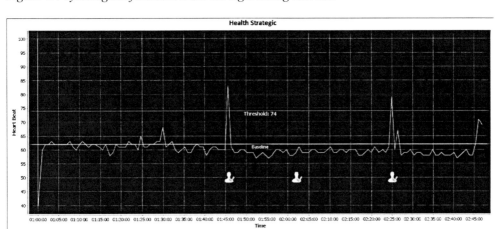

having its own domain. Each value is considered valid over a time interval identified by a *start* and *end* time-point. A set of timelines are used to describe the temporal evolution of the represented world, usually called the domain. To describe consistent temporal behaviours of a domain, the timeline-based approach makes use of the concept of *compatibility* (Muscettola et al., 1992).

A *compatibility* specifies requirements among set of values either on the same timeline or on different timelines. In particular it involves (a) a *reference* value and one or more *target* values, that are other values on the same or on other timelines (b) some *relations*, which are constraints limiting the domain of reference value or target value arguments (e.g. a relation can specify that reference and target values would be separated by a given temporal distance). We call a value *v* admissible if there exists a compatibility having *v* as a reference value and all temporal requirements are satisfied. A value *v* can also be made admissible through unification with an already admissible value *v'* such that *v* = *v'*. Finally, a timeline-based domain is called *admissible* if all values of the domain are admissible and if, for each timeline, no different values overlap in time.

Timelines are used to maintain information about trainee features. In particular, various variables have been modelled through different value types:

- **Personality traits** are modelled through predicates of the form personality trait(x) where x is an integer ranging from 0 to 10;
- **Leadership style** through predicates of the form leadership style(x) with x being a Boolean variable assuming value 0 for socio-emotional and 1 for task oriented leadership style;
- **Background experience** through predicates of the form background experience(x) where x is an integer assuming values 0 for low experience, 1 for medium experience and 2 for high experience;

- **Self-efficacy** through predicates of the form *selfefficacy(x)* with *x* being an integer ranging from 0 to 10;
- **Stress and anxiety** through predicates respectively of the form *stress(x)* and *anxiety(x)* where *x* is an integer ranging from 0 to 100.

Additionally a timeline called **profile** with predicates of the form *profile(x)* with *x* being an integer ranging from 0 to 100 model an aggregate classification of the current trainee status and is used to both define different aggregations of trainee variables that may be of interest (i.e. to create different trainee profiles that consider different variables) and consequently to trigger particular behavioural plans suitable for the particular category or for a given profile. In particular the key connection between Behavioral and Crisis planners is represented by a timeline **induced_stress** that is used by the crisis planner to modulate lesson stimuli presented to trainees. Once allowed values are defined, we define compatibilities for each value. Static variables do not change over time so compatibilities for their values are of the form:

$$pred(x) \rightarrow (this\ duration[H-O, H-O]$$

where *pred* is the corresponding variable predicate (e.g. personality trait, leadership style, etc...), *this* refers to the reference value, *duration* is a constraint on the duration of the reference value, H is the planning horizon and O is the planning origin.

For each dynamic variable a compatibility is added to the system:

$$pred(x) \rightarrow \begin{cases} pro\ profile(y) \\ this\ during\ pro \end{cases}$$

where *pro* is a label identifying the target value *profile(y)* inside the synchronization and *this during pro* is a constraint requiring that the reference value must appear during the *pro* target value. These compatibilities have the result that, whenever a new value is added to the corresponding dynamic variable, a profile value is also added to the profiles variable with a free y argument. Based on specific person-alisation rules, profile value compatibilities allow both the definition of the current profile and the synthesis of suggestions for training customisation.

Example. In order to explain how trainees are assigned to profiles during training, let us suppose that a trainee x answers an anxiety question and that, consequently, an event rep-resenting an updated level of anxiety is added to his (or her) anxiety timeline. The applied compatibility has a structure similar to the following:

$$x \ anxiety(y) \rightarrow \begin{cases} pro \ profile(z) \\ this \ during \ pro \end{cases}$$

As explained before, this compatibility assures that every time we have an anxiety update, an event, named *pro* locally to the rule, is added to the *profile* timeline of trainee x, the new anxiety value must appear "during" pro (triggering event's starting point is constrained to be [0, +inf] *before pro*'s starting point while pro's ending point is constrained to be [0, +inf] *before* triggering event's ending point). Once the event *pro* is added to current Event Network the solving procedure is called and itself requests a compatibility application.

Let's assume now that the following re-quirements, representing trainee associations to different profiles, are defined inside the Behavioural Modeller:

$$r_r : (a \ value = 0 \wedge be \ value = 0 \wedge pro \ value = 0)$$
$$r_1 : (a \ value = 1 \wedge be \ value = 0 \wedge pro \ value = 1)$$
$$\dots$$

where a stands for anxiety, and be for back-ground experience. Hence the previous require-ments basically state: if anxiety value is equal to 0 and background-experience is equal to 0 then the profile must be equal to 0; if anxiety

value is equal to 1 and background-experience is equal to 0 then the profile must be equal to 1; etc... in enacting such requirements the association of trainees to profiles can change. Profile information is then passed on to the Crisis Planner, which updates the values of other timelines associated with trainee x according to a set of training actions:

$$a_r : (pro \ value = 0 \wedge is \ value = 1 \wedge \dots)$$
$$a_1 : (pro \ value = 1 \wedge is \ value = 0 \wedge \dots)$$
$$\dots$$

The idea behind these personalisation rules, for example, is to associate a low anxiety value with a high induced stress value and vice versa. The resulting compatibility is:

$$x \ profile(y) \rightarrow \begin{cases} a \ anxiety(v_{\mu}) \\ be \ background \ experience(v_1) \\ is \ induced \ stress(v_2) \\ this \ during \ a \\ this \ during \ be \\ this \ during \ is \\ r_r \vee r_1 \vee \dots \\ a_r \vee a_1 \vee \dots \end{cases}$$

Finally, the induced stress compatibility selects proper events from the Crisis Knowledge Base and presents them to the trainee, in order to generate an appropriate stress level, with the aim of maximising the learning process.

4. AFFECTIVE STATE MANIPULATION AND CONTROL

The Behavioural Framework, as described in the previous section, provides the mechanism to determine the behavioural and emotional characteristics of a trainee within the Pandora system, and to then monitor their behaviour and emotions as they progress through the training scenario, and the decisions they are required to make during that process. It also describes the mechanisms to control the levels of stress imposed on the trainees through the Crisis Planner, in other words the background levels of stress inherent in the set of events that make up the crisis scenario along the prescribed timeline. The Behavioural Framework also initiates the use of the Affective State Framework to manipulate and control the induced level of stress. In essence therefore, the Affective State Framework provides the systemic emotional intelligence to manage and manipulate the emotions of the trainees, to make the training more realistic and valuable. Through this facility we have the potential to individually personalise the training experience for each trainee, in terms of their own psychological makeup, to ensure that they are appropriately tested to determine their decision-making performance under stress, their ability to negotiate appropriately in a multi-agency situation under stress, and their planning and communication skills in such an environment. This process is controlled by the Pandora Emotion Engine, which is described in section 4.1, explicitly using affective markup of assets and information management and manipulation techniques to create affective ambience, described in sections 4.2 and 4.3.

4.1. The Pandora Emotion Engine

The Emotion Engine provides an Engaging Interaction Framework and effectively acts as a middleware component of the Pandora Architecture, interpreting and filtering instructions from the Crisis Simulation Framework, the Behavioural Framework, and the Trainer Support Framework, providing rendering instructions to the Simulation Environment Builder Framework. This section discusses discussed the architecture of the emotion engine and provides an overview of the interfaces and flow of information between the main components. The Emotion Engine architecture can be broken down in to two primary components: the Non-Playing Character (NPC) Framework and the Affective State Framework. An overview of how they, and their sub-components, interact

internally and also with external components is provided in Figure 5.

The types of NPC, and the roles they perform, were described earlier in 2.1. The NPC framework consists of two sub-components. An NPC Repository Manager, which provides access to a local NPC repository that stores the specification for each NPC in order to allow them to be rendered in a variety of multimedia forms, from a pure text representation through to a fully rendered 3D avatar. It provides an interface to input, export (both using a standard XML avatar description language) and manipulate NPCs. The second sub-component is an NPC Customisation Engine, which allows NPCs to be configured to set the level of expertise, experience, emotional type, communication skills etc. NPCs can be configured for a particular training scenario or introduced on the fly during training and controlled directly by the trainer if needed.

The Affective State Framework has three components. The Event Asset Store Manager, which provides an interface for input, output and manipulation of assets stored in a local Multimedia Asset Store. This store not only records the asset but other associated details such as its type, nature of the asset, how it may be combined with other assets, its duration, meta-tags in an XML emotion mark-up language, an indication of the effective level that it could be expected to engender in trainees if used in isolation.

The second component is the Affective State Elaboration component, which takes as input the NPC and Asset rendering information provided by the Event Asset Selector. When this input is received it calculates the actual value of the affective trajectory, based on the current trainee emotional and behavioural state and the desired state provided by the Behavioural Framework via the Event Asset Selector. This calculation can be for an individual trainee or all trainees. This is the point at which the emotional intelligence of the system is applied, taking the inferred behavioural and emotional state of the trainees from the behavioural framework, and linking this to the desired

Figure 5. Emotion engine component diagram

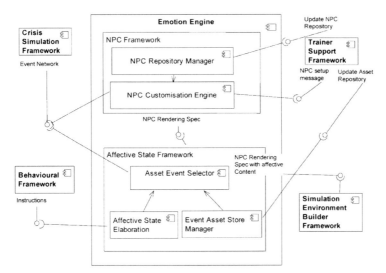

state, which may be provided from the crisis framework, automatically calculated within the behavioural framework, or input directly by the trainer. The trajectory between the current and the desired state is then calculated, at an individual and group level, and passed to the event asset selector.

The third component is the Event Asset Selector which provides a mash-up facility to build rendering specifications for the Environment Simulation Engine, developing combinations of multimedia assets and NPC behaviours to engender required affective states, individually and collectively, in the trainees. It takes its input from the Crisis Framework, the Behavioural Framework, the NPC Framework, the Event Asset Store Manager and the Affective State Elaboration. This next section discusses the interfaces between the components and the flow of information through the emotion engine as an event is processed. Prior to the actual execution of a training session, the trainer might carry out a number of tasks such as accessing: the NPC Repository Manager to input a new NPC; the NPC Customisation Engine to configure one or more NPCs for a particular scenario; the Event Asset Store Manager to introduce new multimedia assets into the asset store. Once

a scenario has begun execution, the Emotion Engine can be bypassed, however it is invoked for one of more of the following three reasons: if the event being processed requires NPCs; if assets are needed from the Event Asset Store; or if there is a requirement to change affect from the Behavioural Framework.

If an NPC is needed then the NPC Framework Customisation Engine will receive one input at run-time, an NPC Event Specification from the Crisis Framework. This specification describes the parameters for an NPC planned event e.g. Event id, Trainee id(s) or group, NPC id, default affective level, pre-canned asset id or trainer input, state of the world (e.g. all phones in the world are dead), Timeline timestamp etc. Secondly, it will receive an NPC setup message from the Trainer Support Framework. The NPC framework has only one output, which is used as an input to the Affective State Framework: the NPC rendering specification. This is an XML construct describing the rendering information for the NPC characters and the asset content to be associated with them for the current event in the scenario. Within the Affective State Framework, the Event Asset Selector takes inputs from the NPC Framework, containing the NPC Rendering information, the Behavioural

Framework, containing trainee behavioural/ emotional state and target state information, and the Crisis Engine, containing current event information. An affective calculation service and asset information are provided to the Event Asset Selector by the Effective State Elaboration Event Asset Store Manager respectively. Although the Behavioural Framework information can be sent through at any time, the affective trajectory can only be applied when NPC/Asset information is being output for rendering, so the Behavioural Framework inputs will be stored in an Event Log until the next event is required, when it will be applied, as it carries the highest priority. Event input will only arrive as a separate input if the event has no NPC involvement, in which case there will be no NPC Rendering information as an input.

There is, therefore, a single process flow through the Event Asset Selector, which is as follows:

- Input comes either from the NPC Framework or the Crisis Engine;
- The relevant assets are retrieved from the Event Asset Store, with relevant meta-data;
- A decision is then taken, based on the behavioural/emotional input stored in the event log, whether or not to call the Affective State Elaboration component to produce affective input to revise the NPC and Asset rendering data;
- The Event Log is then updated to show the latest event and timestamp for which data is being output;
- The NPC and Asset rendering output is then produced, including the affective revisions if required, and this forms the output to the Simulation Environment Builder Framework.

4.2. Developing Affective Markup: EmotionML

Many different models and representations of emotion and the processes concerned with the elicitation and effects of emotions have been proposed and implemented in software systems. The choice depends on various factors including the purpose of the software system and the underlying theory of emotion on which the system is based. Emotion, which has many ambiguous and contrasting definitions, is used in, and brings together, a number of fields such as psychology, physiology, linguistics, cognitive science and neuroscience. All of these have contributed to the conclusion that emotions play a key role in learning and decision-making (Ahn and Picard 2006), and work on emotional intelligence has clearly demonstrated a relationship to effective leadership [Palmer et al 2001], which as shown earlier, directly relates into the Pandora learning environment. Marsella et al. (2010) characterises the different types of computational models that can be used to represent emotion by reflecting on the use to which they can be put and the impact they have in the following areas of research:

1. Emotion research in psychology;
2. Artificial Intelligence (AI);
3. Human-Computer Interaction (HCI).

In Pandora, our focus is predominantly in the area of HCI, taking input from the psychological assessments of trainees prior to the training and using biometric sensors during training as part of the input required to assess current stress levels, so that they can be manipulated during the training simulation. Representation of emotions in a computer is challenging, as psychologists tend to describe emotions using abstract terms and concepts whereas a computational model requires a precise, formal definition, the construction of which can often reveal gaps in or assumptions in existing knowledge (Marsella et al., 2010). It is however important that computational models use well-founded semantics to represent emotional constructs and processes.

Within HCI, there are a variety of approaches to representing and understanding emotions in a learning situation, for example the use of Bayesian networks to aid the understanding of students' plans and their reasoning during the learning process in order to provide interactive help (Conati, 2002). Appraisal theory (Scherer, 2005) suggests that our emotions are created as a result of our appraisal or evaluation of a particular situation and this explains why people can react differently to the same stimuli. Much of the work on modelling emotions has focused on appraisal variables, i.e. which stimuli yield particular emotions in certain situations, and this has lead to the development of computational appraisal models (Marinier et al., 2009) who propose "an abstract cognitive theory of behaviour control (PEACTIDM) and a detailed theory of emotion (based on an appraisal theory), integrated in a theory of cognitive architecture" explaining why cognition and emotion are interdependent and that both need each other.

Dimensional theories argue that emotion should be represented as a continuum rather than as discrete points. Mehrabian and Russell (1974) proposed a three-dimensional "PAD" model where the three dimensions correspond to pleasure - a measure of how pleasant an emotion might be (ranging from agony to ecstasy), arousal – the intensity of the emotion (ranging from sleep to intense excitement) and dominance – measure of power or control i.e. how dominant the emotion is (ranging from submissive to total dominance). Computational models of dimensional theories often include algorithms describing how they change over time, e.g. having experienced an intense emotion, it is followed by a slow decay to some neutral or resting state, taking into account for example, the personality of the person being modelled. An advantage of computational models is that they can aid the testing of psychological theories, as models, and can be run with different experimental parameters without involving real subjects. A significant focus in affective computing concerns the design of avatars able to exhibit affective states in order to provide realistic believable interactions. An important aspect of recognising emotions in an avatar is the appropriate display of facial expressions and many studies have been undertaken in this area such as that by Mosera et al. (2007) which demonstrated that avatars can elicit a response similar to that provided by a real human face

and concluded that they could be used in training programs, however there are still noticeable differences in various types of brain responses when comparing real and simulated faces.

Understanding emotions is important not only to understand how humans interact with machines but also as computers are increasingly being used to observe and interpret human emotions. It has therefore become important to be able to represent and process emotions in a standard way. Emotion Markup Language (EmotionML) is an XML-based language designed to represent emotion in a machine-readable manner. It is going through the W3C standards process and is currently at the "Working Draft" stage (W3C, 2011). EmotionML is intended to be used as a plug-in language i.e. to be used in conjunction with other XML languages such as SMIL. The main areas in which it is expected that EmotionML will be applied are:

1. Annotation of data and media;
2. Recognition of emotion expressed by people;
3. Simulation of emotion by technological artefacts.

All three of these areas are relevant to Pandora, and so from the inception of the project, EmotionML was considered as a likely technology for use in its implementation. Detailed consideration of how EmotionML could be used to implement aspects of Pandora revealed a several potential issues with the version 1.0 or the draft standard. Three of these are outlined below:

1. EmotionML considers scales (e.g. for representing intensity of emotion) to be continuous, linear values. This may not be adequate to capture important information in Pandora. In some cases scales may need to be logarithmic or take into account the notion of a "tipping point". In other cases it may be important to be able to represent discrete values;

2. EmotionML allows for different vocabular-
    ies (e.g. for representing the category of
    emotion). The need for this is the lack of
    agreement amongst professionals, such as
    psychologists, about a single vocabulary.
    The problem of having a multiplicity of
    vocabularies, especially with none being
    specified as a default, is that of interoper-
    ability. As Pandora moves beyond a pilot
    project it is likely it will need to interact
    with external systems e.g. to use media
    originated and annotated externally and
    so interoperability will be important;
3. EmotionML allows for emotions to be
    tagged with a timestamp. In Pandora data
    received from monitoring trainee affective
    state will be received in a stream throughout
    training and it will be useful to be able to
    represent the identification of emotion as
    starting at a time offset within the session.

These issues and a description of planned
use-cases for EmotionML in implementing
Pandora were discussed at a W3C EmotionML
Workshop in October 2010 and were taken
into account when revising the draft standard,
although there is still some work to do to finally
resolve these issues (MacKinnon, Windall, &
Bacon, 2010; W3C, 2011).

4.3. Creating Affective States: Information and Multimedia Environment Manipulation

Since we have established a mechanism by
which we can encode affect in a markup form,
we can then apply it to information and multimedia assets, where we believe that the use of
that information or those assets will impact the
"genuine subjective feelings and moods" (Russell & Carroll, 1999) of the trainees. Affective
state manipulation has long been the province
of the storyteller, where the creation of a sto-
ryline that is engaging and immersive results
in the "suspension of disbelief" where the most
extreme of actions and emotions can enthral
and affect the viewer/listener/reader (Kintsch,
1980; Carroll, 1990; Brewer & Lichtenstein,

1982). More recently, the affective computing
and serious games communities have invested
considerable effort in the development of research on the detection of emotion in human
interaction, and in the accurate representation
of emotion through avatars, in support of affective state management. While a number of
the techniques for emotion detection (Calvo
& D'Mello, 2010) might well prove useful in
future versions of the Pandora system, when
it runs as a fully virtual, fully autonomous
environment, our initial work has focused on
the combination of physiological monitoring,
trainee self reporting, decision-modelling
and trainer analysis. Existing techniques for
physiological monitoring, reported by Calvo
and D'Mello, have focused around electrical
responses from brain, heart, muscles and skin,
and for the Pandora system we have chosen to
focus on cardiac-somatic features (Andreassi,
2007). Within the current model for the Pandora
system, which has been designed explicitly to
reflect the training requirements of Gold Commanders, a number of interactions will take place
in the physical environment, between human
trainees, which will have a direct impact on
decision-making, stress levels, and emotional
condition. The combination of physiological
monitoring, psychological self-reporting, feedback from decision-making within the scenario,
and external trainer observation, allows the
system to manage and manipulate affective
state irrespective of whether interactions occur
in the physical or digital environment. Existing
work in the serious games community (Yannakakis, 2008) has demonstrated the value of
the combination of physiological monitoring,
specifically heart, combined with self-reporting,
in affect detection, and Pandora has developed
on this approach.

With regard to accurate representation of
emotion through avatars, in the Pandora system, we find ourselves in the situation where,
although the system is being realised in a digital
environment, the deployment of the system will
occur in computer-supported physical space,
augmented reality space, and full virtual reality
space. Accordingly, emotive affect cannot be

purely founded in avatar-based representations of emotions impacting the trainees, although we will use such techniques in the fully virtual space, and, to some extent, in the augmented reality space. Our work on avatar-based representation of emotions is strongly influenced by current work in this area by the serious games community (McQuiggan et al., 2008; Spires, 2008; Johnson & Friedland, 2010). However, we have not been able to identify any affective computing or serious games affective management systems that offer the ability to dynamically manage the training environment, including dynamic real-time changes to the scenario and narrative, to manipulate trainee affective state, in particular decision-making under stress, in the combined physical and augmented reality environment we require to meet our Gold Commander training requirements. This places us in the position of trying to find other mechanisms to achieve our desired goal of affecting trainee emotions and behaviours to determine their performance under stress.

Within the film and TV community, there is a considerable body of knowledge and experience in the use of auditory and visual effects, combined with information management and manipulation, to create affective ambience (Tan, 1994; Bruno, 2001). In fact, whole genres of film have been identified with the techniques utilised to induce affective impact on the audience, most notably *film noir*, and it is those techniques which the Pandora project seeks to draw upon to achieve affective impact on the trainees. Techniques using special effects, both auditory and visual, can be used to create general ambience, however one key technique used heavily in film and TV is not available to us, background music. The project has therefore focused effort on the visual representation of emotion through avatars (Picard, 2000), the representation of emotion through speech (Cowie & Cornelius, 2003; Batliner et al., 2007), the use of special effects, and the use of information management and manipulation. Whilst there is a considerable body of knowledge on information overload, missing or incomplete information, and dealing with conflicting information within

the database and HCI communities (Angeles & MacKinnon, 2005; Sharp et al., 2007), the use of these to generate stress to affect users is novel and represents a contribution of the project to the body of knowledge.

Alongside the concepts of information manipulation and management to impact on the behavioural and emotional performance of the trainees, the Pandora system has also investigated and implemented the creation of rule-based multimedia mashups. In essence, these are combinations of multimedia assets, tagged for emotional affect and linked to identified events in the crisis scenario, that can, in combination, have a greater affect on the trainees and therefore induce a change in the emotional trajectory of the individual or group, associated with a request to achieve such a change sourced from the Behavioural Framework. The information presented to the trainees within the Pandora environment can come through a variety of media channels, direct from non-playing characters, or through environmental conditions, and the multimedia mashup rules not only define the combinatorial characteristics for the multimedia assets, but also define the media channel usage, any environmental factors, and can link to specified NPC characters, particularly if initiated by the trainer:

- **Example Mashup Rule:**
  ◦ Identify power series of assets that can be run at the current event node;
  ◦ Identify all combinations of asset mashups that meet the affective trajectory requirement identified by the Behavioural Framework;
  ◦ Constrain the mashups list by removing all combinations with conflicting assets, and/or media channel conflicts;
  ◦ If the list is 0, repeat for lower affective level, until mashups list is 1 or greater;
  ◦ If list is >1, select mashup randomly & if affective level < required trajectory, run all mashups consecutively to create information overload stress;
  ◦ If mashup list = 1, use information manipulation rules.

- **Example information manipulation rules:**
  - ○ **Information overload rule:** flood all available channels with information but short duration to reduce time for analysis, leading to cognitive overload;
  - ○ **Missing information rules:** report one or more media channels as disabled, so only make available from the other channels. Remove one information asset from the relevant media channel randomly;
  - ○ **Information corruption rules:** Use background effects to override information presentations. Degenerate quality of video and/or audio dynamically to reduce information quality.

As a result, trainees can be subjected to a bewildering barrage of multimedia information, or a frustrating absence of complete information, on which to base important decisions and to develop strategic plans, and these factors induce the stress we wish to impose on the trainees to make the training scenarios more realistic. Basing this in the concepts of emotional intelligence, and building an AI capability, using inference of behaviour and emotional state and rule-based management of information, utilising the techniques described above, is also novel and represents a contribution to the body of knowledge.

The project has finalised the prototype development phase, delivered a robust prototype system, and undertaken full-scale testing and experimental evaluation of the system. Testing took the form of standard software unit, module, sub-system and system tests, user interface tests, and protocols and rule instantiation tests. Experimental evaluation took the form of field trials run at the UK Government Emergency Planning College, and these are reported in Section 5. More detailed evaluation results and statistical analyses will appear in the project final report, which will be a publicly published document. On completion of the final reporting phase of the project, formal protocols and rule specifications will emerge from the project, for inclusion into relevant standards and commercial specifications.

5. FIELD TESTING AND EVALUATION

During the later stages of the project we produced increasingly robust versions of the Pandora training tool, and were able to undertake an intensive test in a 3-day evaluation session using real strategic level Crisis Managers (Gold Commanders). This event took place at the Emergency Planning College (UK Cabinet Office) in York in February 2012. The sessions involved 13 Gold Commanders and 3 different trainers. The user reaction was extremely positive especially with respect to both the flexibility offered by the planning technology in creating different courses of actions and in recreating engaging and realistic interactions. The knowledge and skills of the 13 Gold Commanders ranged from novice to very experienced.

The Gold Commanders were trained in three separate groups, each group using the Pandora system for one day. Trainees were asked to fill in several questionnaires throughout the day in order to gather their reaction to a number of aspects in the system on a scale from 0 to 6 (where 6 is high). The aspects reported on were as follows:

1. Learning climate;
2. Self-perception of learning;
3. Security and privacy;
4. Technology Acceptance;
5. Oral instructions;
6. Tutorial;
7. User Interface.

The feedback received from all three groups was exceptionally positive. The bulk of the scores were in the 3-6 range, with A to D having no scores below 3. With only 13 users, a significant statistical study would not be appropriate and a considerable quantity of qualitative feedback was therefore gathered as well. Some quotes from the trainees were:

I like the flexibility of the system – it enables real decision making.

I think it's brilliant, really good.

What a clever bit of kit.

Real potential to understand your own ability and potential.

Really good system overall, simple to use, I was very impressed, easy to manipulate and do what you want.

It has massive potential.

Some comments regarding requested improvements to the system were received, and these tended to focus around the user interface and the desire for enhanced features. There were no negative comments in relation to the fundamental approach to training taken by the system, all trainees were extremely positive in this regard.

The trainers were equally positive. Despite some initial scepticism about the use of the Holter to monitor heart rate, the trainers found this incredibly useful as a guide to how stressed the trainees really were when they were they were not showing any outwardly recognisable symptoms of stress, and also how trainees reacted differently to the same stimuli. Some comments from the trainers were:

I can deliver training to Senior Directors across the country simultaneously using this system.

Being able to let people see the consequences of their mistakes in advance is valuable experiential learning.

Easy to use.

Flexible system – and truly dynamic.

Total classroom control.

My Executive Level customers would enjoy and welcome the opportunity to train using this system.

When can we have it and how much will it cost?!

It is clear that the fundamental approach taken by Pandora worked extremely well, all trainees were fully immersed in the environment throughout the entire training session and went away energised from their experience. Both students and trainers felt the system provided a completely different perspective on how to set up and structure training events in the future.

A more detailed analysis of the physiological data gathering during the training sessions is outside the scope of the present paper. Nevertheless, it is worth highlighting that a preliminary analysis of the available physiological data, gathered during the evaluation session with real crisis managers, clearly showed the levels of trainee involvement during the training session.

6. SOCIO-ECONOMIC BENEFITS OF THE PANDORA APPROACH

Pandora offers a prototype of an advanced training system, which includes a scenario targeted specifically at Gold Commanders in crisis management scenarios. Since Gold Commanders represent the strategic level of crisis planning, improving the training and thereby the efficacy of their strategic thinking and the design of their remediation plans, will have a significant beneficial effect in the handling of a variety of different crises. Better crisis management will have significant socio-economic impacts, in terms of reduced casualty rates, faster and more efficient remediation, reduced loss of working time, reduced loss of productivity and improved coordination of expensive resources. Additionally, since the project will provide different deployment models for the training scenarios, it becomes possible to train larger numbers both at strategic and tactical levels, utilising distributed virtualised representations of information, and thereby advance the training scenarios into fully immersive digital environments. Whilst such an approach will require the development of more sophisticated affective detection and affective management tools, it will enable the use of varied training scenarios that are too expensive for physical simulations to be realised in virtual form, thereby enabling training activities that are not currently practical. Again this will have significant socio-economic benefits, in the ability of crisis managers to develop more wide-ranging, complex and detailed strategies and remediating actions to deal with the ever-growing range of crises that they might be called on to manage. The use of the Pandora system in different partner countries internationally will also support the sharing of best practices in crisis management, scenario information and experiences and will promote understanding of different response modes related to cultural, legal and social variations, which would be of particular importance when dealing with crises that cross national boundaries.

Whilst the Pandora system has been developed for crisis management training, the e-learning architecture and component model is not specific to this particular situation and could be used for a variety of different training needs, since the key component is a scenario that can be modelled as a set of discrete events against a timeline. We can envisage a large number of different application areas ranging from business planning, through health and social care, to regional infrastructure planning, all of which could be modelled within the Pandora system and then used for simulation and training purposes. In fact, if we consider that the Pandora system offers a visualisation and simulation environment to support event network based scenarios, we can consider its use for almost any timeline-based process. The benefits of the training environment, which includes the modelling of the behaviour of trainees, the potential for customisation of the

immediate training session by the trainer, and the introduction of affective elements to impact the emotions and behaviours of the trainees, provide a range of facilities that could be utilised in different ways. Using the Pandora approach to provide training for a variety of different sectors and scenarios would give organisations and national bodies a significant lead in the use of visualisation and simulation technologies to provide learning experiences that would otherwise be too expensive, too dangerous or simply impracticable for the general workforce. The socio-economic and social impacts of the widespread use of high quality simulation and visualisation in distributed virtual environments to provide realistic learning experiences would be extremely significant.

7. CONCLUSION

The Pandora project has developed a prototype software system to provide a managed training environment for crisis management strategic planning, for Gold Commanders, and has developed an approach to introduce realistic emotional stress levels to this training situation. The use of behavioural modelling, combined with physiological tracking, self-reporting, and feedback from decision-making activities within the scenario, provides an accurate picture of the emotional and behavioural condition of the trainees at any point in the timeline. This system provides the opportunity for trainees to exercise emotional intelligence within group dynamic either within leadership or group support roles, to achieve consensus on decisions and actions or to pursue personal goals.

Given the information provided from the behavioural framework Pandora exhibits systemic emotional intelligence in, the use of information manipulation and management techniques, combined with multimedia asset mashups and auditory and visual effects. These can impact realistically on the stress levels of the trainees to provide the required conditions to test their decision-making under stress, their ability to negotiate pragmatically under stress, and their ability to develop effective, flexible and realistic strategic plans.

As described above, the system is currently under test and evaluation by crisis managers and should see a public and commercial release in 2012. Research undertaken for the project indicates that there is no equivalent system available at this time, and the emotional intelligence approach adopted in this project, combined with the timeline planning model, represent contributions to the body of knowledge in this area.

The underpinning systemic infrastructure developed for the Pandora project will be applicable to a number of other domains, where timeline-based planning, event network decision-making, and affective impacts would be of value. At the time of writing, the project partners are investigating a number of potential new areas of application for the Pandora infrastructure, including military, health and local authority planning, and organisational strategy. A further stage of development will be the production of an authoring tool, based on the protocols and processes identified in the current project, to enable the easy creation of new scenarios in any chosen domain.

ACKNOWLEDGMENT

The authors would like to thank colleagues from the other partners in the Pandora project for their contributions to the work presented, those partners being CEFRIEL (Italy), XLAB (Slovenia), FUB (Italy), UEL (U.K.), ORT (France) and EPC (U.K.). We would also wish to thank the EU for funding this work under FP7-ICT-SEC-2007-1 grant number 225387.

REFERENCES

Ahn, H., & Picard, R. W. (2006). affective cognitive learning and decision making: The role of emotions. In *Proceedings of the 18th European meeting on Cybernetics and Systems Research (EMCSR 2006)*.

Andreassi, J. L. (2007). *Human behaviour and physiological response*. Taylor & Francis.

Angeles, P., & MacKinnon, L. M. (2005). Quality measurement and assessment models including data provenance to grade data sources. In *Proceedings of the ATINER Conference 2005*, Athens, Greece.

Atkin, A. (2004). *Playing at reality: Exploring the potential of the digital game as a medium for science communication*. (PhD Thesis). the Australian National University.

Bacon, L., Windall, G., & MacKinnon, L. (2011, September 6-8). The development of a rich multimedia training environment for crisis management: using emotional affect to enhance learning. In *Proceedings of the 18th Association for Learning Technology Conference (ALT-C 2011)*, University of Leeds, UK. DOI: 10.3402/rlt.v19s1/7780. Retrieved from http://repository.alt.ac.uk/id/eprint/2159. ISBN 978-91-977071-5-2

Baffes, P., & Mooney, R. (1996). Refinement-based student modelling and automated bug library construction. *International Journal of Artificial Intelligence in Education, 7*, 75–117.

Bales, R. (1958). Task roles and social roles in problem solving groups. In E. E. Macoby, & T. M. Newcomb (Eds.), *Readings in social psychology*. New York, NY: Holt, Rinehart and Winston.

Bandura, A. (1986). *Social foundations of thought and actions. A social cognitive theory*. Englewood Cliffs, NJ: Prentice Hall.

Barrick, M. R., & Mount, M. K. (1991). The big five personality dimensions and job performance: A meta-analysis. *Personnel Psychology, 44*, 1–26. doi:10.1111/j.1744-6570.1991.tb00688.x.

Barta, W. D., & Kiene, S. M. (2005). Motivations for infidelity in heterosexual dating couples: The roles of gender, personality differences, and socio-sexual orientation. *Journal of Social and Personal Relationships, 22*, 339–360. doi:10.1177/0265407505052440.

Batliner, A., Steidl, S., Hacker, C., & Noth, E. (2007). Private emotions versus social interaction: A data-driven approach towards analysing emotion in speech. *User Modeling and User-Adapted Interaction, 18*(1-2), 175–206. doi:10.1007/s11257-007-9039-4.

Brewer, W. F., & Lichtenstein, E. H. (1982). A structural-affect theory of stories. *Journal of Pragmatics, 6*, 473–486. doi:10.1016/0378-2166(82)90021-2.

Bruno, G. (2001). *Atlas of emotion: Journeys in art, architecture, and film*. New York, NY: Verso.

Calvo, R. A., & D'Mello, S. (2010). Affect detection: An interdisciplinary reveiw of models, methods and their applications. *IEEE Transactions on Affective Computing, 1*(1), 18–37. doi:10.1109/T-AFFC.2010.1.

Carberry, S., & De Rosis, F. (2008). Introduction to special Issue on Affective modelling and adaptation. *User Modelling and User-Adapted Interaction, 18,* 1-2, 1-9.

Carroll, N. (1990). *The philosophy of horror.* London, UK: Routledge.

Chan, W.-H. (2007, May 7). Serious games=serious training. *FCW.com.*

Conati, C., Gertner, A., & Vanlehn, K. (2002). Using bayesian networks to manage uncertainty in student modeling. *Journal of User Modeling and User-Adapted Interaction, 12*(4), 371–417. doi:10.1023/A:1021258506583.

Conati, C., & Maclaren, H. (2009). Modeling user affect from causes and effects. In *Proceedings of the First and Seventeenth International Conference on User Modeling, Adaptation and Personalization.*

Conway, M., & Giannopoulos, C. (1993). Dysphoria and decision making: Limited information use for evaluations of multi-attribute targets. *Journal of Personality and Social Psychology, 64,* 613–623. doi:10.1037/0022-3514.64.4.613 PMID:8473978.

Cortellessa, G., D'Amico, R., Pagani, M., Tiberio, L., De Benedictis, R., Bernardi, G., & Cesta, A. (2011, June 28-July 1). Modeling users of crisis training environments by integrating psychological and physiological data. In *Proceedings of the Twenty-fourth International Conference on Industrial, Engineering and Other Applications of Applied Intelligent Systems,* Syracuse, NY (pp.79-88).

Costa, P. T. Jr, & McCrae, R. R. (1992). *Revised NEO personality inventory (NEO PI–R) and NEO five-factor inventory (NEO FFI) professional manual.* Odessa, FL: Psychological Assessment Resources.

Cowie, R., & Cornelius, R. (2003). Describing the emotional states that are expressed in speech. *Speech Communication, 40,* 1–2, 5–32. doi:10.1016/S0167-6393(02)00071-7.

Eysenck, M. W. (1982). *Attention and arousal, cognition and performance.* New York, NY: Springer. doi:10.1007/978-3-642-68390-9.

Funder, D. C. (2007). *The personality puzzle* (4th ed.). New York, NY: Norton.

Goleman, D., Boyatzis, R. E., & McKee, A. (2002). *Primal leadership: Realizing the power of emotional intelligence.* Harvard Business Press.

Graven, O. H., & MacKinnon, L. M. (2006). Exploitation of games and virtual environments for elearning. In *Proceedings of ITHET 7th Annual International Conference,* Sydney, Australia. IEEE Press.

Graven, O. H., & MacKinnon, L. M. (2008). Prototyping a games-based environment for learning. In *Proceedings of eLearn 2008.* Las Vegas, NV: AACE Press.

Hadley, C. N., Pittinsky, T. L., Sommer, S. A., & Zhu, W. (2009). *Measuring the efficacy of leaders to assess information and make decisions in a crisis: The C-LEAD scale. The Leadership Quarterly, 22*(4), 633-648. ISSN 1048-9843

Hannah, S. T., Avolio, B., Luthans, F., & Harms, P. D. (2008). Leadership efficacy: Review and future directions. *The Leadership Quarterly.* doi:10.1016/j.leaqua.2008.09.007.

Hedlund, J., Forsythe, G. B., Horvath, J. A., Williams, W. M., Snook, S., & Sternberg, R. J. (2003). Identifying and assessing tacit knowledge: Understanding the practical intelligence of military leaders. *The Leadership Quarterly, 14,* 117–140. doi:10.1016/S1048-9843(03)00006-7.

Johnson, W. L., & Friedland, L. E. (2010). Integrating cross-cultural decision-making skills into military training. In D. Schmorrow, & D. Nicholson (Eds.), *Advances in cross-cultural decision making.* Boca Raton, FL: CRC Press.

Judge, T. A., & Ilies, R. (2002). Relationship of personality and to performance motivation: A meta-analysis. *The Journal of Applied Psychology, 87,* 797–807. doi:10.1037/0021-9010.87.4.797 PMID:12184582.

Keinan, G. (1987). Decision making under stress: Scanning of alternatives under controllable and uncontrollable threats. *Journal of Personality and Social Psychology, 52*(3), 639–644. doi:10.1037/0022-3514.52.3.639 PMID:3572731.

Kintsch, W. (1980). Learning from text, levels of comprehension, or: Why would anyone read a story anyway. *Poetics, 9,* 877–898. doi:10.1016/0304-422X(80)90013-3.

Leonard, H. (2004). Leadership in crisis situations. In J. Bums, G. Goethals, & G. Sorenson (Eds.), *The encyclopedia of leadership.* Berkshire Publishing Group, Great Barrington.

Liu, H., Arafa, Y., Boldyreff, C., & Dastbaz, M. (2011, November 2-3). Cost-effective virtual world development for serious games. *The 3rd IEEE International Games Innovation Conference (IGIC 2011)*, City of Orange, CA.

MacKinnon, L., Bacon, E., & Windall, G. (2010, October 5-6). Tracking and influencing trainee emotions in a crisis-planning scenario. In *Proceedings of the W3C Workshop on Emotion Markup Language*, Paris, France.

Marinier, R. P., Laird, J. E., & Lewis, R. L. (2009). A computational unification of cognitive behavior and emotion. *Cognitive Systems Research, 10*(1), 48–69. doi:10.1016/j.cogsys.2008.03.004.

Marsella, S., Gratch, J., & Petta, P. (2010). Computational models of emotion. In K. R. Scherer, T. Bänziger, & E. Roesch (Eds.), *A blueprint for an affectively competent agent: Crossfertilization between emotion psychology, affective neuroscience, and affective computing*. Oxford, UK: Oxford University Press.

McQuiggan, S., Mott, B., & Lester, J. C. (2008). Modeling self-efficacy in intelligent tutoring systems: An inductive approach. *User Modeling and User-Adapted Interaction, 18*, 81–123. doi:10.1007/s11257-007-9040-y.

Mehrabian, A., & Russell, J. A. (1974). *An approach to environmental psychology*. Cambridge, MA: The MIT Press.

Mosera, E., Derntla, B., Robinson, S., Finkd, B., Gurb, R. C., & Grammere, K. (2007). Amygdala activation at 3T in response to human and avatar facial expressions of emotions. *Journal of Neuroscience Methods, 161*(1), 126–133. doi:10.1016/j.jneumeth.2006.10.016 PMID:17126910.

Mumford, M. D., Zaccaro, S. J., Harding, F. D., Jacobs, T. O., & Fleishman, E. A. (2000). Leadership skills for a changing world: Solving complex social problems. *The Leadership Quarterly, 11*, 11–35. doi:10.1016/S1048-9843(99)00041-7.

Muscettola, N., Smith, S. F., Cesta, A., & D'Aloisi, D. (1992). Coordinating space telescope operations in an integrated planning and scheduling architecture. *IEEE Control Systems, 12*(1), 28–37. doi:10.1109/37.120450.

Northouse, G. (2007). *Leadership theory and practice* (4th ed.). Thousand Oak, CA: Sage.

Ochalla, B. (2007, June 29). Who says video games have to be fun? The rise of serious games. *Gamasutra*. Retrieved June 26, 2012, from www.gamasutra.com

Paglis, L., & Green, S. (2002). Leadership self-efficacy and managers' motivations for leading change. *Journal of Organizational Behavior, 23*, 215–235. doi:10.1002/job.137.

Palmer, B., Walls, M., Burgess, Z., & Stough, C. (2001). Emotional intelligence and effective leadership. *Leadership and Organization Development Journal, 22*(1), 5–10. doi:10.1108/01437730110380174.

Picard, R. W. (2000). Towards computers that recognize and respond to user emotion. *IBM Systems Journal, 39*, 705–719. doi:10.1147/sj.393.0705.

Raghunathan, R., & Pham, M. T. (1999). All negative moods are not equal: Motivational influences of anxiety and sadness on decision making. *Organizational Behavior and Human Decision Processes, 79*(1), 56–77. doi:10.1006/obhd.1999.2838 PMID:10388609.

Russell, J. A., & Carroll, J. M. (1999). On the bipolarity of positive and negative affect. *Psychological Bulletin, 125*, 3–30. doi:10.1037/0033-2909.125.1.3 PMID:9990843.

Salas, E., Driskell, J., & Hughs, S. (1996). The study of stress and human performance. In J. Driskell, & E. Salas (Eds.), *Stress and human performance*. Lawrence Erlbaum Associates.

Salgado, J. F. (1997). The five factor model of personality and job performance in the European community. *The Journal of Applied Psychology, 82*, 30–43. doi:10.1037/0021-9010.82.1.30 PMID:9119797.

Scherer, K. R. (2005). Appraisal theory. In T. Dalgleish, & M. J. Power (Eds.), *Handbook of cognition and emotion*. Chichester, UK: John Wiley & Sons, Ltd. doi:10.1002/0470013494.ch30.

Schwarz, N. (1990). Feelings as information: Informational and motivational functions of affective states. In T. E. Higgins, & R. M. Sorrentino (Eds.), *Handbook of motivation and cognition: Foundations of social behaviour* (pp. 527–561). Guilford.

Sharp, H., Roger, Y., & Preece, J. (2007). *Interaction design: Beyond human computer interaction*. Wiley.

Shute, V. J., & Psotka, J. (1996). Intelligent tutoring systems: Past, present and future. In D. Jonassen (Ed.), *Handbook of research on educational communications and technology*. Scholastic Publications.

Spielberger, C. D. (2010). State-trait anxiety inventory. *Corsini Encyclopedia of Psychology, 1*.

Spires, H. A. (2008). 21st century skills and serious games: Preparing the N generation. In L. A. Annetta (Ed.), *Serious educational games* (pp. 13–23). Rotterdam, The Netherlands: Sense Publishing.

Stajkovic, A. D., & Luthans, F. (1998). Self-efficacy and work related performance: A meta-analysis. *Psychological Bulletin, 124,* 240–261. doi:10.1037/0033-2909.124.2.240.

Tan, E. S. H. (1994). Film-induced affect as a witness emotion. *Poetics, 23,* 7–32. doi:10.1016/0304-422X(94)00024-Z.

Thoreson, C., Bradley, J., Bliese, P., & Thoreson, D. (2004). The big five personality traits and individual job performance growth trajectories in maintenance and transitional job stages. *The Journal of Applied Psychology, 89*(5), 835–853. doi:10.1037/0021-9010.89.5.835 PMID:15506864.

Van Vianen, A., & De Dreu, C. (2001). Personality in teams: Its relationship to social cohesion, task cohesion, and team performance. *European Journal of Work and Organizational Psychology, 10*(2), 97–120. doi:10.1080/13594320143000573.

W3C. (n.d.). *Emotion markup language (EmotionML) 1.0* (Working Draft 7). Retrieved June 26, 2012, http://www.w3.org/TR/emotionml/

Yannakakis, G. N., Hallam, J., & Lund, H. H. (2008). Entertainment capture through heart rate activity in physical interactive playgrounds. User modelling and user-adapted interaction. *Special Issue: Affective Modelling and Adaptation, 18*(1-2), 207–243.

Lachlan MacKinnon, BSc, PhD, FBCS, CITP, MIEEE, MACM, MAACE, is Professor of Computing Science (Strategic Development), Head of the Department of Smart Systems Technology, and Head of the Department of Creative Digital Technologies, in the School of Computing & Mathematical Sciences, University of Greenwich, U.K. He is also Visiting Professor of Information and Knowledge Engineering at the University of Abertay Dundee, U.K. (where he was formerly Head of the School of Computing & Creative Technologies), and Visiting Professor of Games & Multimedia Technology at Buskerud University College, Kongsberg, Norway. Professor MacKinnon is currently Chair of the UK national Committee of the Council of Professors and Heads of Computing (CPHC), and Chair of the Education Committee of the BCS Academy of Computing. He is Chair of the Executive Committee of the British National Conference on Databases, and a member of the UK National Committee of the British Human Computer Interaction Group. His research interests are in computing policy, information and knowledge engineering, smart systems, games and creative technologies, eHealth and eLearning, and computer security.

Liz Bacon, BSc, PhD, CEng, CSci, FBCS, CITP, FHEA, is Professor and Dean of the School of Computing and Mathematical Sciences at the University of Greenwich, Chair of the BCS Academy of Computing, a BCS (Chartered Institute for IT) Vice President and Trustee and is a past Chair of the Council of Professors and Heads of Computing. She is / has been involved in many professional activities during her career such as working with e-skills UK, the Science Council, Parliamentary IT Committee (PITCOM), EQANIE (European Quality Assurance Network for Informatics Education), the National HE STEM Programme and being an ICT Thought Leader for the University of Cambridge International Examinations. Liz is a joint Director of the eCentre research group and has been involved in e-learning research for more than 10 years, this includes work on personalisation, serious games and enterprise development. She is an experienced systems designer and developer, with the bulk of her research and practice activity being directly industry facing, through knowledge transfer and consultancy.

Gabriella Cortellessa (MS Computer Science Engineering 2001, PhD Cognitive Psychology 2005) is a research scientist at ISTC-CNR. Her research spans on Mixed-Initiative Problem Solving, Design of Interactive Intelligent Systems, Evaluation Methods for Intelligent Systems. She has been part of the CNR team that worked with ESA for ten years developing the user interaction front-end for several deployed systems. She has been work-package leader in PANDORA, working on user modeling and engagement monitoring for interactive crisis training and she is currently pursuing the same research interest focusing on the personalized monitoring technology for old people. She has been one of the promoters of the SPARK Workshop Series, on Scheduling and Planning Applications held in conjunction with ICAPS, and is in the program committee of several AI conferences like IJCAI'09-11 and ICAPS'09, ECAI'10 and ICAART'11-12.

Amedeo Cesta (MSc Electronic Engineering, 1983, PhD in Computer Science, 1992: University of Rome "La Sapienza") is a senior research scientist in Artificial Intelligence at CNR (National Research Council of Italy) and Group Lead at ISTC (Institute for Cognitive Science and Technology). He has founded and currently coordinates the Laboratory on Planning and Scheduling Technologies (PST). He has conducted research in several AI areas like Multi-Agent Systems, Intelligent Human-Computer Interaction, Planning & Scheduling always pursuing the synthesis of innovative Decision Support Systems. He is currently exploring the integration of planning and scheduling techniques in new applicative areas (e.g., crisis managers training) and the synthesis of new cognitive aids for old people by integrating ICTs and robotics. He has been the Technical Manager of the PANDORA project and has worked at the integration of planning and cognitive technology in the project crisis simulation environment.

96   International Journal of Distance Education Technologies, 11(2), 96-109, April-June 2013

Affective Realism of Animated Films in the Development of Simulation-Based Tutoring Systems

Hiran B. Ekanayake, Stockholm University, Sweden & University of Skövde, Sweden & Department of Computation and Intelligent Systems, University of Colombo School of Computing, Colombo, Sri Lanka

Uno Fors, Department of Computer and Systems Sciences, Stockholm University, Stockholm, Sweden

Robert Ramberg, Department of Computer and Systems Sciences, Stockholm University, Stockholm, Sweden

Tom Ziemke, School of Humanities & Informatics, University of Skövde, Skövde, Sweden

Per Backlund, School of Humanities & Informatics, University of Skövde, Skövde, Sweden

Kamalanath P. Hewagamage, University of Colombo School of Computing, Colombo, Sri Lanka

ABSTRACT

This paper presents a study focused on comparing real actors based scenarios and animated characters based scenarios with respect to their similarity in evoking psychophysiological activity for certain events by measuring galvanic skin response (GSR). In the experiment, one group (n=11) watched the real actors' film whereas another group (n=7) watched the animated film, which had the same story and dialogue as the real actors' film. The results have shown that there is no significant difference in the skin conductance response (SCR) scores between the two groups; however, responses significantly differ when SCR amplitudes are taken into account. Moreover, Pearson's correlation reported as high as over 80% correlation between the two groups' SCRs for certain time intervals. The authors believe that this finding is of general importance for the domain of simulation-based tutoring systems in development of and decisions regarding use of animated characters based scenarios.

Keywords: Affective Realism, Animated Scenarios, Emotion, Game Simulator, Psychophysiology, Skin Conductance Response

DOI: 10.4018/jdet.2013040105

INTRODUCTION

Simulation-based training brings many advantages over conventional training, such as highly relevant and experiential training contexts (Bell, Kanar, & Kozlowski, 2008). One of the potential applications of simulation-based systems is in treatment/rehabilitation of mentally disordered offenders (MDOs). Currently, most risk analysis and treatment/rehabilitation of MDOs typically takes place within clinical settings and risk estimation is based on verbal descriptions. These methods are weak in identification of social and cultural factors and different kinds of triggers for provoking violence. Moreover, MDOs often have reduced ability to understand and react to verbal descriptions of situations (Murphy, 2006; Rogers, Dziobek, Hassenstab, Wolf, & Convit, 2007). To overcome these limitations simulation systems with video-based scenarios that patients can interact with have been developed (Wijk, Edelbring, Svensson, Karlgren, Kristiansson, & Fors, 2009). Similar systems have been applied for rehabilitation of men sentenced for domestic violence, where the clients can train to understand their own and their spouse's emotional and physical reactions in certain situations in order to re-learn how to avoid violent reactions (Sygel Jakobsson, Fors, & Kristiansson, 2010; Sygel Jakobsson, Kristiansson, & Fors, 2011). Although, these systems are able to engage the users to a satisfactory degree, they have limitations too: they are expensive when real actors are employed; the scenarios are neither open for changes nor flexible enough to adapt to the patient; and they are unable to engage patients towards expected emotional reactions. The aim of our research is to address these issues using state of the art technologies for game development and psychophysiological measurements available today.

The utilization of games and game technologies for purposes beyond entertainment is referred to as serious games (Ritterfeld, Cody, & Vorderer, 2009; Brennecke, 2009; Backlund, Engström, Johannesson, & Lebram, 2010; Mitchell & Savill-Smith, 2004). In particular, much attention has been paid to visualization technologies and several studies have been conducted to examine the physical realism and pedagogical value of game simulators (Backlund et al., 2010; Backlund, Engstrom, Hammar, Johannesson, & Lebram, 2007) and the difference between simulators and their corresponding real world contexts (Nählinder, 2009). However, Hudlika (2009) identifies a lack of affective realism in games, i.e. games' capability of generating affectively realistic social interactions between game characters and players. Some key requirements for game engines to achieve this are: capability to recognize players' emotions and, capability to adapt gameplay and game character behaviors to emotions. Affective feedback games and biofeedback games are examples of approaches aiming for affective realism by using invisible physiological responses (e.g. heartbeat rate variations) and behavioral responses (e.g. gestures, facial expressions, postures) of the players (Gilleade, Dix, & Allanson, 2005; Bersak, McDarby, Augenblick, McDarby, McDonnell, McDonald, & Karkun, 2001; Kim, Bee, Wagner, & André, 2004; Fairclough, 2007; Yannakakis & Hallam, 2008).

The psychophysiological indices are considered to offer several advantages over other methods in recognition of emotions, as their changes are continuous and can also be used to determine psychological variables beyond the emotional domain, such as cognition and motivation (Fairclough, 2007; Ekanayake, Karunarathna, & Hewagamage, 2009). Our current study basically relies on galvanic skin response (GSR), also known as the electrodermal activity (EDA), of subjects. EDA is a widely used response system in psychophysiological research and its applications can be found in basic research examining attention, emotion, and information processing to more applied clinical research. The tonic level of skin conductance or resistance in the absence of phasic response is known as the skin conductance level (SCL) or skin resistance level (SRL), whereas phasic increases in conductance or decreases in resistance on top of tonic level are known as skin conductance responses (SCRs) or skin resistance responses (SRRs). A tutorial over-view of EDA discussing physical, inferential and psychosocial aspects of EDA can be found in Dawson, Schell, and Filion (2000).

Our research focused on developing a game-based simulation system with virtual actors (animated characters) and using bio-feedback to adapt the scenarios to an individual patient being treated in the rehabilitation of MDOs. As a basis for the above vision, the current study has compared two film clips, one with real actors based scenarios and the other one with animated characters based scenarios, to see whether they are similar in evoking psychophysiological activity in subjects for the events in the films. Subjects' reactions were measured using GSR. This paper presents the methodological approach we followed, results we obtained, and a discussion of concluding remarks, limitations and future work.

METHODS

System Design

The proposed system design is based on the idea of presenting scenarios showing an individual or groups of individuals carrying out their ev-eryday activities such as preparing and having a family dinner, chit-chatting about everyday events, etc. However, those scenarios also con-tain events at certain time intervals that are very challenging to the patient in terms of emotional and physical expressions, including quarrel and violence. The length of the film is dependent on the reactions of the patient and the choices that the patient makes at critical instances in the film. In the existing system (Wijk et al., 2009), a patient's reaction is measured using a questionnaire in which the patient manually makes a choice among the options displayed on the screen. Based on the patient's choice of action the next video scenario is presented which shows the consequence of the patient's reaction. However, due to the limitations of questionnaire based evaluation such as unreli-ability of self-reported emotional information and requirement to interrupt the experience, au-

tomatic recognition of emotional reaction based on psychophysiological signals is proposed (Picard et al., 2004). Moreover, to eliminate higher costs when real actors are used, it has been suggested to create animated films with virtual characters.

The current study is based on a simplified version of the abovementioned architecture. Two films, real actors' based and animated char-acters' based, both having the same story and using the identical sound track, were employed. The beginning of the story consists of a neutral family situation between a man and a woman which later develops into a tense and violent situation as a result of the man misinterpreting the woman. In the story, the man is supposed to be an MDO. Table 1 summarizes the story and approximate timing of selected scenes in respect to both real actors' and animated films. Figure 1 shows screenshots representing typical content of visual scenes in the two films.

The aim of the study is to quantitatively determine whether both types of films, and to what degree, elicit emotional and physiological reactions of the users and possible correlations in those measurements. To guide our investigation, we have set up the psychological expectation of scenarios as follows.

The user should already from the begin-ning (around minute 2) detect that the man is not behaving well (this would hopefully elicit some small emotional and physical reactions). When the woman comes home around minute 4 and he starts to behave nasty with her, the user should probably be more emotionally engaged and also show more physical reactions. Finally, from minute 8 and to the end, when the man is starting to rape her (but does not succeed) and then putting a knife at the neck, the users should get very emotionally aroused and show strong physical reactions.

Subjects

A total of 26 voluntary healthy male subjects (mean age 23.9 years and S.D. 5.3) participated in the study. All subjects gave their written and informed consent prior to recording. They also

Table 1. Content and timing of certain scenes in the two films (both film types are using the same sound track and displays approximately the same visual content at all times)

Story Content	Timing of the Scenes (in Minutes)
A couple is living together with one child of their own. The woman has from an earlier relation also an older child, which stays every second week with her father and her mother (this woman) respectively. Now the woman has got a new position at her job, and is for the first time ever going on a business trip. The man does not like this and the introduction shows that he is patronizing her and also shows examples of him disliking that she is moving forward in her career.	0:00 – 1:50
The couple agrees to have dinner the next evening when she comes home around 8 pm.	2:00
However, she does not turn up at 8 pm the day after, and when the man is trying to call her on her cell phone, she does not answer. The man is getting more and more upset after each call he makes. This scene ends up with him starting to drink some beers.	3:00 – 3:40
When she finally turns up around 9 pm, he is rather upset and angry with her. She tries to explain that she missed the bus and did not hear the phone.	3:40 – 6:30
He is getting even angrier and takes her purse and finds the cell phone. He discovers that she has called her ex-boyfriend and gets very angry.	6:40 – 7:40
He starts to grab her, takes her arms behind the body and starts to get very aggressive.	7:50 – 8:40
She runs into the bedroom to get away, but he runs after her and starts to fight and make an attempt to rip her clothes off.	8:45 – 8:58
She kicks him and runs to the kitchen to get away but he runs after and starts to threaten her with a knife and holds the knife towards her neck.	9:00 – 9:15
Suddenly the police ring the door bell (called by the neighbors) and say that they will break in to the apartment if the door is not opened. The scene and film ends with the man letting the woman go and then their child stands in front of them looking worried...	9:15 – 9:45

certified that they were not suffering from any mental illnesses; not taking any medication, or having any alcohol or substance abuse. The real actors' film group consisted of 14 subjects (mean age 23.6 years and S.D. 4.4) and the animated film group (mean age 24.2 years and S.D. 6.3) consisted of 12 subjects. An ANOVA of age showed no significant age difference between the two groups [$F(1,22)=0.26$; $p=0.62$].

Procedure

The experiment took place in a lab environment at the Department of Computer and Systems Sciences (DSV), Stockholm University, where disturbances from sound and other distractions were minimized. The films were approximately 10 minutes long (real actors' film 9:44 minutes

and animated film 9:29 minutes). Although, they differ by the visual content, both had the same story and sound track.

GSR was recorded using the BIOPAC MP150 data acquisition system and AcqKnowledge software at a sampling rate of 2000Hz. The electrode placement used was volar surfaces on the medial phalanges of the left hand (Dawson et al., 2000). Additionally, electromyography (EMG) towards the orbicularis oculi muscle of the right eye and electroencephalography (EEG) using Emotiv EPOC neurofeedback headset were also recorded for future analysis.

Before watching the film, each participant relaxed for about two minutes while closing their eyes. The Camtasia screen recorder recorded the film being shown, subject's facial appearance,

Figure 1. Screenshots from four scenes of the film clips. A, One of the first scenes where the man is fondling the child; B, The woman has just arrived home from the trip; C, The man is starting the quarrel and is holding the arms of the woman; D, One of the last scenes where the man is threatening the woman with a knife.

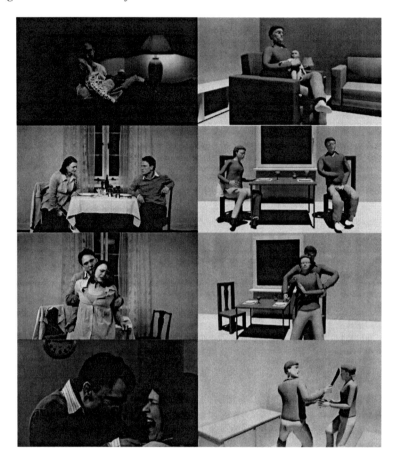

and a marker value shown on top-left side of the screen which is used to synchronize the film timeline with all other biophysical data (see Figure 2).

Analysis

All data analysis was conducted in MATLAB (version 7.6.0 R2008a; The Mathworks, Natick, MA). Recorded GSR signals were first resampled at 128Hz to match the sampling rate of other biophysical data streams. Unfortunately, due to technical and some other problems such as signals not being synchronized, noise in the

signals due to background events and low quality signals due to bad electrode contact, GSR data of eight subjects had to be eliminated from further analysis. Therefore, the final group sizes were eleven in the real actors' film group and seven in the animated film group. GSR data of the remaining subjects were range corrected to reduce individual differences in GSR. Next, the pulse location (valley), skin conductance level (SCL) at that location, rise time, amplitude (at peak), and recovery time of SCR pulses of each GSR recording were captured using an automated feature recognition algorithm.

Figure 2. Camtasia screen recorder capturing the film being shown, subject's facial appearance and marker value for synchronization

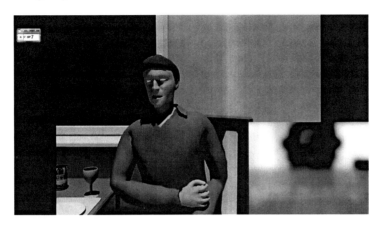

Figure 3 shows a GSR recording before and after range correction and extraction of SCR features are applied.

To compare the two groups (real actors' film and animated film) two approaches were used. Since it is very difficult to differentiate between event-related SCRs and nonspecific SCRs due to the constraints of the experiment, only the first 60 SCRs for each subject, which is based on the SCR amplitude when they were arranged in the decreasing order of amplitude, is considered. Next, in the first approach, the number of SCRs falling within 10 seconds intervals, termed as SCR score, for the duration of the film, is counted for each subject's recording. An additional calculation was performed to correct the effects of the duration difference between the two types of films. To fulfill the second approach, a similar procedure was used, but instead of calculating the number of SCRs falling in a 10 seconds time interval the summation of SCR amplitudes was calculated. Finally, before comparing the two groups using ANOVA and t-test, group averages were calculated for each 10 seconds time segment. The Pearson's correlation coefficient was calculated between the two groups' mean SCR score and mean SCR amplitude both for the overall film durations as well as considering a moving time window of 60 seconds from the beginning to the end of film durations.

Figure 3. Original GSR signal (left) and GSR signal after the range correction with features has been extracted (right)

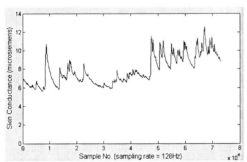
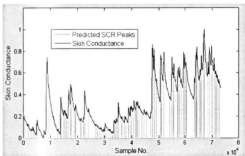

RESULTS

As mentioned in the analysis, due to technical problems, GSR data of eight subjects had to be eliminated from further analysis. The resulting group sizes were eleven in the real actors' film (mean age 22.2 years and S.D. 2.4) and seven in the animated film group (mean age 25.1 years and S.D. 8.0).

Comparing Real Actors' Film Group and Animated Film Group on Mean SCR Scores

Figure 4 shows the graphical representation of the two groups' mean SCR scores. A single factor ANOVA showed no significant difference between two groups' mean SCR scores [F(1,112)=0.0001; p=0.992]. Figure 5 shows the ANOVA box plot summarizing the results. A separate paired two sampled t-test also revealed there was no significant difference between the means of the two groups [t(56)=0.01326; p=0.989].

A graphical representation of Pearson's correlation coefficients between the two groups' SCR scores calculated for 60 seconds consecu-tive time intervals from the beginning to the end of the film durations is shown in Figure 6. It is apparent that the correlation coefficient between the two groups varies at larger percentages during the course of film durations, sometimes reaching as high as 80%. The overall correlation coefficient between the two groups resulted in only 44.07%.

Comparing Real Actors' Film Group and Animated Film Group on Mean SCR Amplitudes

A single factor ANOVA comparing the two groups' mean SCR amplitudes revealed that there is a significant difference between the mean amplitudes [F(1,112)=15.95; p=0.00012]. A graphical representation of SCR amplitudes of the two groups is shown in Figure 7, whereas Figure 8 summarizes the ANOVA statistics. A separate paired two sampled t-test also confirmed that the means of SCR amplitudes significantly differs in the two groups [t(56)=5.86; p= 2.48711E-07].

Figure 9 shows the Pearson's correlation coefficients between the two groups' mean SCR amplitudes calculated for each 60 seconds

Figure 4. SCR scores of the two groups within each 10 second time intervals

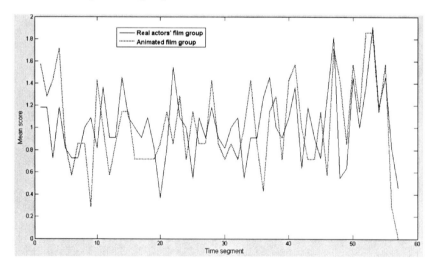

Figure 5. A box plot of ANOVA comparing SCR scores of the two groups: Real actors' film group (column 1) and animated characters' film group (column 2)

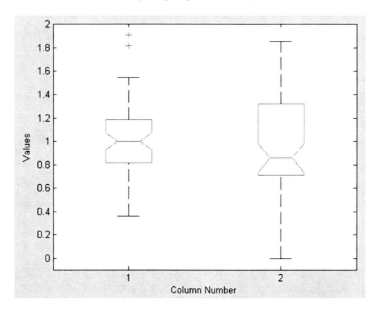

Figure 6. Correlation coefficients between the two groups SCR scores using a moving window of 60 seconds time frame

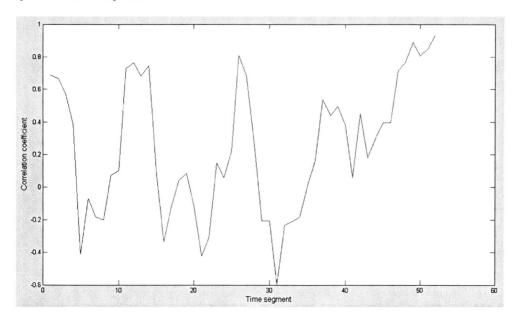

Figure 7. SCR amplitudes of the two groups within each 10 second time intervals

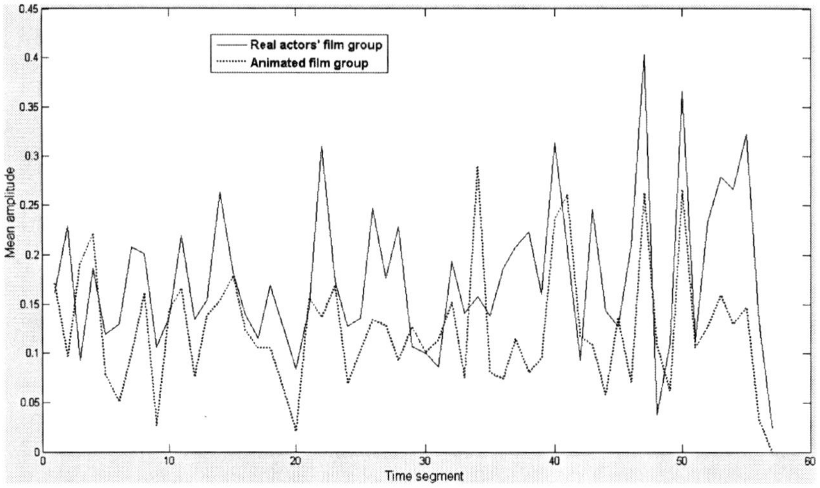

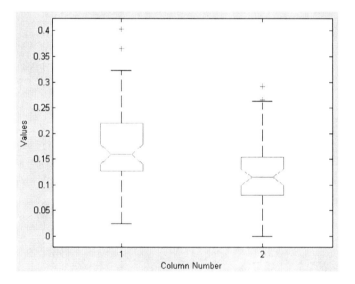

Figure 8. A box plot of ANOVA comparing SCR amplitudes of the two groups: Real actors' film group (column 1) and animated characters' film group (column 2)

time intervals from the beginning to the end of film durations. Once again it reports correlation coefficients as high as over 80% during certain time intervals. However, the overall correlation coefficient between the two groups is only 54.9%.

CONCLUSION

Our effort in comparing real actors based scenarios and animated characters based scenarios in a controlled laboratory setting using the skin conductance responses (SCRs) revealed very

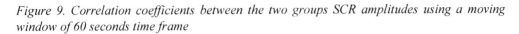

Figure 9. Correlation coefficients between the two groups SCR amplitudes using a moving window of 60 seconds time frame

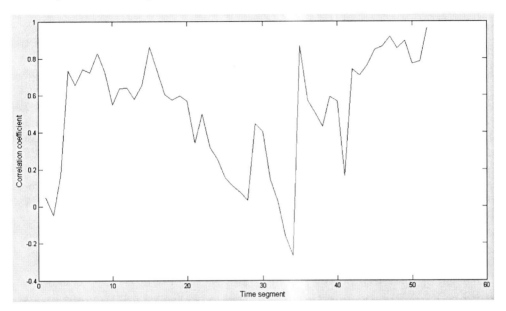

interesting relationships between the two. First, both ANOVA and t-test showed no significant difference between the two groups' mean SCR scores. However, when the SCR amplitudes were taken into account, both ANOVA and t-test showed that the mean SCR amplitudes of the two groups differ significantly. Reasons for getting these seemingly contradictory or complementary results can be argued for in the following way: the fact that there is no significant difference between the mean SCR scores of the two groups reveals that both types of scenarios are equally capable of triggering psychophysiological activity of subjects. However, the fact that there is a significant difference between the two groups' mean SCR amplitudes reveals that intensity wise the psychophysi-ological activities of the two types of scenarios differs from each other. The ANOVA box plot in Figure 8 shows that the mean SCR ampli-tudes of the animated film group are slightly lower than that for the real actors' film group, suggesting that animated scenarios are weaker than real actors' based scenarios in evoking psychophysiological activity.

Meanwhile, Pearson's correlation coef-ficient between the two groups for the overall film length of both SCR scores and amplitudes resulted in very low values (44.07% and 54.9%) suggesting that there is no linear correlation between the two groups' psychophysiological activity. However, when the correlation coef-ficient is calculated using a moving window size of 60 seconds, it showed that the correlation coefficient varies, and, as a result, it showed up to about 80% correlation coefficient during certain time intervals between the two groups' psychophysiological activity. For instance, starting from about minute 7 both groups show similar patterns of SCR scores (Figure 4) and SCR amplitudes (Figure 7). This is a very strong indication that both groups, during certain time intervals, were experiencing the films similarly despite the difference in their visual content. Moreover, when referring to the psychological expectation of the story, the scenario of the abovementioned time period corresponds to the most critical part of the story in which the user is expected to elicit very strong emotional reactions. Both figures 4 and 7 show comparatively high scores and amplitudes during this time period and thereby signal that the psychological expectation of the story has been fulfilled. However, SCR scores and SCR amplitudes of the two groups report dissimilar patterns as well. For instance, the SCR score of the animated film group at the beginning of the film is higher than that of the real actors' film group. A plausible interpretation is that when someone is exposed to an unfamiliar type of content (animation in this case), there is a possibility that the person becomes triggered for some time by its unfamiliarity. However, the primary aim of our study was to investigate whether the two types of scenarios, in general, were similar in evoking psychophysiological activity in subjects for the events in the films i.e. whether and to what degree SCR scores and amplitudes were similar in the two groups. Therefore, giving interpretations for the patterns are beyond the scope of our current investigation. Moreover, we do not know how other dimensions such as the story and the sound track have influenced the subjects independent of the visual content, which can be a topic for future research. Additionally, the technique we employed to calculate the correlation, the Pearson correlation, is attributed with certain assumptions such as homoscedasticity of the data (Hayes, 2005, pp. 296-300). In Pereda, Quian Quiroga, and Bhattacharya (2005), the authors present other techniques for measuring independence between two time series such as cross-correlation, a measurement of the linear correlation between two variables as a function of their delay time. Incorporating such techniques may improve accuracy of measurements of independence between the two groups.

Our method has certain other limitations. First, although we planned for a total of 26 subjects, because of technical and some other problems, we ended up with 18 subjects in total and not having groups of equal group sizes. Next, during our analysis, we stuck to certain assumptions: we used a range correction procedure for skin conductance to overcome individual

differences proposed by Dawson et al. (2000); only a maximum of 60 SCRs were counted when calculating SCR scores and amplitudes to overcome non-specific SCRs; SCR scores and amplitudes were calculated for a time interval of 10 seconds assuming that a time window of that length is suitable to study emotional reactions of the body (also suggested in Healey & Picard, 1998); and Pearson's correlation coefficients were calculated for a dynamic window length of 60 seconds, so that at most 10 pairs of values are considered when calculating a correlation coefficient. Another issue in our method is the quality of the animated scenarios. It has been noted that the quality of graphics and physical realism of motion are not very satisfactory compared to what can be achieved using today's state of the art animation technologies.

SCRs are caused by at least two or three pathways from the brain and not all of them are associated with emotions (Dawson et al., 2000). However, from SCRs being used in similar studies, such as Wahlund, Sorman, Gavazzeni, Fischer, and Kristiansson (2010), we are certain that our methodology and results are credible.

Nevertheless, we believe that the methodological approach and the results presented in this paper are of general importance for the domain of simulation-based tutoring systems in development of and decisions regarding future tools for identification of and rehabilitation of MDOs. In general, our implications are that animated scenarios can serve as a flexible and low cost alternative visualization approach to real actors based scenarios if developed considering other design aspects, such as the story, as well as human psychophysiological responses. Regarding future work, it is our conviction that the EEG, EMG, and questionnaire data that we collected will also lead us to further findings informing us as how to proceed in our effort of developing a game-based simulation system with virtual actors and using biofeedback to adapt the scenarios to the individual patient being treated.

ACKNOWLEDGMENT

This work was supported by NeLC project of SPIDER program of Sweden. The authors wish to acknowledge the support from Dr. Andreas Olsson at the Department of Clinical neuroscience, Karolinska Institutet, Dr. Kjell Näckros, DSV, Stockholm University, Dr. Marianne Kristiansson from Department of Forensic Psychiatry, National Board of Forensic Medicine, Sweden, and all participants in the experiment.

REFERENCES

Backlund, P., Engstrom, H., Hammar, C., Johannesson, M., & Lebram, M. (2007). Sidh - a game based firefighter training simulation. In *Proceedings of the 11th International Conference on Information Visualization (iV07)*, Zurich, Switzerland.

Backlund, P., Engström, H., Johannesson, M., & Lebram, M. (2010). Games for traffic education: An experimental study in a game-based driving simulator. *Simulation & Gaming, 41*(2), 145–169. doi:10.1177/1046878107311455.

Bell, B. S., Kanar, A. M., & Kozlowski, S. W. J. (2008). Current issues and future directions in simulation-based training in North America. *International Journal of Human Resource Management, 19*(8), 1416–1434. doi:10.1080/09585190802200173.

Bersak, D., McDarby, G., Augenblick, N., McDarby, P., McDonnell, D., McDonald, B., & Karkun, R. (2001). Intelligent biofeedback using an immersive competitive environment. In G. Abowd, B. Brumitt, & S. Shafer (Eds.), *UbiComp 2001, LNCS* (Vol. 2201). Heidelberg, Germany: Springer.

Brennecke, A. (2009). *A general framework for digital game based training systems.* Retrieved from http://books.google.lk/books?id=sQINSQAACAAJ

Dawson, M. E., Schell, A. M., & Filion, D. L. (2000). The electrodermal system. In J. T. Cacioppo, L. G. Tassinary, & G. L. Bernston (Eds.), *Handbook of psychophysiology* (pp. 200–223). Cambridge, UK: Cambridge University Press.

Ekanayake, H. B., Karunarathna, D. D., & Hewagamage, K. P. (2009). Determining the psychological involvement in multimedia interactions. *The International Journal on Advances in ICT for Emerging Regions, 2*(01), 11–20.

Fairclough, S. H. (2007). Psychophysiological inference and physiological computer games. In *Proceedings of the Brainplay '07: Brain-Computer Interfaces and Games*, Salzburg, Austria.

Gilleade, K. M., Dix, A., & Allanson, J. (2005). Affective videogames and modes of affective gaming: Assist me, challenge me, emote me. In *Proceedings of DiGRA '2005*, Vancouver, Canada.

Hayes, A. F. (2005). *Statistical methods for communication science*. Mahwah, NJ: Lawrence Erlbaum Associates.

Healey, J., & Picard, R. (1998, May). Digital processing of affective signals. In *Proceedings of the ICASSP*, Seattle, WA.

Hudlicka, E. (2009). Affective game engines: Motivation and requirements. In *Proceedings of the 4th International Conference on Foundations of Digital Games*, Orlando, FL.

Kim, J., Bee, N., Wagner, J., & André, E. (2004). Emote to win: Affective interactions with a computer game agent. *GI Jahrestagung, 1*, 159–164.

Mitchell, A., & Savill-Smith, C. (2004). *The use of computer and video games for learning, a review of the literature* (pp. 1–93). London, UK: Learning and Skills Development Agency.

Murphy, D. (2006). Theory of mind in Aspergers syndrome, schizophrenia and personality disordered patients. *Cognitive Neuropsychiatry, 11*(2), 99–111. doi:10.1080/13546800444000182 PMID:16537236.

Nählinder, S. (2009). *Flight simulator training: Assessing the potential.* (Doctoral dissertation, Linköping University), Available from DiVA (209999).

Pereda, E., Quian Quiroga, R., & Bhattacharya, J. (2005). Nonlinear multivariate analysis of neurophysiological signals. *Progress in Neurobiology, 77*(1-2), 1–37. doi:10.1016/j.pneurobio.2005.10.003 PMID:16289760.

Picard, R., Papert, S., Bender, W., Blumberg, B., Breazeal, C., & Cavallo, D. et al. (2004). Affective learning: A manifesto. *BT Technology Journal, 22*(4), 253–264. doi:10.1023/B:BTTJ.0000047603.37042.33.

Ritterfeld, U., Cody, M., & Vorderer, P. (2009). Serious games: Explication of an oxymoron: Introduction. In U. Ritterfeld, M. Cody, & P. Vorderer (Eds.), *Serious games: Mechanics and effects* (pp. 3–9). New York, NY: Routledge.

Rogers, K., Dziobek, I., Hassenstab, J., Wolf, O., & Convit, A. (2007). Who cares? Revisiting empathy in Asperger syndrome. *Journal of Autism and Developmental Disorders*, *37*(4), 709–715. doi:10.1007/s10803-006-0197-8 PMID:16906462.

Sygel Jakobsson, K., Fors, U., & Kristiansson, M. (2010). A new, interactive, computer simulation concept for treatment and evaluation of men convicted of domestic violence. In *Proceedings of the International Association of Forensic Mental Health Services,* Vancouver, Canada.

Sygel Jakobsson, K., Kristiansson, M., & Fors, U. (2011). A computer simulation model for treatment of men convicted of domestic violence-a prospective controlled observational study. In *Proceedings of the International association of forensic mental health services (IAFMHS) Conference,* Barcelona, Spain.

Wahlund, K., Sorman, K., Gavazzeni, J., Fischer, H., & Kristiansson, M. (2010). Attenuated subjective ratings and skin conductance responses to neutral and negative pictures in non-psychopathic mentally disordered offenders with various diagnoses. *Psychiatry Research*, *180*(1), 30–34. doi:10.1016/j.psychres.2009.09.009 PMID:20493542.

Wijk, L., Edelbring, S., Svensson, A. K., Karlgren, K., Kristiansson, M., & Fors, U. (2009). A pilot for a computer-based simulation system for risk estimation and treatment of mentally disordered offenders. *Informatics for Health & Social Care*, *34*(2), 106–115. doi:10.1080/17538150903014395 PMID:19462270.

Yannakakis, G. N., & Hallam, J. (2008). Entertainment modeling through physiology in physical play. *International Journal of Human-Computer Studies*, *66*(10), 741–755. doi:10.1016/j.ijhcs.2008.06.004.

Hiran Ekanayake is a lecturer in the Department of Computation and Intelligent Systems at University of Colombo School of Computing (UCSC) in Sri Lanka since 2006 and currently reading for his PhD attached to both Stockholm University and University of Skövde in Sweden. He received his B.Sc. (Honors) in Computer Science from University of Colombo in 2003 and MPhil from UCSC in 2009. His research interests include affective computing, serious games, cognitive robotics and psychological aspects of human learning. For his PhD he is investigating human psychophysiological signals and physical behavioral patterns of multimodal nature to develop an assessment methodology to capture meaningful engagement and development of task specific competency of human learners in complex game-based virtual training environments such as driving simulators.

Uno Fors received his PhD in medical informatics at Karolinska Institutet (KI) 1990. Fors was appointed as professor in medical simulation at KI 2007 but moved to Stockholm University in 2010, where he now is vice head of department and professor in IT, simulation and learning at the department of computer- and systems sciences at Stockholm University (SU). Fors has published more than 55 papers in scientific journals and 100 conference publications and serves as reviewer of many international journals within healthcare, education and informatics. Fors has initiated and led more than 20 larger projects within e-health, simulation and medical education. The research areas of most interest are healthcare informatics and healthcare education, but with an emphasis on simulation and virtual cases for learning, assessment and clinical use. Of special interest are studies focusing on emotional engagement, learning outcomes and clinical applications.

Robert Ramberg got his PhD in cognitive psychology at the department of psychology, Stockholm University and now holds a position as professor at the department of computer- and systems sciences at Stockholm University (SU). Ramberg also holds a position as research director at the Swedish Defense Research Agency doing research on flight simulation and training. He has published numerous articles in journals and refereed conferences. He has served as program committee and editorial board member for several international conferences as well as acted as reviewer for several international journals within the field of technology enhanced learning and collaboration. Of particular interest to his research are theories of learning (socio-cultural perspectives on learning and cognition), pedagogy and how these theories must be adapted when designing and evaluating technology enhanced learning and training environments and more specifically how artifacts of various kinds (information technology and other tools) mediate human action, collaboration and learning.

Tom Ziemke is full professor of cognitive science in the School of Humanities & Informatics, University of Skövde, Sweden, and chairman of the university's Informatics Research Centre. He received his PhD in 2000 from the University of Sheffield, UK. His main research interest is embodied cognition, i.e. the role of the body in cognition, emotion, and social interaction. He was coordinator of a large-scale European project called ICEA ("Integrating Cognition, Emotion and Autonomy", 2006-2009), was/is principal investigator in a number of other European projects in the area of cognitive systems, and is a member of the executive committee of EUCogIII ("3rd European Network for the Advancement of Artificial Cognitive Systems, Interaction and Robotics", 2011-2014). He is associate editor of the journals Cognitive Computation *and* New Ideas in Psychology, *and has edited two books on embodied cognition and social interaction.*

Per Backlund has a background in the fields of teaching, cognitive science, and information systems development. He holds a BSc in cognitive science and an MSc in computer science from the University of Skövde and a PhD in information systems from Stockholm University in 2004. His research interests are in serious games, in particular, how games and game technology can be used for training and dissemination of information. This includes analyzing the needs of clients to see how game technology and game design can contribute to achieve their goals.

K. P. Hewagamage obtained his BSc in Computer Science (First Class Honors) from the University of Colombo and the Doctor of Information Engineering from Hiroshima University in Japan. Professor Mohan Award for the outstanding computer science graduate in 1994, the best paper award at IEEE International Conference of Visual Languages in 1999, an award for the excellence in research by the University of Colombo in 2004 and 2006, are some of awards received for his academic activities. He has more than 90 publications in International peer reviewed Journals and Conference Proceedings. He is a senior member of IEEE, an academic advocate of ISACA and a member of ACM. Dr. Hewagamage is a senior lecturer in computer science at the University of Colombo School of Computing (UCSC) and the coordinator of e-Learning Centre, UCSC. He is a visiting researcher of Stockholm University, Sweden and Shimane University, Japan.

Words that Fascinate the Listener:
Predicting Affective Ratings of On-Line Lectures

Felix Weninger, Institute for Human-Machine Communication, Technische Universität München, Munich, Germany

Pascal Staudt, Institute for Human-Machine Communication, Technische Universität München, Munich, Germany

Björn Schuller, Institute for Human-Machine Communication, Technische Universität München, Munich, Germany

ABSTRACT

In a large scale study on 843 transcripts of Technology, Entertainment and Design (TED) talks, the authors address the relation between word usage and categorical affective ratings of lectures by a large group of internet users. Users rated the lectures by assigning one or more predefined tags which relate to the affective state evoked in the audience (e. g., 'fascinating', 'funny', 'courageous', 'unconvincing' or 'long-winded'). By automatic classification experiments, they demonstrate the usefulness of linguistic features for predicting these subjective ratings. Extensive test runs are conducted to assess the influence of the classifier and feature selection, and individual linguistic features are evaluated with respect to their discriminative power. In the result, classification whether the frequency of a given tag is higher than on average can be performed most robustly for tags associated with positive valence, reaching up to 80.7% accuracy on unseen test data.

Keywords: Emotion Recognition, Linguistic Features, Online Lectures, Technology-Entertainment and Design Talks (TEDTalks), Text Classification

INTRODUCTION

Sensing affect related states, including interest, confusion, or frustration, and adapting behavior accordingly, is one of the key capabilities of humans; consequently, simulating such abilities in technical systems through signal processing and machine learning techniques is believed to improve human-computer interaction in general (Schuller & Weninger, 2012) and computer based learning in particular (Aist, Kort, Reilly, Mostow, & Picard, 2002; Forbes-Riley & Litman, 2010). Important abilities of affective tutors or lecturers, besides emotional expressivity (Huang, Kuo, Chang, & Heh, 2004), include the choice of appropriate wording, which has been found to be highly important in computer

DOI: 10.4018/jdet.2013040106

based tutoring to support the learning outcome (Narciss & Huth, 2004). Furthermore, there is increased evidence for the influence of affect related states on the learning process (Craig, Graesser, Sullins, & Gholson, 2004; Bhatt, Evens, & Argamon, 2004; Forbes-Riley & Litman, 2007). In particular, previous studies highlighted the relation between system responses in a tutoring dialogue and student affect (Pour, Hussein, Al Zoubi, D'Mello, & Calvo, 2011); it turned out, for example, that dialogue acts of an automated tutor influence student uncertainty (Forbes-Riley & Litman, 2011). However, these studies do not take into account the linguistic content of lectures as a whole; hence, we aim to bridge this gap by addressing the automatic assignment of categorical affective ratings by a large audience to on-line lectures from the TED talks website (www.ted.com/talks). This prediction is based on learning the relation between linguistic features of the speech transcripts and the ratings given by the audience, which comprises many thousands of internet users in our case. Such automatic predictions can be immediately useful to evaluate the quality of lectures given by a distant education system, and to gain insight into which lecture topics or lecturing strategies are related to certain affective states. The aspect of predicting the induced affect from the lecturers' speech has—to our knowledge—not been addressed in a systematic fashion so far: Rather, in (Forbes-Riley & Litman, 2011), features from student responses to the system and abstract goals of the dialogue manager are used to analyze student affect. In this respect, that study is somewhat related to sentiment analysis (Schuller & Knaup, 2010) or opinion mining (Turney, 2002), where the goal is to deduce the affect of the users from written reviews. However, in our study we aim at predicting the users' affective ratings based on the lectures themselves. This also distinguishes our contribution from the large body of literature on prediction of (ordinal-scale) movie ratings—for a recent study on the public Internet Movie Database (IMDB), we refer to (Marovic, Mihokovic, Miksa, Pribil, & Tus, 2011). In that field, in contrast to our study, the vast majority

of approaches seem to be exploiting similarities in user profiles rather than features of the rated objects (*instances* in terms of machine learning), such as in (Marlin, 2003).

Finally, in contrast to many previous studies focusing on singular affects or ratings on a single 'good or bad' scale, we investigate the multi-label categorical ratings from the TED talks website which are given by internet users through assignment of tags to each talk. The tag set is determined by the creators of the TED talks website. These tags are on the one hand directly associated with the emotion evoked in the audience (e. g., 'obnoxious', 'funny'); on the other hand, they can refer to perceived attributes of the speaker resulting in a certain affect of the audience (e. g., 'courageous', which may result in 'feeling moved'). Third, the tags may describe the argumentative structure of the talk (e. g., 'long-winded', 'unconvincing'), which is arguably reflected in affective states such as 'boredom' or 'confusion' which are often investigated in the context of tutoring (Pour et al., 2011; Forbes-Riley & Litman, 2011). For the most part, these tags refer to emotion-related states (e.g., confusion, feeling inspired) rather than full blown 'Big 6' emotions, while 'obnoxious' (arguably, the 'strongest' of the 14 tags) could roughly correspond to disgust. Furthermore, in most cases, tags can be classified into those inducing positive or negative valence (e.g., 'confusing' and 'long-winded' for negative valence, and 'inspiring' or 'fascinating' for positive valence).

On lectures from the TED talks website, a slightly tongue-in-cheek analysis has been performed as to the relation of linguistic content and the user ratings (www.get-tedpad.com). This analysis is based on n-gram language modeling, and simplifies the categories to a 'good/bad' classification; still, we are not aware of a scientifically rigorous study on this topic.

In the remainder of this article, we first detail our evaluation database, which contains 843 TED talk transcripts of roughly two million words. There, we also explain how we turn the analysis of categories into a dimensional problem by defining binary classification tasks, which we consider relevant for practical applications in lecture evaluation. Then, the experimental setup and results, including feature extraction and classifiers, are laid out. Finally, feature relevance analysis is performed and conclusions are drawn.

EVALUATION DATABASE

Overview

The TED talks web site offers over thousand lectures from a wide range of topics. The speakers have a maximum of 18 minutes to talk. The language is English. The lectures are released under the Creative Commons BY-NC-ND license and are thus freely available for research. Transcripts are available for a majority of the lectures. For this study, we collected all 843 transcribed lectures which were available at the time of data collection (April 2011); we expect this number to be further increasing in the future. While audio and video are available in addition to the transcript, we use text data exclusively in this study. In a real-life system for affect classification, one cannot always rely on ground truth transcripts, but one would have to use automatic speech recognition (ASR) instead. Yet, as our study focuses on linguistic features for a novel affect classification paradigm, we thereby eliminate ASR inaccuracy as a confounding factor.

The TED website allows the users to rate each talk by selecting up to three of 14 predefined tags; the number of times that a certain tag has been assigned to a single talk will be called *tag frequency* in the following. In the collected data set, on average, the total amount of tags given is 1,695. This number indicates that each talk is rated by a few hundred users at least, supposing non-malicious system use. Since the ratings are anonymous, no information is available on the background of the raters; however, since all talks are given in English, a certain familiarity of the raters with the Western culture can be assumed safely. The available tags are shown in Table 1 along with statistics on the tag frequency.

One can see that the average tag frequencies vary strongly for different tags. For instance, the tag 'inspiring' is assigned 290 times per talk on average while 'confusing' is only assigned 18 times. The maximum tag frequency of 13,989 occurs for 'jaw-dropping' while 'long-winded' was assigned only 238 times at most. Overall, it is evident that positive tags seem to be assigned much more frequently than negative or neutral tags.

Subdivision

We split the corpus of 843 TED talks into a training, validation and test set. While the instances in the training set are used to build a model for classification, the disjoint test set is used to evaluate its ability to label unseen test data (cf. the section 'Automatic Classification Experiments' below). The validation set is used to optimize design decisions or 'hyperparameters' in the process of building classification models on a set that is disjoint from both the training and the test set. While the precision of the estimated model parameters is generally expected to increase with larger training sets, the statistical significance of the evaluation decreases with smaller validation and test set sizes. Taking into account these requirements, we split the corpus of 843 TED talks into a training, validation and test set of roughly equal sizes, following a straightforward protocol to foster reproducibility. Defining s_j as the unique ID given by the website to talk j modulo 3, we assigned all lectures j with $s_j = 0$ to the training, all with $s_j = 1$ to the validation and those with $s_j = 2$ to the test set. Since the talk ID depends on the order in which the lectures were published, this splits the corpus in a way that the distribution of newer and older lectures is nearly the same in all three sets—this ensures a near equal amount of user ratings in practice, since influence factors such as popularity can be assumed as random when following this partitioning strategy. In the result, 277 lectures are contained in the training, 285 in the validation, and 281 in the test set. The slightly differing numbers of lectures per set are due to the fact

Table 1. Minimum, maximum and mean tag frequency per tag in the TED talks database

Tag	Tag Frequency		
	Min	Max	Mean
Positive			
Jaw-dropping	0	13,989	176
Funny	0	7,185	113
Courageous	0	5,497	90
Fascinating	2	8,729	231
Inspiring	3	10,601	290
Ingenious	0	2,334	121
Beautiful	0	6,000	105
Informative	0	3,680	210
Persuasive	0	4,965	171
Neutral/Negative			
OK	2	348	58
Confusing	0	526	18
Unconvincing	0	2,020	51
Long-winded	0	238	34
Obnoxious	0	1,026	24

that the talk IDs are not continuous, probably since some of the lectures have been removed from the website.

Obtaining Dimensional Ratings

Unlike categorical annotation schemes often followed in emotion recognition (Schuller, Batliner, Steidl, & Seppi, 2011), the tags given by the users are not mutually exclusive. Hence, we treat the tags as dimensions in this study; an optimal way to assess and handle the possible interdependencies between those tags remains to be investigated in future research.

Thus, for each talk, a '14-dimensional' annotation is obtained from the tag frequencies. An essential part of this transformation is normalization: The total number of tags assigned to a talk strongly depends on the time that the talk has been already available at the website, and on the general popularity of the talk, which in turn may depend on the topic. In fact, the total number of tags assigned to a talk varies from 96 to 46 k.

Therefore, to obtain an annotation independent of both the total number of ratings and the overall frequency of the tags, we first calculate the 'relative tag frequency' r_{ij} for each talk:

$$r_{ij} = \frac{n_{ij}}{N_j}$$

where n_{ij} is the frequency of tag i for talk j and N_j is the total number of tags assigned to talk j. With this relative measure we set a threshold for each tag i, which allows to define a discrete class label $c_i(j) \in$ { yes, no } indicating whether the tag i is assigned to talk j more frequently than 'it could be expected' or not. From an application point of view, this class label determines whether an automatic system should assign the tag i to the talk j. More precisely, the labels $c_i(j)$ are computed by discretizing r_{ij} at the median m_i of the r_{ij} among all lectures in the data set, i.e., $c_i(j) = $ yes if and only if $r_{ij} > m_i$.

It is notable that in our study, ratings are obtained from thousands of anonymous users while in fields such as personality analysis or emotion recognition often a carefully chosen set of annotators is employed to get a stable ground truth (Schuller et al., 2011). We are aware of the fact that quality control is a non-trivial issue; however, we argue that in contrast to ratings by large groups of paid subjects as done in crowdsourcing (Parent & Eskenazi, 2011), there is no incentive to produce 'random' ratings in our case. The fact that a user may—intentionally or not—assign the same rating multiple times can even be seen as valuable information (emphasis) as long as such behavior does not occur excessively.

AUTOMATIC CLASSIFICATION EXPERIMENTS

The discrete class labels which are assigned to each talk allow viewing the prediction of user ratings as text classification problems. In general text classification, the goal is to automatically assign category labels to textual documents by means of linguistic features, such as occurrence of certain keywords. In our study, we consider one binary (yes/no) text classification problem per tag. We take a purely data-based approach where the relation of linguistic features and certain tags, including their relevance for classification, is learned fully automatically from a large set of training documents (cf. above).

Linguistic Features

This study focuses on the set of words and bag of words (BoW) models: In the set of words model, only binary features exist, which indicate the presence (1) or absence (0) of a word. In contrast, in a BoW model, features correspond to word counts. It has been observed that more sophisticated contextual models do not achieve fundamental improvements in comparison to the resulting blow-up of the feature space

(Sebastiani, 2002). In addition, we considered the TF x IDF approach (term frequency times inverse document frequency). In this model, the first factor (TF) measures the frequency of a 'term' (in our case, a word) in a lecture. The second factor (IDF) is used to enhance precision, assuming that using terms which occur in a high percentage of the documents lead to many 'false positives' (Salton & Buckley, 1988). In our experiments, we compute the IDF factor on the training set. The size of the feature space, corresponding to the vocabulary size of the training set, is 36 k. Hence, there is a need for classifier that can handle large feature spaces efficiently (cf. the subsequent section); furthermore, we investigate feature selection methods (cf. below).

Classifiers

The classification algorithms used for the experiments are implemented in the Weka toolkit (Hall et al., 2009; Witten & Frank, 2011) for straightforward reproducibility. Naïve Bayes (NB) is designed for binary (set of word) features while Multinomial Naïve Bayes (MNB) handles multinomial features, i.e., word counts as in the bag of words model (McCallum & Nigam, 1998). Naïve Bayes classifiers are a popular technique for text classification, because they are fast and easy to implement (Rennie, Shih, Teevan, & Karger, 2003). They are probabilistic classifiers which consider the probability $P(\hat{c}|\mathbf{d})$ that a document, represented as a vector $\mathbf{d}$, is assigned to the class $\hat{c} \in \{$ yes, no $\}$. By Bayes' theorem, this probability can be expressed as:

$$P(\hat{c}|\mathbf{d}) = \frac{P(\hat{c})P(\mathbf{d}\mid\hat{c})}{P(\mathbf{d})}$$

where $P(\hat{c})$ is the prior probability of class $\hat{c}$, and $\mathrm{P}(\mathbf{d}\mid\hat{c})$ is approximated from the corresponding relative frequencies measured in training data, following the 'naïve' assumption of conditional independence of the features.

For classification, the class maximizing (3) is selected; with respect to this maximization, the term $P(\mathbf{d})$ is constant and can hence be neglected. Due to the feature independence assumption, both types of NB models can be trained very efficiently even with a high number of features, and it has been shown that while the assumption of feature independence might be violated in real-life applications, there are many data sets in which strong dependencies exist among attributes, yet Naïve Bayes achieves high accuracy (Domingos & Pazzani, 1997); for a possible explanation of this behavior we refer to the study by Zhang (2004).

Besides, we use Support Vector Machines (SVM) (Vapnik, 1995) with linear kernel, trained with the Sequential Minimal Optimization (SMO) algorithm especially suited for the sparsity of our linguistic features, i.e., the situation where each feature has only few non-zero values among the instances (Platt, 1999). Linear support vector machines define a hyperplane which separates positive and negative instances in the vector space of features, while maximizing the margin, i.e., the distance between the hyperplane and the nearest positive example respectively negative example. Mathematically, if the 'yes' and 'no' classes are mapped to 1 and −1, SVM classify an instance $\mathbf{d}$ by means of:

$$\hat{c}\left(\mathbf{d}\right) = \operatorname{sgn}(\mathbf{w}^{T}\mathbf{d} + b)$$

where sgn is the sign function, and $\mathbf{w}$ and b can be interpreted as a weight vector for the individual features and the classifier bias, respectively. Both these parameters are learnt from training data. Linear SVM are popular for text classification since they are robust to overfitting to high dimensional input spaces as their complexity is not determined by the number of features, but on the separation of the training examples by the margin, and text classification problems are likely to be linearly separable (Joachims, 1998).

For each of the three classifiers, the hyper-parameters of the linguistic feature extraction methods were optimized on the validation set.

For all of the classifiers it turned out to be beneficial to convert all words to lower case, and remove stopwords (e.g., *the, for, but*) according to Weka's (Hall et al., 2009) built-in list of English stopwords. Since every classifier was able to deal with the resulting number of features, no periodic pruning or selection of the top words ranked by frequency is applied. For the NB classifier, the performance of simple binary features could not be further improved by modifications such as multiplication of with the IDF. As expected, MNB showed the highest performance for TFs instead of binary features. Furthermore, it appeared beneficial to transform the TFs to their logarithm, without measuring IDF; finally, normalization of the feature vectors to unity Euclidean length turned out to be advantageous. SVM surprisingly showed better effectiveness when only classifying by binary word presence. Moreover, in contrast to MNB, taking into account the IDF achieved better accuracy here. An overview over the combinations of classifier and linguistic features is given in Table 2.

Feature Selection

In text classification, besides removal of stopwords, often task-specific relevant features are selected. In this study, we apply two frequently used criteria to assess the relevance of features: the χ^2 statistic, measuring the statistical dependence between class labels and occurrence of terms, and information gain, quantifying the 'bits' of information obtained for the prediction of the class label by knowing whether a term occurs in a training instance (Gabrilovich & Markovitch, 2004; Yang & Liu, 1999; Yang & Pedersen, 1997). As these methods are supervised, i.e., they require class labels, feature selection criteria are evaluated on the training set only.

Results and Discussion

With the features parameterized as above and the default classifier hyperparameters defined in Weka, classifiers are trained on the union of

Table 2. Parameterization of linguistic feature extraction for each classifier, optimized on the validation set. Normalization refers to enforcing unity Euclidean length of feature vectors.

Classifier	Features	Normalization
NB	0/1	No
MNB	Log. TF	Yes
SVM	0/1 x IDF	Yes

training and validation set, and evaluated on the test set. For each of the tags the unweighted average recall (UAR) of the three different classifiers is measured. That is, the percentage of correctly classified instances (recall) is measured for both the 'yes' and 'no' classes and the unweighted average is taken. This measure is arguably better suited to imbalanced classification problems than conventional accuracy (Witten & Frank, 2011; Schuller et al., 2011): As the discretization threshold for the class labels is computed on the whole data set, the test set is not necessarily balanced for all tags; in our data set, the 'most imbalanced' tag in the test set is 'obnoxious', for which 153 instances exist in the 'no' and 128 in the 'yes' class. Table 3 shows the UAR of the binary classification tasks for the 14 tags.

Overall, the results are encouraging: We observe remarkable performances of up to 80.7% UAR for 'funny' (by MNB) and 80.2% UAR for 'fascinating' (by SVM). Furthermore, for all except three tag / classifier combinations, results are observed significantly above chance level UAR (50%, p < .05 according to a one-tailed z-test). As a rule of thumb, 57% UAR have to be surpassed to ensure significance, which is not given for 'confusing' (MNB and SVM) as well as 'obnoxious' (NB). Still, for each tag, there is at least one classifier that performs above chance.

Regarding the choice of the classifier, we observe that SVM outperform NB and MNB in six of the fourteen tags. MNB is observed most effective for five other tags while NB surpasses both MNB and SVM for three tags. Significant differences (p < .05) are, however, only encountered in two

cases: For 'funny' and 'obnoxious', MNB outperforms NB by about 7% absolute UAR. This could indicate that TF instead of binary feature representation is particularly effective for these 'emotional' tags.

Conversely, examining the results among tags, it is evident that the effectiveness strongly varies. Particularly, the tag with the highest UAR and the one with the lowest UAR differ by more than 20% absolute UAR for any of the three classifiers. The highest average UAR across all classifiers is achieved for the tag 'beautiful', which delivered an average UAR of 77.6%. With 56.8% average UAR, the tag 'confusing' lagged behind all others. In general, it is obvious that categories with a positive meaning consistently lead to better classification effectiveness, as can be seen from the mean UAR across positively associated tags and all classifiers (74.9% UAR) as opposed to negatively associated or neutral ones (60.3% UAR). This surprising fact is however understandable when one considers that the classifiers for positive and negative tags are built on different amounts of data: Remember that either there is a clear bias of the users towards assigning positive tags—or, a lack of 'bad' lectures in general, cf. Table 1. Furthermore, tags such as 'confusing', 'unconvincing' or 'long-winded' arguably carry a high level (pragmatic) meaning that can hardly be captured by term frequency features in general. This phenomenon will be further discussed in the subsequent section.

Results using feature selection are shown exemplarily for the tag *beautiful* in Figure 1. In that case, feature selection can improve the results by up to 2% absolute, which is however

Table 3. Unweighted average recall (UAR) for each tag and for the three classifiers. The highest UAR per tag is typed in bold face. 'Mean' denotes average UAR across classifier, and average UAR across positive / negative tags.

UAR [%]	Classifier			
Tag	NB	MNB	SVM	Mean
Positive				
Jaw-dropping	68.3	68.0	**71.6**	69.3
Funny	73.4	**80.7**	76.1	76.7
Courageous	73.3	77.5	**78.8**	76.5
Fascinating	76.1	76.3	**80.2**	77.5
Inspiring	69.4	**73.3**	71.7	71.5
Ingenious	74.1	**74.4**	73.7	74.0
Beautiful	75.2	78.0	**79.6**	77.6
Informative	72.4	75.7	**77.5**	75.2
Persuasive	73.3	76.2	**77.6**	75.7
			Mean	74.9
Neutral/Negative				
OK	**63.0**	60.9	61.1	61.7
Confusing	**57.8**	56.9	55.6	56.8
Unconvincing	60.2	**61.5**	61.0	60.9
Long-winded	**63.8**	61.1	63.2	62.7
Obnoxious	55.4	**63.0**	60.8	59.7
			Mean	60.3

not significant (p > .05) according to a one-tailed z-test. Furthermore, the optimal number of features for SVM classification is above 20 k. Similar results were obtained for the other tags; for none, significant UAR improvements could be obtained. This is in contrast to the behavior of feature selection reported in recent studies on sentiment analysis, e. g., (Schuller, 2011), where large performance gains could be obtained by feature selection, and the optimal number of features was observed at two orders of magnitude below; arguably, the task to predict user ratings is more multi-faceted than sentiment analysis, requiring a larger of number of features. Again, this motivates a closer look at relevance of individual features, as performed in the next section.

FEATURE RELEVANCE

In Table 4, we show for four selected tags the most discriminative words, corresponding to the binary word features with the highest positive or negative feature weight in an SVM classifier which was built on training and validation set TF features normalized to have the range [0, 1]. From the definition of linear SVM classification (cf. above), it follows that whenever a word corresponding to a feature with a positive weight occurs in a lecture, it will contribute to the classifier's decision to label the lecture as a 'yes' (1) instance, and vice versa, negative weights will foster a decision for the 'no' (-1) class. Hence, words corresponding to high absolute feature weights are most important for the model's decision between the two classes.

Figure 1. Feature selection: Unweighted average recall (UAR) for the Beautiful tag, with increasing numbers of features (total feature space: approx. 36 k features). No FS: No feature selection (cf. Table 3).

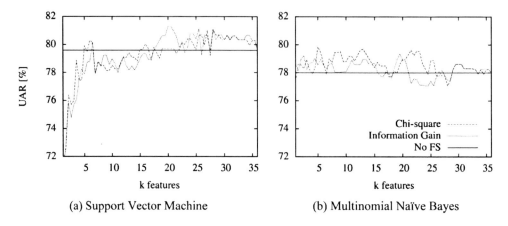

(a) Support Vector Machine   (b) Multinomial Naïve Bayes

For the tag *fascinating* (80.2% UAR), it seems that that on the one hand music is likely tagged as 'fascinating', on the other hand it is striking that many of the words that are indicative for a positive ('yes') example can be connected with forms or appearance ('size', 'shape', 'dots', 'holes', 'patterns' and 'object'). One possible explanation could be that topics like nature, astronomy, architecture or art tend to be rated as fascinating by many people. Clearly, for the 'no' instances, words associated with society and economy are among the 'top ten', such as 'communities', 'campaign', 'management' or 'poverty'. Overall, this suggests a strong dependence of the rating on topic—it appears that the classifier learns an implicit model for topic classification. Next, when examining the most relevant words for the tag 'courageous' (78.8% UAR), results are more mixed: Among the positive feature weights, one notices a few topic-dependent ones such as 'political' and 'justice', but also words that are related directly or in a broader sense to 'courage', such as 'support' and 'fear' (the opposite of courage). Conversely, however, we observe that highly negative feature weights are given for words that can be considered 'non-political': music and wine.

Among the words indicative of 'persuasive' lectures (77.6% UAR), we find some that can be interpreted as being characteristic of the argumentation style—pointing out 'difference(s)', the 'average', or 'effective' (means)—but cannot be attributed to a single topic; neither can the words with negative feature weights which include 'photo', 'ultimate' or 'invisible'.

Finally, the results for the 'negative' tag 'unconvincing', which with 61.0% UAR lags behind the tags with positive meaning, suggest some overfitting to particularly 'convincing' or 'unconvincing' training examples: What strikes is the fact that numbers appear among the top ten words of the tag 'unconvincing' for both positive and negative feature weights. In general, as could be expected from the model performance, the results are much harder to interpret. For instance, the fact that the word 'technological' has a high weight for 'unconvincing' is surprising.

Generally, one should keep in mind that these ten words are just a fractional amount of all relevant features. In fact, the very high number of relevant features is an essential characteristic of text classification tasks (Joachims, 1998). To further shed light on the importance of the top-ranked features, the positive and negative feature weights in the order of their absolute values are shown in Figure 2, for the 'fascinating' and 'obnoxious' tags. We observe that weights decay rapidly for 'fascinating'

Table 4. The ten most discriminative words, in the order of their absolute feature weight in the SVM, for classifying into 'yes' (tag frequency above median) and 'no' instances

yes	no	yes	no
music	decline	fear	music
objects	communities	invited	wine
experiments	responsibility	political	web
surface	campaign	answers	fairly
size	father	women	blue
shape	solutions	support	pattern
patterns	conference	village	historical
evolution	initiative	woman	objects
dots	management	prepared	blocks
holes	poverty	justice	binary
(a) 'fascinating'		**(b) 'courageous'**	
yes	no	yes	no
average	built	music	16
groups	music	alternative	teachers
lose	beautiful	changing	school
difference	artificial	technological	dead
differences	ultimate	perception	training
country	june	marketing	forgot
staring	enter	decade	inspiring
effective	photo	truck	child
issue	invisible	35	jail
aids	motion	broader	impression
(c) 'persuasive'		**(d) 'unconvincing'**	

Figure 2. Absolute feature weights of the most relevant features in linear SVM classification

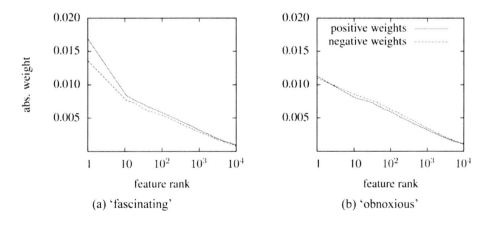

(a) 'fascinating'   (b) 'obnoxious'

(which displays the highest UAR for SVM classification), indicating that the 'top' words are strongly indicative of the class, while weights are generally lower and decrease slower for 'obnoxious', which exhibits lowest performance in classification.

CONCLUSION AND FUTURE WORK

We have introduced a novel paradigm for textual affect classification: the automatic prediction of subjective user ratings in affective dimensions given to on-line lectures. These affective dimensions were deduced from the frequency of 14 prototypical adjectives (tags), assigned to a large database of transcripts of TED talks. Our results suggest that especially positive tags can be assigned robustly. Examinations of the classifier models reveal that for some tags, this might be due to implicit topic classification. Thus, future work could focus on multi-modal integration to combine linguistic features with acoustic and video features. Certainly, it could be believed that, e.g., incorporating prosodic anchors of charismatic speech (Rosenberg & Hirschberg, 2005) would benefit generalization of the models. Yet, first experiments with automatic classification based on the acoustic feature set of the 2011 Audio/Visual Emotion Challenge (Schuller et al., 2011) resulted in only 55.5% UAR across the 14 tags on the test set—interestingly, the maximum of 65.8% UAR was obtained for the tag 'long-winded'. Overall, this indicates that the methodologies for human affect recognition from speech cannot be transferred directly to the task at hand, in contrast to the linguistic features investigated in this article. Besides acoustics, useful video features that influence the audience's affect might include 'low level' global motion (optical flow) or histogram features, or 'higher level' features based on pre-classification, such as action units, gestures or body posture—the latter, however, might prove challenging to extract in real-life, web quality recordings such as the TED talks database.

Furthermore, having demonstrated the principal usefulness of linguistic features for the task at hand, we will investigate the effect of using ASR instead of ground truth transcripts in order to show how the proposed text classification methods could be applied in a real-life system. For affect recognition, it is well known that ASR inaccuracies can considerably impact performance (Wöllmer, Weninger, Steidl, Batliner, & Schuller, 2011). In that sense, the proposed evaluation database will serve as a challenging testbed for robust speech recognition algorithms.

REFERENCES

Aist, G., Kort, B., Reilly, R., Mostow, J., & Picard, R. (2002). Experimentally augmenting an intelligent tutoring system with human-supplied capabilities: Adding human-provided emotional scaffolding to an automated reading tutor that listens. In *Proceedings of the International Conference on Multimodal Interfaces (ICMI)*, Pittsburgh, PA: IEEE.

Bhatt, K., Evens, M., & Argamon, S. (2004). Hedged responses and expressions of affect in human/human and human/computer tutorial interactions. In *Proceedings of Cognitive Science* (pp. 114–119). Chicago, IL: CogSci.

Craig, S., Graesser, A., Sullins, J., & Gholson, B. (2004). Affect and learning: An exploratory look into the role of affect in learning with AutoTutor. *Journal of Educational Media, 29*(3), 241–250. doi:10.1080/1358165042000283101.

Domingos, P., & Pazzani, M. (1997). Beyond independence: Conditions for the optimality of the simple Bayesian classifier. *Machine Learning, 29*, 103–130. doi:10.1023/A:1007413511361.

Forbes-Riley, K., & Litman, D. (2007). Investigating human tutor responses to student uncertainty for adaptive system development. In *Proceedings of Affective Computing and Intelligent Interaction* (pp. 678–689). Lisbon, Portugal: ACII. doi:10.1007/978-3-540-74889-2_59.

Forbes-Riley, K., & Litman, D. (2010). Designing and evaluating a wizarded uncertainty-adaptive spoken dialogue tutoring system. *Computer Speech & Language, 25*(1), 105–126. doi:10.1016/j.csl.2009.12.002.

Forbes-Riley, K., & Litman, D. (2011). Benefits and challenges of real-time uncertainty detection and adaptation in a spoken dialogue computer tutor. *Speech Communication, 53*(9-10), 1115–1136. doi:10.1016/j.specom.2011.02.006.

Gabrilovich, E., & Markovitch, S. (2004). Text categorization with many redundant features: Using aggressive feature selection to make SVMs competitive with C4.5. In *Proceedings of The Twenty-First International Conference on Machine Learning (ICML)* (pp. 321–328). Banff, Canada: AAAI.

Hall, M., Frank, E., Holmes, G., Pfahringer, B., Reutemann, P., & Witten, I. H. (2009). The WEKA data mining software: An update. *SIGKDD Explorations, 11*(1), 10–18. doi:10.1145/1656274.1656278.

Huang, C.-C., Kuo, R., Chang, M., & Heh, J.-S. (2004). Fundamental analysis of emotion model for designing virtual learning companions. In *Proceedings of the 4th IEEE International Conference on Advanced Learning Technologies (ICALT)* (pp. 326–330). Joensuu, Finland: IEEE.

Joachims, T. (1998). Text categorization with support vector machines: Learning with many relevant features. In C. Nédellec & C. Rouveirol (Eds.), *Proceedings of the 10th European Conference on Machine Learning (ECML)* (pp. 137–142). Chemnitz, Germany: Springer.

Marlin, B. (2003). Modeling user rating profiles for collaborative filtering. In *Proceedings of Neural Information Processing Systems (NIPS)*. Vancouver, Canada: Neural Information Processing Systems Foundation.

Marovic, M., Mihokovic, M., Miksa, M., Pribil, S., & Tus, A. (2011). Automatic movie ratings prediction using machine learning. [Opatija, Croatia: IEEE.]. *Proceedings of MIPRO, 2011*, 1640–1645.

McCallum, A., & Nigam, K. (1998). A comparison of event models for Naive Bayes text classification. In *Proceedings of the AAAI-98 Workshop on Learning for Text Categorization* (pp. 41–48). AAAI Press.

Narciss, S., & Huth, K. (2004). How to design informative tutoring feedback for multi-media learning. In D. L. H. Niegemann, & R. Brunken (Eds.), *Instructional design for multimedia learning* (pp. 181–195). Münster, Germany: Waxmann.

Parent, G., & Eskenazi, M. (2011). Speaking to the crowd: Looking at past achievements in using crowdsourcing for speech and predicting future challenges. In *Proceedings of the Annual Conference of the International Speech Communication Association (INTERSPEECH)* (pp. 3037–3040). Florence, Italy: ISCA.

Platt, J. C. (1999). Fast training of support vector machines using sequential minimal optimization. In *Advances in kernel methods: Support vector learning* (pp. 185–208). Cambridge, MA: MIT Press.

Pour, P. A., Hussein, M. S., Al Zoubi, O., D'Mello, S., & Calvo, R. A. (2011). The impact of system feedback on learners' affective and physiological states. In *Intelligent Tutoring Systems* (Vol. 6094, pp. 264–273). Pittsburgh, PA: Springer. doi:10.1007/978-3-642-13388-6_31.

Rennie, J. D., Shih, L., Teevan, J., & Karger, D. R. (2003). Tackling the poor assumptions of naive bayes text classifiers. In *Proceedings of International Conference on Machine Learning (ICML)* (pp. 616–623). Washington, DC: AAAI.

Rosenberg, A., & Hirschberg, J. (2005). Acoustic/prosodic and lexical correlates of charismatic speech. In *Proceedings of the Annual Conference of the International Speech Communication Association (INTERSPEECH)* (pp. 513–516). Lisbon, Portugal: ISCA.

Salton, G., & Buckley, C. (1988). Term-weighting approaches in automatic text retrieval. *Information Processing & Management, 24*(5), 513–523. doi:10.1016/0306-4573(88)90021-0.

Schuller, B. (2011). Recognizing affect from linguistic information in 3D continuous space. *IEEE Transactions on Affective Computing, 2*(4), 192–205. doi:10.1109/T-AFFC.2011.17.

Schuller, B., Batliner, A., Steidl, S., & Seppi, D. (2011). Recognising realistic emotions and affect in speech: State of the art and lessons learnt from the first challenge. *Speech Communication, 53*(9/10), 1062–1087. doi:10.1016/j.specom.2011.01.011.

Schuller, B., & Knaup, T. (2010). Learning and knowledge-based sentiment analysis in movie review key excerpts. In A. Esposito, A. M. Esposito, R. Martone, V. Müller, & G. Scarpetta (Eds.), *Toward autonomous, adaptive, and context-aware multimodal interfaces: Theoretical and practical issues* (Vol. 6456, pp. 448–472). Springer. doi:10.1007/978-3-642-18184-9_39.

Schuller, B., Valstar, M., Eyben, F., McKeown, G., Cowie, R., & Pantic, M. (2011). AVEC 2011 – The first international audio/visual emotion challenge. In *Proceedings First International Audio/Visual Emotion Challenge and Workshop (AVEC 2011)* (pp. 415–424). Memphis, TN: Springer.

Schuller, B., & Weninger, F. (2012). Ten recent trends in computational paralinguistics. In A. Esposito, A. Vinciarelli, R. Hoffmann, & V. C. Müller (Eds.), *Proceedings of the 4th COST 2102 International Training School on Cognitive Behavioural Systems* (pp. 35-49). Springer.

Sebastiani, F. (2002). Machine learning in automated text categorization. *ACM Computing Surveys, 34*(1), 1–47. doi:10.1145/505282.505283.

Turney, P. D. (2002). Thumbs up or thumbs down? Semantic orientation applied to unsupervised classification of reviews. In *Proceedings of the 40th Annual Meeting on Association for Computational Linguistics (ACL)* (pp. 417–424).

Vapnik, C., & Cortes, V. (1995). Support vector networks. *Machine Learning, 20,* 273–297. doi:10.1007/BF00994018.

Witten, I. H., & Frank, E. (2011). *Data mining: Practical machine learning tools and techniques* (3rd ed.). Amsterdam, Netherlands: Elsevier.

Wöllmer, M., Weninger, F., Steidl, S., Batliner, A., & Schuller, B. (2011). Speech-based non-prototypical affect recognition for child-robot interaction in reverberated environments. In *Proceedings of the Annual Conference of the International Speech Communication Association (INTERSPEECH)* (pp. 3113–3116). Florence, Italy: ISCA.

Yang, Y., & Liu, X. (1999). A re-examination of text categorization methods. In *Proceedings of the ACM Conference on Research and Development in Information Retrieval (SIGIR)* (p. 42-49). New York, NY: ACM.

Yang, Y., & Pedersen, J. O. (1997). A comparative study on feature selection in text categorization. In *Proceedings of the International Conference on Machine Learning (ICML)* (pp. 412–420). San Francisco, CA: AAAI.

Zhang, H. (2004). The optimality of naive Bayes. In *Proceedings of the Florida AI Research Society (FLAIRS)*. Miami, FL: AAAI.

Felix Weninger received his diploma in computer science (Dipl.-Inf. degree) from Technische Universität München (TUM), one of Germany's repeatedly highest ranked and among its first three Excellence Universities, in 2009. He is currently pursuing his PhD degree as a researcher in the Intelligent Audio Analysis Group at TUM's Institute for Human-Machine Communication, focusing his research on multi-source speech and audio recognition, including signal separation and robust back-ends for automatic speech recognition and paralinguistic information retrieval. Mr. Weninger is a member of the IEEE and (co-)authored more than 30 publications in peer reviewed books, journals and conference proceedings in the fields of speech and music signal processing, machine learning, and medical informatics.

Pascal Staudt received his BSc degree in Electrical Engineering and Information Technology from Technische Universität München for his study on text classification in affective dimensions. At the moment he is a graduate student in the Audio Communication and Technology program at Technische Universität Berlin. His research interests include audio synthesis, signal processing and multimedia content analysis.

Björn Schuller received his diploma in 1999 and his doctoral degree for his study on Automatic Speech and Emotion Recognition in 2006, both in electrical engineering and information technology from TUM. He is tenured as Senior Lecturer in Pattern Recognition and Speech Processing heading the Intelligent Audio Analysis Group at TUM's Institute for Human-Machine Communication since 2006. Best known are his works advancing Human-Computer-Interaction, Semantic Audio and Audiovisual Processing, Affective Computing, and Music Information Retrieval. Dr. Schuller is president-elect of the HUMAINE Association and member of the ACM, IEEE and ISCA, and (co-)authored 4 books and more than 270 publications in peer reviewed books (21), journals (39), and conference proceedings in the field of signal processing, and machine learning leading to more than 2,700 citations - his current H-index equals 28.

International Journal of Distance Education Technologies

An official publication of the Information Resources Management Association

Mission

The *International Journal of Distance Education Technologies* (IJDET) publishes original research articles of distance education four issues per year. IJDET is a primary forum for researchers and practitioners to disseminate practical solutions to the automation of open and distance learning. This journal is targeted to academic researchers and engineers who work with distance learning programs and software systems, as well as general participants of distance education.

Subscription Information

IJDET is published quarterly: January-March; April-June; July-September; October-December by IGI Global. Full subscription information may be found at www.igi-global.com/ijdet. The journal is available in print and electronic formats.

Institutions may also purchase a site license providing access to the full IGI Global journal collection featuring more than 100 topical journals in information/computer science and technology applied to business & public administration, engineering, education, medical & healthcare, and social science. For information visit www.igi-global.com/isj or contact IGI at eresources@igi-global.com.

Copyright

Correspondence and questions:

Editorial:	Fuhua Lin	**Subscriber Info:**	IGI Global
	Editor-in-Chief		Customer Service
	IJDET		701 E Chocolate Avenue
	E-mail: oscarl@athabascau.ca		Hershey PA 17033-1240, USA
			Tel: 717/533-8845 x100
			E-mail: cust@igi-global.com

IJDET is indexed or listed in the following: ABI/Inform; ACM Digital Library; Aluminium Industry Abstracts; Australian Education Index; Bacon's Media Directory; Burrelle's Media Directory; Cabell's Directories; Ceramic Abstracts; Compendex (Elsevier Engineering Index); Computer & Information Systems Abstracts; Corrosion Abstracts; CSA Civil Engineering Abstracts; CSA Illumina; CSA Mechanical & Transportation Engineering Abstracts; DBLP; DEST Register of Refereed Journals; EBSCOhost's Academic Search; EBSCOhost's Academic Source; EBSCOhost's Business Source; EBSCOhost's Computer & Applied Sciences Complete; EBSCOhost's Computer Science Index; EBSCOhost's Computer Source; EBSCOhost's Current Abstracts; EBSCOhost's Science & Technology Collection; Electronics & Communications Abstracts; Engineered Materials Abstracts; ERIC – Education Resources Information Center; GetCited; Google Scholar; INSPEC; JournalTOCs; KnowledgeBoard; Library & Information Science Abstracts (LISA); Materials Business File - Steels Alerts; MediaFinder; Norwegian Social Science Data Services (NSD); PsycINFO®; PubList.com; SCOPUS; Solid State & Superconductivity Abstracts; The Index of Information Systems Journals; The Standard Periodical Directory; Ulrich's Periodicals Directory

CPSIA information can be obtained at www.ICGtesting.com
Printed in the USA
BVOW052045100613

322955BV00005B/10/P